I'LL BE THERE

Vignettes of an Intrepid Traveller

Caroline Kennedy

Copyright @ Caroline Kennedy 2023

All Rights Reserved

*For Mayumi and Jasmine
and in memory of Elisar,
the greatest part of my journey was with you.*

*To my grandchildren, Ronan, Ione & Sienna, hoping you will
create your own adventures one day.*

*And thanks to all those family members and friends
who shared parts of the journey with me.*

*Thanks also to my editor, Richard Roper
and to my reader, Robert Isenberg*

Chapters

Introduction 1
Chapter 1: A Wanderer Is Born 4
Chapter 2: The Early Years 7
Chapter 3: Summers in Mallorca, Winters in Scotland 11
Chapter 4: The Swimming Team 16
Chapter 5: The Reluctant Debutante 20
Chapter 6: New York, New York 23
Chapter 7: Carnegie Hall Days 28
Chapter 8: An Evening with Frank Sinatra 42
Chapter 9: Tiptoeing Through the Tulips 45
Chapter 10: Blinded By the White 49
Chapter 11: Andy Edie & Baby Jane 69
Chapter 12: In the Company of Writers 73
Chapter 13: The First of the Free Spirits 78
Chapter 14: A Stint at the BBC 88
Chapter 15: 11,000 Miles & 8 Time Zones 94
Chapter 16: A Twist of Fate 110
Chapter 17: In Search of the Maharishi 119
Chapter 18: Nothing Can Go Wrong 132
Chapter 19: Art, Politics & Explosions 141
Chapter 20: From Mere Mortal to Living Goddess 149
Chapter 21: Tired Of Waiting 162
Chapter 22: A Date with the Pope 171
Chapter 23: The Boy Wonder of Tarlac 178
Chapter 24: Two Arrivals 203
Chapter 25: The Offending Emeralds 211
Chapter 26: An Edifice Complex 216
Chapter 27: Payback Time 221
Chapter 28: A Floundering Marriage 226

Chapter 29: It's Rita Again! 229
Chapter 30: A Number One Best Seller 234
Chapter 31: The War in Dubrovnik 240
Chapter 32: The Stalker 247
Chapter 33: A Campaign of Terror 252
Chapter 34: An Honorary Man 258
Chapter 35: Why Newfoundland? 268
Chapter 36: Farewell to the Pearl of Dubrovnik 276
Chapter 37: Theatre In My Blood? 278
Chapter 38: Paradise Lost 281
Chapter 39: A Difficult Romance 285
Chapter 40: The Bombshell 307
Chapter 41: Losing My Son 311
Chapter 42: The World is a Book 317

Introduction

"Will you raise your right hand and swear after me, I will not assassinate the President of the United States!" The American Vice-Consul in London peered at me over his half-moon glasses.

I looked at him, trying to suppress a giggle.

Let me say here, this was not the beginning of my life. But it was to be the beginning of my wandering life.

It was December 1963, a month after the most popular modern President, John F Kennedy, had been shot in Dallas. By 1963 "the times", according to Bob Dylan, "were a-changing." The generation gap was never so apparent, never so bitter and never so wide.

"Our parents don't understand us," had been the complaint of countless generations of young people before us but it was never as true as it was in the early Sixties. To our parents who grew up in the austerity of the Great Depression, a global pandemic and two world wars, Dylan's lyrics presented an alien and frightening battle cry, challenging as they did everything that seemed, reasonable, orderly and disciplined in their way of life. Suddenly millions of teenagers all over the world, who perceived they were "misunderstood" by their parents, were able to recite a new mantra.

Constraints on literature, art, theatre, television, film, fashion and sex were being loosened from their moralistic shackles of previous decades. There was no turning back now. This was the defining moment. Respect for authority and for politicians who, in our eyes, had got it all wrong for so long, evaporated almost overnight. The permissive society was being born and we were there assisting at its birth. Even conventional religion suffered as we turned east for answers, knowledge and spiritual fulfilment.

The two capitals of this innovation were both in Britain, "Swinging London" and Liverpool. After all, between them, they had produced the Beatles, the Rolling Stones, Mary Quant, Carnaby Street, the King's Road, Biba, Vidal Sassoon, the mini skirt, the mini car, TV satire and colour television. Youth in almost every country looked to us for innovation and inspiration. They emulated our sound, copied our look and mimicked our way of life. We were never prouder than we were in the Sixties. We were the blessed generation.

In December 1963, with my own particular mantra from Dion's "The Wanderer" ringing in my ears, the world beckoned and I was ready.

"Would you please raise your right hand and swear after me, I will not assassinate the President of the United States!" the Vice-Consul repeated.

I giggled again, "You're joking?"

The Vice-Consul loomed large in front of me. He pulled himself up to his full height, six foot two or three I would guess, and spluttered, "Miss Kennedy, this is no laughing matter. I want you to raise your right hand and....."

"Yes, yes, I understand. But honestly, am I likely to admit to you if I was planning to do that?"

From the opposite side of his desk, the Vice-Consul frowned. He was beginning to lose patience with me. He reached over to grab my right hand. And, after a brief but obvious mental exercise as to which of my two hands that might be, raised it above my shoulder and repeated the phrase.

"I swear I shall not assassinate the President of the United States!"

Still amused, but anxious to fulfill this one last requirement to obtain my all-important green card, I had little choice but to do his bidding. I mumbled the words. In the end, he was easy to satisfy. He had, I guessed, discharged his duty, as he saw fit. From now on, he must have reassured himself that, if ever Caroline Kennedy was caught red-handed attempting to kill Lyndon Johnson or indeed any successive United States President, he, the Vice-Consul, could always protest, "But she swore to me she wasn't going to do it!"

He beamed with the kind of pride that comes only with victory, lowered my right hand and pumped it vigorously.

"Good luck in the United States, Miss Kennedy!" He smiled graciously.

As I turned to leave, he coughed. I looked back.

"I just wanted to say," he added, "they'll just love your accent over there!"

As I closed the door to his office I breathed a sigh of relief. I had leaped my final hurdle. I had been accepted into the United States with one shake of the Vice-Consul's hand. I was on my way to the Big Apple.

So, after having discovered how carefully immigration applicants are vetted, imagine how astounded I was to find myself, a few months later, actually shaking hands with President Johnson with, apparently, not a single Secret Service Agent in sight.

It was summer of the following year, 1964. I had been attending an informal Democratic fund-raising barbeque, hosted by the actor Paul Newman and the President's daughter, Linda, in the magnificent grounds of one of those rambling Long Island heritage homes.

Within minutes of my arrival I found myself rubbing shoulders with Senator Ferdinand Edralin Marcos, the Philippines presidential candidate. As a woman, I should probably have had some feminine intuition here for, in a few years' time, I was to become an outspoken adversary of both him and his wife Imelda. I would write exhaustively on the ill-gotten gains of their conjugal dictatorship and I would clash, more than once with their eldest daughter Imee, on television in Manila. But there was no way of knowing then what a central part of my early life they and their country would become. So I shook hands, smiled politely, made some innocuous comment on the evening and moved on.

It was then that I almost bumped into Lyndon Baines Johnson. My first thought on encountering the President was that, had I brought one, I could have easily disguised a gun wrapped up in my Texas-sized T-bone steak. Perhaps the Vice Consul had been right in making me swear not to assassinate the President. For right here, right now, I realized, nobody would have even noticed. In one swift move, I could have taken out Lyndon Baines Johnson before anyone had a chance to recognize what was happening. But, instead, all I could do was make small talk, "Lovely evening, beautiful garden, delicious food," that kind of thing.

Here I was, a fledgling journalist with an opportunity to discuss serious politics, civil rights or the Vietnam War with the President of the United States, and I stood, like a frightened rabbit in the headlamps, too coy to ask him anything.

Too embarrassed to linger, like the words to the Burt Bacharach song, I simply "walked on by."

Caroline Kennedy
Culver City 2023

Chapter 1
A Wanderer Is Born

Nothing changed the day I was born. The war was still raging in Europe and the Pacific. Britain was still being bombed on a nightly basis. And eggs, milk, meat, sugar, bacon, tea and cheese were still being strictly rationed. But I knew nothing of all this.

I arrived on April 30th, 1944 in Godalming, Surrey. It was just five weeks ahead of the Normandy invasion which came to be known as D-Day. But I knew nothing of that too. My mother said she also remembered very little about my birth. Like most mothers of her generation, she received the "sleeping gas", nitrous oxide and, just as she had been for her three previous babies, she was totally comatose when her fourth and final child made her entrance into the world. (A decade later midwives began to suggest that it might be safer for mothers to be awake and actively involved in the birthing experience!)

And so here I was, the fourth child of my parents, Geoffrey Farrer Kennedy, a civil and consulting engineer, and Daska Marija Ivanovic, an auburn-haired beauty from what is now Croatia, who was dubbed by the UK Press as "the Pearl of Dubrovnik". They had met through a mutual friend, Chester Beatty, who was the founder member of my father's Cambridge University jazz band. Chester was also a friend of my mother's older brother, Vane. And when Vane invited Chester to Dubrovnik for a summer holiday, my father was invited to come along too. The love affair between my father and mother swiftly blossomed and they were married at Caxton Registry Office in London in 1937.

Now that I had arrived, I needed a name. My mother insisted on Bella after her Jugoslav grandmother. However, as she was to remind me several times over the course of my life, Bella meant "beautiful" and so, on the way to the Church my father had misgivings.

"But what if she doesn't turn out to be beautiful? What then?" he asked nervously.

I doubt it would ever have entered my mother's head that any of her four children would turn out to be anything less than beautiful. But, for the sake of compromise, she did agree at the last minute to call me Caroline, after the opulent yacht owned by a friend of theirs the philanthropist and founder of the Victrola gramophone, Eldridge Reeves "E.R." Johnson, that sailed into my mother's home port of Dubrovnik every summer.

And so, as my godmother, Olga Horstig, cradled me in her arms in the twelve-century parish church of St. Peter & St. Paul in Godalming, I was baptized, Caroline Bella Kennedy.

Missing from this ceremony were my older sisters, 5 year-old twins Marina and Tessa. As a precaution for their own safety, and like many other British children during the war, the twins had been evacuated two years earlier. They had flown to the US in the care of my Jugoslav grandparents, Bozidar and Milica Banac, and were heralded by the newspapers upon their arrival at Idlewild Airport in New York as "*the first pair of twins to fly the Atlantic*". They spent the rest of the war in the company of my grandparents, my Aunt June and our cousin, Bozo, in a sprawling house in Nyack, Long Island.

Sadly, these evacuations created not only disruption within families and communities but, in many cases, complete estrangement for several years. Sometimes, as in my sisters' case, this forced separation came at a very impressionable young age when children and parents were supposed to be bonding. As a consequence of their absence, I did not get to meet my older siblings until I was two years old.

My mother, father and two-year-old brother, Alexander, remained at *Orchards*, a gabled house in Godalming, designed by the renowned British architect Edwin Lutyens. *Orchards* was surrounded by extensive gardens, complete with pergola and rose garden, created by the equally famous British horticulturist and photographer, Gertrude Jekyll.

Even at the height of the war, my father was never conscripted into the Armed Forces. The government needed civil and consulting engineers to work for the war effort and my father's firm, Kennedy & Donkin, was tasked to do just that. This meant that my father was commuting daily to his office in Caxton Street, London, which put an immediate strain on my parents' relationship. My mother hated the countryside. Used to a carefree life of luxurious travel, five- star hotels and expensive restaurants, she found it difficult to adapt to the tranquility and drabness of postwar Britain while looking after two young children. So, when I was 6 months old, my parents employed Daphne Summersell, an 18-year-old graduate from the highly respected Norland College of Nursing, to be the full-time nanny for Alexander and me. This was probably the best choice they ever made together. "Daphie", as she came to be known to us, was loving, warm, kind, honest, capable, uncomplaining, loyal and very caring.

Over the next three years, my mother became increasingly discontented with country life. She loved the city, she loved being close to her mother and older brother and, with President Tito of Jugoslavia having banned her and her family from ever returning to their birthplace, London had become their adopted home. She desperately wanted her own family to move there. My father, on the other hand, could only feel at home surrounded by nature and in the chaotic company of children, dogs, cats, hens, rabbits, guinea pigs, horses and donkeys. In a very short time, it became a rift that could not easily be healed.

In 1948, on a summer holiday, in a villa overlooking Lake Lugano, my father, his four children and Daphie waited for my mother to join them. She sent a telegram announcing that she wouldn't be coming. From that moment my father knew the marriage had ended. I only learned this many decades later, when Daddy was terminally ill himself. He, Daphie and I drove from the UK to the Swiss Alps, a place he truly loved. We visited many of the spots which had come to be his favourite haunts over his lifetime. On that trip he told us he wanted to spend at least one night in a hotel overlooking Lake Lugano. And the following morning I found him weeping silently on the balcony gazing out over the lake. Daphie ushered me out of the room and whispered that directly across the lake from their balcony was the house where we had all spent the summer of 1948, when my mother had sent the telegram announcing she would not be joining us, that the marriage had ended. I guess this was the first time my father had had a chance to exorcise this most painful moment of his life.

For me and my brother, my parents' break-up was not too difficult to accept. After all, Daphie had taken care of us since I was a baby. But, for my sisters, it was understandably more difficult. Our mother had been the only mother they had known.

During her time in London, Mummy had converted from her Serbian Orthodox denomination to Catholicism. And, in 1948, during a visit to the Vatican to request the annulment of her marriage to Geoff, she quietly married the man with whom she had recently fallen in love, a swash-buckling former Royal Scots Greys cavalry officer, Neil "Billy" McLean, whose base was London but whose adventurous life would lead him to many remote countries all over the world, working undercover for the British government.

Chapter 2
The Early Years

Following the marriage break-up, our family moved to Tilford, a village in Surrey. The house was called *Pinewood*, a bungalow with an enormous, multi-levelled garden. As a single father of four, Daddy came to depend on Daphie more and more. And, in 1952, they were married. To me, their marriage seemed so natural and inevitable. Nothing changed as Daphie had been in my life from the start. I felt very blessed. I had two mothers, both of whom loved me and I loved them.

Sadly, as a consequence of my mother leaving home when I was four, I have very few early memories of her. The divorce courts in England were not as kind to her as the divorce courts in Jugoslavia had been to my grandmother, Milica, when she left my grandfather to marry the Jugoslav shipping magnate Bozidar "Dundo" Banac. Milica had been awarded custody of her three children, Vane, Daska and Vladimir. Thus, I think my mother truly believed that she, too, would gain custody of her four children when her divorce became final. But, tragically for her, my father was awarded custody of the four of us until the age of 16. The Judge gave my mother permission to see us only for one week at Christmas, one week at Easter and three weeks in the summer. She was devastated. It was a pain she lived with all her life. Of course, it was only after I had children of my own that I could even begin to understand the gaping hole it must have left in her heart all those years.

Needless to say, when she was allowed to see us she spoilt us all terribly to a point where, as an uncomprehending child, I thought my mother must be extremely rich and extravagant and my father extremely poor and frugal! The contrast between their two homes was immense. With my father and Daphie we lived simply in a bungalow in the country. Because of food rationing, we grew our own vegetables, harvested our own fruits and were expected to eat everything that was put on our plates, including stewed tripe and onions, mutton stew and dumplings and bread slathered with beef dripping. We also cared for countless animals, both inside and outside the home.

In complete contrast, in my mother's opulent four-storey Gloucester Square house near Hyde Park, it seemed like there was no rationing at all. There were frequent trips to Harrods, Selfridges and Fortnum & Mason to buy our groceries. Also there were imported goods from Paris and New York. And, if we didn't feel like finishing our food, we could simply leave it. There were no live animals in my mother's home, only her impressive ceramic dog collection gracing almost every step on the four flights of stairs.

With Daphie, we learned to cook, sew, knit and, even, darn socks. With my mother we learned to appreciate paintings, opera, fashion and fine food. There really couldn't have been more of a contrast.

My father and stepfather, too, were vastly different. My father was a responsible family man whereas that could never be said of my stepfather. My father loved being surrounded by children. My stepfather was easily irritated by them. My father worked hard and relaxed by making up stories for us, going for nature walks in the countryside or playing the piano for us and his friends. My stepfather travelled to remote countries for weeks, or even months at a time, more often than not forgetting his responsibilities at home. My father had an occasional cigar or whiskey after dinner, owned and cherished a vintage Bentley and was a self-taught jazz pianist. My stepfather enjoyed smoking cigars and drinking post-prandial liqueurs throughout the day, never owned a car and had little appreciation of music. The only similarity was they were both good raconteurs. I learned my sense of responsibility, honesty, love of nature and love of family from my father. I learned my love of adventure, my appreciation of other cultures and a desire to be a free spirit from my stepfather.

In my early years in Tilford, I was surrounded by animals, including one Welsh Mountain pony, a golden retriever, two cats, two donkeys, several chickens, one bantam hen, umpteen rabbits and guinea pigs and five ponds containing goldfish, frogs and newts. These ponds, covered in purple, pink and white water lilies attracted their own wildlife, hosts of brightly-coloured dragonflies, iridescent blue kingfishers, passing ducks and geese and the occasional solitary heron in search of an easy meal.

Our garden included enormous brightly-hued rhododendron bushes that provided perfect hiding places for our many games of hide-and-seek. Down one side of the garden was a mature wood, full of snowdrops, lilies of the valley, bluebells and bracken. On the far side of the house was an extensive vegetable garden where we tended carrots, cabbages, tomatoes. lettuces, asparagus, onions, peas, runner beans and potatoes. Among them, pear and apple trees had been planted. Alongside there was a large soft-fruits cage, with raspberries, strawberries, redcurrants, blackcurrants and gooseberries.

How Daphie had time to tend to all these as well as caring for my father and four children, I have no idea. I still marvel at the stamina she possessed. Like my father, she was never happier than being surrounded by children, donkeys and dogs while, at the same time, harvesting, freezing and bottling her own fruits and vegetables. Her summer puddings, apple crumbles and gooseberry fools became legendary within the family and beyond.

Every weekend we would go for nature walks to local beauty spots, accompanied by our two Labradors, Honey and Treacle. Daddy would point out edible mushrooms, poisonous toadstools, the various species of trees and wildflowers, nuts and berries, birds and butterflies. Sometimes we would clamber over crumbling stiles, and walk through fields blazing with wild red poppies, bright yellow mustard flowers and deep blue cornflowers. Sometimes we would walk through the local woods with carpets of bluebells under our feet. But, wherever our walks would take us, being the youngest I always lagged behind everyone else. Inevitably, Daddy would have to stop to wait for me to catch up. And, while waiting, if he was close to a patch of clover, he would search for one with four leaves. Amazingly, he rarely failed to find one. Even today, his grandchildren, still remember his uncanny knack of being able to pluck a four-leaved clover from a patch when we could all spend hours searching and always fail to find one. Every evening, when it was time for bed, Daddy would find time to make up a bedtime story. Once we were drowsy he would tuck us up in bed, kiss us goodnight and then he would sit down at the piano and play his favourite jazz melodies until we fell asleep.

Then there were the birthday parties. My father loved birthdays. And he excelled at them. He could spend hours preparing for them, setting up the buns on strings, apples in bowls of water, wrapping the present for "pass the parcel", blowing up countless balloons, making up funny stories, playing the fool and screening old 8mm Charlie Chaplin, Felix the Cat and Our Gang movies. These were always accompanied by howls of laughter from my friends, no matter how many times they had watched them. At the end of the day, like every other day, he would sit down at the piano and we would have a singalong.

Two years after Daddy and Daphie's marriage, Daphie gave birth to a boy, Christopher. I was 10 years old and having been "the baby" of the family until then, I was thrilled at the arrival of my little brother. I was old enough not to be jealous of the attention he received and yet young enough to enjoy playing with him, feeding him and getting him dressed. He was "my baby" and I probably treated him as such, even with the passing of the decades.

Three years later, in 1957, Daphie gave birth to a second boy, Anthony. Daddy now had three sons and three daughters. And that number, he decided was enough. Daphie, who had been looking after the four of us like we were her own children, now had her own. She was overjoyed and, although outwardly, she never showed any difference between her affections for any of us, I know she was, understandably, thrilled finally to be a "real" mother.

Now with an expanded family, we moved from *Pinewood* to *Lowsley House*, a large, white-stuccoed family home in Liphook, Hampshire, complete with swimming pool, tennis court, stables, apple orchard and vegetable garden. Cattle and sheep grazed in the surrounding fields and, much to the amusement of us children, our neighbour was Boris Karloff, the actor whose iconic role had been to play the monster in the 1931 Frankenstein movie!

The nature walks continued, to nearby hiking trails with poetic names such as, *Weavers' Down, Waggoners' Wells* and *The Devil's Punchbowl*. In Spring we would walk through the bluebell woods on Telegraph Hill. In summer we would barbecue by the pool, swim and play tennis. And, in winter, we would taboggan down the slopes near the home of Sir Arthur Conan Doyle (author of *Sherlock Holmes*) in Hindhead. In winter, too, Daddy and Daphie would swim every morning before breakfast. When ice formed on the surface of the pool, they simply placed logs to break it up and swam between the logs! They were strong. They were hardy. And they were devoted. They were a team, a truly loving team and, without knowing it back then, I was grateful for their example.

But, first and foremost, their wish was to provide a stable, happy family home for us children and, later, their many grandchildren. Towards the end of my father's life, I asked him where he had learned to be such a loving parent and grandparent.

"I guess it was a reaction to my own family," he said. "Neither of my parents were very demonstrative. They were very formal and Edwardian. They were quite wrapped up in their own lives. And, as for my grandfather, I don't remember ever receiving a handshake, let alone a kiss from him. He was very distant and cold. He hardly ever spoke to me at all."

I was saddened that he had never thought to share this with me before. And it made me appreciate him even more. So, when I look back on my life now, I know that it was a mix of all their attributes that made me the inquisitive wanderer I became. I realize now how blessed I was. Sadly, I can't be sure I acknowledged it at the time. As a child, I simply accepted what I had as normal.

Chapter 3
Summers in Mallorca, Winters in Scotland

In 1947 my mother's older brother, Vane Ivanovic, bought a house in Formentor, Mallorca. This was several years before the island became a popular tourist destination for many Europeans seeking the sun. Every summer my mother brought the four of us out for three weeks to the house in Formentor, which came to be known as *Casa Ivanovic*. In those days, there was no airport there. We took a normal flight from London to Barcelona and then boarded a small bi-plane to Palma, landing in a field and scattering grazing sheep and goats. On arrival we passed by a rudimentary immigration desk, in a makeshift terminal, carrying our luggage straight from the plane to my Uncle's pink Cadillac Estate Wagon, which was waiting for us outside.

In Formentor, days would begin early for some. My Uncle Vane, formerly an Olympic hurdler was also an avid spearfisherman, even publishing a book in 1952, entitled, *Modern Spearfishing*. Family members and guests who shared his passion would go out on the boat with him at dawn and return with the daily catch around lunchtime after a sumptuous picnic breakfast on board his boat, the Taro. In those days, Formentor Beach was our own personal domain. Situated over the opposite side of the bay from *Casa Ivanovic*, we often swam across to the beach and had the place to ourselves for as long as we wanted. As children, we spent much of our time in the water. Even on days when there was a giant swell and large waves broke over the rocks, our parents calmly watched us as we were swept off the bathing platforms and into the raging sea. It was exhilarating and terrifying at the same time.

Lunches were long and languorous affairs as our parents and friends spent hours talking, swilling the remnants of their wine, sipping liqueurs, smoking cigars and watching my Uncle Vane deftly turn the making of Turkish coffee into a spectator sport. By the time lunches were over, everyone was ready for the compulsory two-hour siesta, after which there would be more swimming until it was time to change for the evening meal.

Occasionally, when the cook had the evening off, we would drive into Puerto de Pollensa at night for dinner. At that time there were only a couple of hotels, restaurants and shops along the sea front. Even so, these evenings in the Port were a welcome diversion. The car ride there and back was a hair-raising experience. Several of us children piled onto the luggage rack on the roof of the car and held on for dear life! Thinking back, I can't imagine how our parents permitted this dangerous exercise. Alcohol consumption combined with the numerous hairpin bends on the unlit mountain road back to Formentor, would have presented a challenge even to the most skilled driver. Narrow in width and with no barrier along the outer edge, cars, buses and trucks regularly teetered off the side of the mountain, ending up on the rocks below. It was a miracle we arrived home intact every time. It was terrifying and very treacherous but thrilling to us children.

In the fifties and early sixties, Mallorca and, particularly, Formentor, became home to an eclectic, diverse and, occasionally, dubious cast of characters. Some retreated there for solitude, some to escape the law or prying eyes and some, simply, to party and have fun all summer long. I often thought that for a budding writer such as me, there were all the elements of a novel there waiting to be written. *Maybe one day,* I thought, *I would write it!*

Close neighbours included, Otto Skorzeny, the infamous Austrian-born Nazi SS Officer, best known for his daring rescue of Benito Mussolini from an internment camp in the Abruzzi Mountains and for his steadfast loyalty to the Fuhrer, Adolf Hitler. Then there was the Venezuelan beauty, the wildly flirtatious, Mercedes Herrera Benecerraf, daughter-in-law of an extremely wealthy banking family and niece of Caracas's most notorious millionaire international playboy, Reinaldo Herrera. Our next-door neighbour was Whitney Straight, a former dashing fighter pilot and racing driver who, after the war, became Chairman of Rolls Royce and CEO of British Airways. Beside the Hotel Formentor lived Barbara Goalen, once known as Britain's "most photographed woman" A highly-paid post-war model, Barbara still retained the wasp-like figure and the striking sculpted looks of her glory days. Completing the set, in a grand house, above Casa Ivanovic, lived a rich Austrian widowed countess, Veronika Kloiber, who thought nothing of flying over the world-famous conductor, Herbert Von Karayan, and members of the Berlin Philharmonic for an impromptu musical evening in her garden, complete with huge tins of imported caviar, French champagne and a midnight fireworks display.

Neighbours slightly further away included the iconic poet, Robert Graves, who, from 1929 till his death in 1985, had made his home in Deya and where scores of poetry junkies could be seen lined up at his gate every day eager to catch a glimpse of him. Then there was Ann Woodward, the notorious New York socialite, who had murdered her husband, Billy, and who was exiled by her matriarch mother-in-law to avoid the gossiping society of Long Island. Ann wintered in St. Moritz and summered in a secluded house in the nearby town of Pollensa. She became a woman of great intrigue to us, in our teenage years, as delectably raunchy stories of her alcohol and drug-fuelled orgies with her young male guests reached us in Formentor. One such story involved her being brought to a hospital in Palma to have a coca cola bottle extricated from her vagina. Whether this was true or simply one of the numerous stories that her notoriety evoked, I don't know. But, as teenagers, we were more than ready to believe it! And I knew Truman Capote would have relished it and added yet another salacious paragraph to his already explosive article about her in his Esquire article, *"La Cote Basque."*

Many years later in 1969 my mother decided to build her own house, across the bay in Malpas. She chose a beautiful coastal property, spread over several acres, with its own bay facing the evening sunsets. The house she created was stunning from all vantage points. She designed it and was involved in every aspect of building it, working closely with a local architect. She selected all the furnishings, many of which she inherited from her mother Milica, who died earlier that year. She named the property, *La Guarda*. From 1970 onwards my siblings and I visited every summer with our children so that they, too, were able to form their own memories of Mallorca.

One summer, Princess Margaret came to stay in Formentor. Naturally, my mother and my Aunt and Uncle scrambled to be the first to send out handwritten letters to the Princess inviting her to come to *Casa Ivanovic* and *La Guarda* for lunch. Without hesitation, and to their delight, the Princess accepted both invitations. Grand preparations were made, menus were discussed, bottles of imported gin were bought, seating arrangements were planned, dresses were selected and the general air of anticipation was tangible. All I remember about the lunch at my Uncle's house was the shrill voice of Princess Margaret asking, "Do you happen to run to mustard in this house?"

This was met with a stunned silence. My aunt and uncle shook their heads. They had thought of absolutely everything the Princess could have possibly wanted but they had not thought of mustard!

At lunch at my mother's house, again we were all asked to dress up as elegantly as we could. "After all," Mummy told us, "We are entertaining Royalty!"

But then we were amused when, rather than changing into a dress herself, Princess Margaret remained in her nylon drip-dry swimsuit throughout the meal. Seated next to my stepfather, Billy, the Princess downed her gin and tonics with gusto, while the others genteelly sipped their wine. And my young daughter, 2-year-old Mayumi, who was used to sitting next to Billy, came up to the Princess and declared, "You naughty girl. You're sitting in my place!"

We weren't quite sure whether to ignore it or to laugh. We waited. Finally, the Princess smiled graciously and apologized to Mayumi but refused to give up her seat. This was just as well as, when she did finally get up from the table, the cushion she had sat on in her drip-dry nylon bathing suit was soaking wet.

My Uncle and Aunt sold *Casa Ivanovic* in the late 80s, having owned it for almost 40 years. My mother, too, sold *La Guarda* in 1995 when it became too much of a responsibility for her and too much of a drain on her resources.

It was not until late September 2022 that I returned to Mallorca. But this time was for the saddest of reasons. My son, Elisar, died of metastatic colon cancer in 2020 and his last wish was for his ashes to be scattered in the bay in front of my mother's house where he had spent so many carefree summers. Sadly, due to the pandemic, it took two years for his wish to be fulfilled. But finally, on October 4 2022, with my daughter Mayumi and her family, my brother Alexander and his wife Doris, my nieces, Natasa and Leonella, and Elisar's friend and collaborator, Ian Powell, we carried out Elisar's final wish. Our friend over many summers, Alan Ponte, kindly lent us his boat for the occasion and provided a truly memorable picnic. Then we all watched in silence as the flowers and ashes, in a white and orange spiral, drifted on the tide towards my mother's bay. Slowly, sinking beneath the surface, they vanished into the depths of the Mediterranean. And, with them, drowned a large portion of my heart and the still vivid memories of all our childhoods.

Winters in Scotland

In 1954, when I was ten years old, my stepfather, Billy, became Member of Parliament for Inverness-shire. And, since, as an MP he was required to be a resident in his constituency, he and my mother rented a Georgian house, *Eskadale* near Beauly, on the Lovat Estate. And it was there we would spend our Easter and winter holidays along with my uncle, aunt and cousins, Bozo, Minja and Andrija.

At one time the Lovat Estate encompassed a large swathe of the Highlands, stretching from the east coast to the west. The Chiefs of the Lovat/Fraser clan who ruled this part of Scotland were a colourful bunch of characters. In 1745 during the Rebellion the then Lord Lovat, known as "*The Fox*", backed the wrong side when Bonnie Prince Charlie's Jacobites lost at the battle of Culloden Moor and, thus, "*The Fox*" became the last peer to be beheaded for treason in England.

The Lord Lovat we knew, Shimi Lovat, our friend and landlord, was the 25th Chief of the Clan Fraser. He was a much-decorated World War II hero, who, with his personal bagpiper at his side, led his commando unit onto the Sword Beach of Normandy, successfully capturing the Pegasus Bridge. This scene was recreated in the 1962 epic war movie, *The Longest Day*, with Shimi being portrayed by Peter Lawford.

As children, we loved the freedom these Scottish holidays offered. We could spend all day away from the house, tobogganing down the snow-covered hills, fishing in the rivers, climbing the *Cuckoo Stones* (the ancient standing rocks) and only returning in the evening for dinner. No one ever worried about our safety. We flushed pheasants out of the local woods in "shooting season". We fished for salmon and trout in the local rivers and lakes. We rode our rented ponies over the heather-covered moors. And then, in the evenings, we would sit around the log fire playing my mother's favourite card game, Canasta, or Mah Jong well into the night.

My stepfather's Highland constituents were not quite sure what to make of my mother and her family. It was during the Cold War so anti-Russian sentiment was very strong at the time. And, because Jugoslavia was then a Communist country, many of them equated it with Russia. There were many comments about Colonel McLean's "Russkie" wife, and others about his family playing some strange card game called, "Canoostie". I could certainly sympathize with their bewilderment. Despite Billy's genuine Highland roots, we were certainly no ordinary Scottish family. The Ethiopians, Yemenis and Pakistanis who had so often frequented Billy's room in our London flat, started visiting him in Inverness-shire. Again, this raised many eyebrows and became the subject of local gossip as only a handful of people who were close to us were aware of their local Member of Parliament's other, more clandestine, life.

Although Mummy dressed conservatively, much like the locals, in tweeds, tartans and twin-sets during the winter months, she often wore her more eye-catching Emilio Pucci slacks and tops during the summer. But she was a good political wife happy to open fetes, shake countless hands, attend rural functions and smile at everyone, She visited sick constituents, she bought birthday presents for local children and she constantly acted as a chauffeur to the elderly. And, despite, disliking the English countryside as much as she did while living with my father, she adapted well to the Highlands, never once complaining about her rural environment.

Not unexpectedly, Billy lost his seat in the Labour landslide election of 1964. Our Scottish holidays were, sadly, a thing of the past. But the lure of the Highlands has never left me. Its wild, deserted landscapes still beckon. And, whenever I hear the bagpipes playing, my Scottish memories just keep flooding back.

Chapter 4
The Swimming Team

When I was approaching 11-years-old, I was sent off to boarding school. The school that Daddy chose for me was *Tortington Park* just outside the historic market town of Arundel in Sussex. Close to the magnificent, medieval castle, the school was less than two hours' drive from *Pinewood*. Despite my initial reservations, I immediately loved everything about the school. I was quick to make friends, I relished Latin, Current Affairs, Drama and Public Speaking. I loved the fact students were allowed to keep pet rabbits, guinea pigs or gerbils, as long as we cleaned them out and only cared for them in our spare time and not in school time. One time I even found a tiny orphaned baby bat and reared it in a discarded rabbit hutch until it was ready to fly away.

Even though I didn't work too hard, my reports always stated that I excelled in all subjects, with the exception of Maths. I might have had a prodigious memory but, sadly, although it worked with words, it never worked with numbers.

The three sports I enjoyed most were fencing, archery and swimming. The first two were so uncommon in British schools that we actually boasted British Olympic champions in both sports. As for swimming, I became a junior champion early on and was immediately selected to be on the school team, even though I was far younger than my team-mates. I loved being on the team. It meant I could miss doing homework, although I was supposed to do it in my spare time.

Our swimming coach was Miss Hockney, or "Hockers", as we called her. Since I was the youngest on the team, Hockers selected one of the seniors, Mary Lyneham, to coach me every lunch hour. I was in awe of Mary who was long-limbed, had pale olive skin, grey eyes and seemed to be popular with everyone. But she was also a bit of an enigma. No one had met her parents. No one knew where she spent her holidays. And no one had been invited to her house to meet her family. I was intrigued and determined to find out more about her.

So, day after day, at lunchtime Mary and I ate our prepared sandwiches by the swimming pool and then had an hour of training. And, later in the day when classes had finished Hockers and the other ten members of our team, met up with us at the pool for our evening training session.

Hockers had also made Mary in charge of the record player. Mary brought it to the poolside every evening, unpacked it from its box, and connected it to the plug on the outside wall of the changing rooms. And, at the end of the evening, she would box it up again and return it to the Headmistress's office.

This then became our daily routine. Slowly, I got to know more about Mary. Her father was in the Army, in Jaipur at the time. Her mother was a normal Army wife. And her older brother had died before the family left for India and was buried in the family burial plot in Plymouth.

"Do you go to India for your holidays then?" I asked Mary one lunchtime, as we ate our sandwiches.

She shook her head. "No, my parents can't afford to bring me there," she replied somewhat wistfully.

"Do they come here then? Or where do you spend your holidays?" I was genuinely curious.

"No, they can't afford that either," she replied. "Sometimes I spend the holidays with my aunt, sometimes with family friends."

I asked her where she was going to spend this summer holiday. And she shook her head. "I don't know. But Hockers, has invited me to stay with her."

There was something here as a twelve year old I didn't quite understand. I could see that Hockers and Mary were very fond of each other. In fact, there had been rumours in school about their blossoming friendship. But, at that age, I didn't know what the rumours meant. All I noticed was that they appeared very relaxed and happy in each other's company.

That summer had a rhythm of its own. Under the coaching of Hockers, our team won several inter-school championships. And we were hailed by the rest of the students and faculty as heroes every time we placed another silver cup on the Championship shelf.

After a particularly exhausting practice one Saturday afternoon, Mary took me to Hockers' rooms. I felt so special as students, particularly jumiors, were never invited to the faculty's private rooms. Mary and Hockers sat on the sofa smoking. The record player was playing Elvis and, to my delight, Hockers' cat, Micky, came to sit on my lap, purring. I sat on the floor playing with him as Hockers and Mary whispered and giggled together.

A few weeks later, when we were just ending our relay race, Hockers approached the edge of the pool. "Right," she said, "that's enough for this evening.

Tomorrow it's a new foe – Cheltenham Ladies College. They're supposed to be excellent. But I know you can beat them. You won't let me down, will you?"

We all shouted "No!" so loudly, as we scrambled out of the pool, that I was sure our voices must have carried all the way to the school dining room.

"Good!" said Hockers, "You are the best! I am so proud of you!"

We chatted excitedly. Mary smiled at me. "And I'm proud of you," she said to me. "You've done wonders!"

Miss Hockney approached us. She casually put her arm around Mary's shoulder.

"And you've done wonders with her, Mary!" she said. "You'll be after my job next!" They both laughed. They appeared so comfortable and at ease together. I was glad Mary was going to stay with Miss Hockney during the long summer holiday.

We started walking towards the changing rooms. As she always did at the end of our training sessions, Mary bent down to unplug the record player. Just at that moment Micky appeared around the corner of the building. For a second Mary's attention was diverted. She smiled at the him. And then it happened. Her wet fingers came into contact with the live pins of the plug as it came away from the wall. Her body went into severe spasms, her beautiful dark grey eyes bulged in their sockets and her limbs went rigid until she finally sank onto the terracotta tiles.

At first we stood transfixed, unable to move. Then someone screamed for an ambulance as Miss Hockney bent down and started to reach out to Mary. Then someone else shouted, "Don't touch her! Don't touch her! She still has the live plug in her hand!" And Miss Hockney jumped back away from Mary's body.

"Call for an ambulance! Quick!" she shouted, her fists clenched, her eyes welling up in tears. One girl rushed towards the school shouting for help.

I can't remember what I did. All I can remember of that moment was willing Mary to live. Over and over again in my mind I was saying, "Please Mary, live, please Mary don't die!"

But fate had decided otherwise. Mary did die. According to Hockers, there was nothing the doctors at the local hospital could do to save her. As Miss Hockney sat by her bedside, Mary struggled for five days, blind, deaf and dumb until her heart finally succumbed.

I was 12. I was just a child. I was also a good swimmer. During the summer, under Mary's dedicated guidance, I had become a far better swimmer. But, more importantly to me, I had become Mary's friend and confidante.

This was the first time in my young life that I had seen death up close. Before this death had never been real, just something people spoke about with sad expressions and muffled voices. And for decades following that dreadful day I suffered nightmares about that moment, that fatal moment Hockers' cat, Micky, appeared around the corner of the changing rooms and Mary Lyneham, her still wet fingers gripping the live electric plug, looked at him one last time and smiled.

The saddest thing of all was that Mary's parents did not even fly to England from Jaipur to attend the funeral. Mary was buried in the small abandoned churchyard next to the school. Only the school faculty, Mary's classmates and members of the swimming team were allowed to attend.

Throughout the service I watched Miss Hockney's face. It seemed to me she was trying hard to conceal her true feelings. To show her grief would be to announce to the rest of the school faculty, that Mary Lyneham was special to her. That Mary Lyneham was, indeed, the swimming teacher's pet. That Mary Lyneham meant more to her than she did to her own parents. I now know for certain that Shirley Hockney truly loved Mary Lyneham. And that Mary Lyneham, the girl without a caring family, accepted that love with immense gratitude.

I can't remember exactly how many years I suffered from flashbacks from this traumatic incident. It affected me deeply and probably impelled me to behave so badly at school that the headmistress, Miss Bevan, finally told my father it would be better to remove me from *Tortington Park*. Today, I suppose, I would have been diagnosed with PTSD. But, at that time, only members of the Armed Forces involved in close combat would be analyzed with that condition. And so, it was ignored and the nightmares and flashbacks just carried on unchecked for several years.

Maybe it was because of this incident that I became totally addicted to books by or about early European adventurers - Magellan, Lawrence of Arabia, Gertrude Bell, Freya Stark. Stories about The Great Game, the Silk Route and early travellers to the NorthWest Frontier and beyond. They acted, I suspect, as a form of escapism, a way of exorcising my mind of Mary's hideous ending. They fired my imagination and made me all the more determined to travel the world.

For me, unlike my friends, there was no talk of going to University. I didn't want to waste any more years on my education when, as I saw it, I could get my education from seeing the world, learning about other cultures and, perhaps, living among remote tribes. Who knows, perhaps I would end up living alongside the Yanomami in the Amazonian rainforest, or among the Bushmen of the Kalahari, or among the Hmong hill tribe of SE Asia. As I saw it, the world was waiting for me and I was ready to experience it. I would be there. A move to London would provide my first stepping stone.

Chapter 5
The Reluctant Debutante

When I left school three months after my 16th birthday, I knew I had a monumental decision to make, whether to continue to live with my father or go to live with my mother in London. While my parents' divorce settlement in 1944, had meant my father had custody of me and my three older siblings until we were 16, we were then given the choice of which parent we wanted to live with.

Five years earlier, my sisters had already made that choice. After a summer holiday in Mallorca with my mother, they decided to return with her to London. I knew Daddy was very hurt by their decision. He referred to it many times afterwards. On the other hand, at aged 16, my brother Alexander had decided to continue to live with Daddy as he was planning to join the family firm of Kennedy & Donkin.

I hated having to choose. I wished the Court had made that decision for me. I knew it was a lose-lose situation. If I chose to live with my mother, I knew my father and Daphie would feel very betrayed. But, if I chose to continue living with my father, my mother would be devastated.

In the end, I decided the prospect of moving to London was too exciting an opportunity to turn down. I dreaded the conversation with Daddy. But I knew I had to face up to it. I decided I wouldn't simply copy the twins. I would talk to him, show him what a painful decision it was for me to make. To this day I still remember our conversation vividly. We both cried copiously. His response, when it came, ripped through me.

"You're casting me off like an old sock! Why?"

It was impossible to explain. I loved my life with him, Daphie and the boys. But, aside from what London had to offer, I also felt Mummy had missed out on sixteen years of my life and I could only imagine how much she had suffered. I wanted to make it up to her in some way.

We sat there for a while, crying silently. Each with our own thoughts. There was nothing left to say. Nothing he could say would dissuade me. Nothing I could say would ease his pain.

In preparation for my arrival, Mummy decorated the small spare room for me in her new duplex flat at 17 Eaton Square to make it look like a conservatory. It had a green trellis all the way up one wall, with a painted backdrop of climbing flowers. There was a green sofa bed and a small desk with a bookshelf under the window that overlooked her garden below.

But, it seemed that no sooner had I moved to London, than my mother decided I should be "finished off" at a Swiss finishing school. So I attended Institut Videmanette near Gstaad, to improve my French. But the draw of London was too much and, after only 3 months, once the ski season had ended, I returned home. A year later, Mummy decided it was time for me to "come out". And, of course, I had to be properly attired for the "coming out season". So she took me to off to Paris, bought me two Dior dresses and "launched" me into a round of stupefyingly dull parties "to meet the right type of man!"

Back in 1956, my sisters' debutante season had been an elaborate affair. The ballroom of the Dorchester Hotel had been transformed into a tropical paradise and remained the talk of London for many years afterward. I had absolutely no wish to follow suit. If I was to have a party it would be a more discreet affair. Much to Mummy's disappointment, I became the quintessential reluctant debutante, attending as few functions as I could. Dressing up for Ascot was my idea of hell, particularly the idea of wearing a hat. Attending daily lunch parties and nightly dances only increased my desire to travel and get away from it all. I didn't want to join the social circuit. I didn't want to settle down with "the right type of man". I simply wanted to travel the world and write.

My stepfather, Billy, sympathized with me. He knew my dreams were focused elsewhere. Living in Eaton Square with him was endlessly fascinating. Visitors from remote countries, like Yemen, Turkmenistan, the Hindu Kush, Ethiopia, Pakistan and the Congo would come and go every day, firing my fertile imagination as they whispered about plotting coups, daring rescues and secret meetings, while leaning back in armchairs, puffing cigars and sipping brandy. I was happy to listen in. I still did not know, at that time, what Billy actually did for a living. On the surface, he was the Member of Parliament for Inverness-shire, that I knew, but neither my family nor his constituents had little clue about what he was really up to. He would disappear for weeks at a time, rarely saying where he was going and never telling us when he would be back. He was enigmatic. He was bold. He was daring. In my young eyes, he was a true adventurer.

I made up my mind that, as soon as my "debut season" was over, I was going to leave. Although I loved "swinging" London, I loved lunches with my friends at The Chelsea Kitchen, I loved evenings at the Cafe des Artistes and I loved paying 20 pence to see a double feature at the Classic Cinema in Chelsea, but it was not where I wanted to be.

The decision about where I would go first on my life's journey arrived when I went to New York for the debutante party of my cousin, Daska. My grandmother, Milica, flew me there first class and I made up my mind that New York would be the first stop on my life's journey.

As the porter placed our luggage on the scale at the airline ticket desk in Paris, the Air France attendant spluttered, "Oh, but I'm afraid, Madam, you're 100 kilos overweight!"

"Don't be afraid, young man!" my grandmother retorted. "And don't speak to me in kilos! Speak to me in dollars!"

The poor young man gulped. My grandmother turned to me and whispered in my ear, slightly too loudly. "He's the silliest little man in the whole wordl. He doesn't know what he's talking about!"

She removed a large bundle of crisp, clean notes from her bag and flung it on his desk. "I think this is enough!"

She grabbed the boarding passes from his hand and flounced off, leaving the attendant waving the bundle of notes, protesting, "Mais c'est trop, Madame, c'est trop!"

After the week in New York, I decided that, as soon as I returned to London, I would apply for my green card. It was the early 60s. My friend, Ming, from my Swiss finishing school, had been inundating me with letters and phone calls to join her in New York.

"It's so easy to find jobs and boyfriends," she wrote. "They just love our English accents!"

Well, I thought, man had made it to the moon. Why shouldn't I make it to the Big Apple? Not realizing that if I did my life would change quite so dramatically.

Chapter 6
New York, New York

As soon as I arrived in New York I moved into a cheap second-floor walk-up apartment on 59th Street, between 3rd Avenue and the 59th Street Bridge, made world-famous by the singer-songwriting team of Simon and Garfunkel. The location of the flat was, in my view, perfect. Half a block from Third Avenue, it was a street boasting literally dozens of junk shops, many of them set behind drab facades, broken shutters and dirty windows. Once inside, however, their dusty interiors revealed bargains galore for an insatiable collector like me. Strolling through them on a lazy Saturday afternoon was my idea of heaven.

The other advantage of living near 59th & Third Avenue, I soon discovered, was that I was close enough to Bloomingdales to make sure I never ran out of cheap underwear, near enough to Howard Johnson's to satisfy my daily craving for any one of their 37 flavours of ice cream. And within walking distance to P.J. Clarkes, the famous Irish pub, to arrange meetings with friends after work in a relaxed environment. Not that I drank in those days. I remained a teetotaller until I was 39.

My flatmate Ming had moved to New York a few months earlier. A few friends and I had given her a leaving party at the Red Lion Pub in London's Mayfair. During the evening a man approached me, who introduced himself to me as "George". He seemed pleasant enough and we all ended the evening at his opulent house nearby. Although there were clues from the many photographs in his living room, that "George" was no ordinary man, we only discovered his true identity the following day. There, gazing out at us from the gossip pages of the Daily Express, was a photo of "George", who was, in fact, the multi-millionaire George Huntington Hartford, heir to the A & P grocery chain. He and I were to remain good friends for many years.

By the 31st December 1963, New York was in the grip of what was to become one of its longest and coldest winters on record. It would continue, almost unabated, until late April. But, despite the big freeze and despite the sense of shock that still pervaded the American psyche over the recent assassination of President Kennedy, it was obvious to a new arrival like me that society-conscious New Yorkers were welcoming in the New Year much as they always had done.

Festively-attired diners drew up in their chauffeured cars to dine at the Rainbow Room, atop the Rockefeller Plaza. They popped champagne corks, snapped crackers, and counted down the seconds to midnight. And, when the Lester Lanin Orchestra struck the hour, they rose from their chairs, linked arms and sang Auld Lang Syne as they did every year. In the early hours of the morning, their collective voices still clearly echoed in the streets below, as Ming, our dates, Rupert and Mandy and I, wrapped in mufflers, fur hats and woolly mittens, were making our way slowly home after saluting in the New Year in front of the giant screen in Times Square.

Although Ming and I had been invited to several parties that night, I had pleaded my case as to where we should go. I felt for my first New Year's Eve in Manhattan I should experience the event as most New Yorkers celebrated it. And Rupert and Mandy, more than a little bored of the party circuit, indulged me by accompanying us to Times Square.

So now, as we battled our way home, heads bowed against the biting wind, we took temporary shelter in the brightly lit doorways of some of New York's most famous stores, Bonwit Tellers, Saks, H.O. Schwarz and Tiffany's. Their Christmas windows, ablaze and seductive with seasonal displays of expensive gifts and merchandise, lit our way as we tiptoed perilously through the ice and snow. And as we reached the corner of each intersection we paused a moment to take in an icy breath before leaping into the street to avoid stepping into the knee-high slush.

For over a month, this freezing, penetrating wind sliced through the cross streets, causing injuries as it drew the breath right out of people's lungs, blew dirt and debris in their faces and knocked the unsuspecting ones clean off their feet. New York hospitals admitted a record number of patients that winter, suffering from broken arms and legs or, like me, with fragments of grit or glass lodged in their eyes.

Those of us lucky enough to reside in our uptown apartments were able to respond to the sub-zero conditions by turning up our heating systems to bask in sweltering, almost tropical, temperatures. But, on a tip from a friend who worked for the Urban League in Harlem, I made my way uptown in the hopes of submitting my first story for a New York newspaper. There, at 6 West 118th Street, I discovered the tenants were not so fortunate.

In fact, one of the tenants, Mrs Addie Lewis, told us few determined journalists shivering outside the long-neglected, poorly maintained Harlem building, "we are so cold we are forced to carry our mattresses into our kitchens."

There, according to Mrs Lewis, they would sleep on the floor huddled around their gas stoves with pans of scalding water placed beside their babies and toddlers in order to keep them warm.

"We have gone on strike," she continued, "because of the filthy, drafty, insanitary conditions. And because we are plagued with rats."

As a few of us journalists scribbled away in our notebooks, she added, "We have plenty of rats. We have plenty of roaches. We have no heat. We only have one radiator and that leaks. And that's the truth of it! Go tell that to your editors!"

A month or so later, I listened to President Lyndon B. Johnson, in his State of the Nation address, as he recognized the appalling circumstances facing an estimated 35 million people living in such squalour. He referred to them as "the forgotten fifth of our nation who are living in substandard conditions" and he vowed to wage a war on poverty.

For my first few weeks in the city, in between hunting around for freelance writing jobs, I attended the Art Students League. As with many art establishments, the school had its share of dilettantes but the majority of the students were serious and the standard was pretty high.

Many of the boys, excited by a fresh face from "Swinging London", invited me out on dates but I resisted. Ming said she had other plans for me. She had been in New York for some time before I arrived on the scene and was determined to guide me around and introduce me to her wide circle of friends. Ming was a party animal and she was keen to convert me to all the pleasures, that New York offered.

"No beatnik art students for you, my girl!" she giggled, "I've got other ideas!"

Ming's boyfriend, Rupert Hitzig, was an ardent young television executive. Pleasant-looking, talented and fun-loving, Rupert was also extremely ambitious. He worked for CBS and his future looked bright. Back then none of us could even imagine how bright that future would be. Within a decade he had established himself as a highly respected producer with movies such as *Electra Glide in Blue, Much Ado About Nothing and Return to Earth* under his belt.

Rupert had introduced me to Manny, a gangly, shy young poet, with a shock of dark blonde hair. Ming's disapproval of "beatnik art students" did not, apparently, extend to beatnik poets! And so, for my first two months in New York, the four of us nightly combed the city's most popular discos.

Probably we would have continued as a foursome if I hadn't met Caterine Milinaire. Caterine, the stunning, raven-haired daughter of the Duchess of Bedford, was the junior editor at Vogue magazine and she was keen to introduce me to the New York fashion scene. Through her, I got my first designing job making decorative Indian-style belts for a boutique named Paraphernalia that was soon to open on Madison & 67th. Paraphernalia would soon become not only a showcase for new designers like Joel Schumacher, Betsey Johnson, Rudi Gernreich, Mary Quant and Foale & Tuffin but also a social venue, a music venue and an art venue.

Clients included Edie Sedgwick, Dionne Warwick, Lesley Uggams and Aretha Franklin.

At a party one night I bumped into another Anglophile, Robert "Sandy" Lesberg and his wife, Betty. Sandy was a big, bearded redhead with plenty of ambition. His wife was a pretty blonde dominated by her husband's huge personality. Sandy took me aside and, with a self-important air, told me, "I need to talk to you Caroline seriously."

"Yes? What about?" I asked. I had a horrible feeling he might divulge the terrible state of his marriage, in my experience a ploy often used by men prior to an attempted seduction. Happily, though it seemed his marriage was still very much intact.

"I have been offered to front a six-hour radio programme every night on 1010 WINS New York. I'm looking for a team to help put it together. Would you be interested?"

I didn't want to sound too eager but it was hard to disguise the excitement I felt. Fed up with the unpredictability of freelancing, I thought this might offer the chance to fulfill my journalistic ambitions with the added bonus of finally producing a regular salary.

"You bet!" I answered, "What would it involve?"

"I need a producer, well, a couple of them actually. It's a lot of time to fill, six hours a night, six nights a week. All talk. I like your accent too, I can't deny that. You might come over well on radio. How does that sound?"

That sounded even better. Me on the radio, I definitely liked the sound of that.

"I think I could handle it," I assured him nonchalantly. "When can we discuss this properly?"

Sandy grabbed my arm, steered me towards Betty and led the two of us out of the room. Outside the building, he hailed a cab and we headed off to Sardi's to discuss the offer "properly".

By the end of the evening, I was hired. I would work alongside Betty as co-producers of "*The Sandy Lesberg Night Time Program*" on 1010 WINS. The job was to start the following week. I was on top of the world. This was giddy stuff for a girl like me. I had only been in New York a couple of months, I had no contacts to speak of and now a top job had simply fallen into my lap. Perhaps the American Vice Consul had been right. I came from the land of Shakespeare, King Arthur and the Lakeland Poets, maybe it was my English accent that had clinched it. I couldn't wait to get home and tell the waiting trio.

"Good for you!" Rupert enthused, "Soon you'll be joining me at CBS!"

"At this rate, who knows, I could be there next year!" I joked.

Manny hugged me, "I'm real proud of you."

I was overworked and underpaid over the next few months. But it was exhilarating. It gave me the opportunity to call people out of the blue, celebrities, politicians, businessmen, artists, actors and writers to invite them on the show. And I couldn't have wished for better employers. Sandy and Betty were a very positive couple - jovial, intelligent and brimming over with enthusiasm. It didn't take us long to establish a successful routine.

The format for the show included nightly political interviews, round table discussions on current topics, celebrity interviews, music reviews, theatre reviews, film and book reviews, a travel section and poetry reading.

I soon discovered that six hours a night, six nights a week was, as Sandy had warned me it would be, a lot of air time to fill. But I threw myself into it with enthusiasm and everyday it became a little easier. My daily routine was fairly simple. I arrived at the office at around 12pm, spent most of the afternoon on the telephone booking guests for the coming shows, helped tape interviews for the latter half of the programme, stayed on during the evening to receive that night's guests and then, when the last guest had left around 5am, made my way home. Some nights, when Betty and I hadn't procured enough guests or guests failed to turn up at the last minute, Sandy interviewed me about subjects as diverse as Swinging London, holiday travel, the New York social scene and contemporary artists. I started receiving fan mail from as far away as Mississippi, Georgia and Delaware, mainly from long-distance truck drivers who "just loved" my English accent.

During a cab strike I hitched my rides uptown with an early morning laundry cart whose driver, Jimmy, took pity on me one day. In the end it became a regular trip.

"It's on my way," Jimmy explained, "and I get to have some company at this hour of the morning."

"Suits us both then," I replied, pleased that I would no longer have to pay exorbitant rates for a cab to take me home every morning.

One Sunday night, my only night off, I made my excuses to Manny, Rupert and Ming and escaped with Caterine and her boyfriend, Dutch photographer Maurice Hogenboom, to a dinner party hosted by Olivier Coquelin, the French entrepreneur. I didn't know it at the time but my life was about to change forever.

Chapter 7
Carnegie Hall Days

I ignored the knowing glances between Olivier and Caterine as he shook my hand. It appeared to be a wink of approval and, for a brief moment, I had the horrible feeling I might have been brought along by Caterine as a "playmate" for Olivier. But, as he made no specific attempts to chat me up on my arrival, that particular thought soon evaporated. He took me by the arm and ushered me into the living room where a group of people were already drinking and chatting. The introductions were brief and I squeezed myself into a sofa beside Howard Oxenberg, the ex-husband of Princess Elizabeth of Jugoslavia.

"From London?" Howard guessed correctly, breaking the ice.

I nodded, "Yes. Do you know it?"

"Only too well. In fact, the last time I was there I met your Queen."

"Really? How?" I asked.

"I was standing in line with Elizabeth, my then wife, waiting to be introduced to her. Very formal it was. Some stuffy dinner at the Palace. Evening gowns, tiaras and all that."

"I know your ex-wife" I said.

"Oh, how so?" He looked intrigued.

I told him about my Serbo-Croatian lineage and how I'd met Elizabeth and most of her relatives in London over the years. In fact, the long family association had started with our respective grandparents.

"So we're almost related then?" he joked.

"Hardly!" I laughed, "No royal blood in my veins!"

I explained that my grandmother and I had visited Elizabeth in the New York hospital when she had given birth to their second daughter, Christina.

"I even babysat Tina and Catherine in London a few times when Elizabeth was living nearby me in the King's Road."

"No kidding!" he laughed, "Quite a handful my girls, I bet?"

As time passed and people began to get hungry, Olivier announced: "I'm sorry, dinner's a bit late. We're waiting for Joe."

That explanation alone was enough to make everyone smile. It was obvious by their expressions that this Joe, whoever he was, made a habit of being late.

So we filed into dinner. The empty chair reserved for Joe just happened to be, or was obviously intended to be, beside me. We were halfway through the meal, listening intently to Olivier's latest plans for a new nightclub, to be called The Hippodrome when the door opened and Joe Dever walked in. What I saw was a middle-aged man, pale skin, blond hair, slightly effeminate, with a very gentle face. What I also noticed was everyone's face light up with surprise and pleasure. Despite being notoriously unpunctual, it was evident that this Joe was a popular man amongst this group of New Yorkers.

Olivier stood up. "Welcome, Joe. You know everyone, of course!"

Joe looked around, nodding at the assembled gathering. Then he looked at me.

"Not me, yet," I said, holding out my hand.

"Joe, this is Caroline Kennedy. Caroline this is Joe Dever. Why don't you sit right there, Joe, next to her?"

Neither Joe nor I knew at that moment that this was a setup, a blind date arranged by Olivier and Caterine. We shook hands and Joe sank down beside me. We were unable to talk for the first half of dinner as the guest on his other side proceeded to monopolize him in a lengthy discussion about a charity event she would be hosting in a few weeks' time.

"You must come and write about it, Joe, please say you will. Just everyone's going to be there. We're hoping to raise $100,000. Guess what, I've got Sally Rand - remember her? - doing her famous fan dance!"

"Sally Rand?! My God, she must be over 80, isn't she?" someone asked, "Does anyone really want to see her dancing nude on stage at that age?"

The charity organizer looked offended. "Darling, she's still got the most faaaaabulous figure, you'd be sooooo jealous. I'll sell you some tickets in a minute, you really must come see her for yourself."

Joe looked at me and shrugged his shoulders. I could see he was bored but, as I soon learned, being a good listener was all part of his job. And he genuinely enjoyed it, which was probably the secret of his popularity. Unlike other New York gossip columnists Joe was not intoxicated by the sound of his own voice, did not have a gargantuan ego, nor was he in the least bit opinionated. He simply listened quietly and people naturally trusted him.

When he eventually managed to extricate himself from the one-sided conversation Joe immediately turned to me. And, as soon as I spoke he knew where I came from. Like many Americans of his generation, he was a great Anglophile and he had particularly fond memories of his time spent in London. Yet again, I thought, the American Vice Consul in London had been right. New Yorkers, and that included Joe Dever, appeared to be entranced by my English accent.

I have little recollection of what we talked about during dinner but it was enough to know that Joe and I would become, at least, good friends. I was nineteen but looked about 15. Joe was already 45 and looked, possibly, older. But to me at that time anyone over 40 tended to look old. I was impetuous, headstrong and excited at being in New York but, although I didn't realize it then, I was totally out of my depth in a city where the majority of society people I'd met so far had struck me as being phony, jaded and materialistic. I discovered immediately that Joe was none of those things. He was very open with me from the start.

"Listen, darling," he told me, "I have no excuses. I'm a hack writer of a trashy gossip column. I know I could do a lot better but right now this is how I make my living."

Joe, I discovered that night, was also a procrastinator and a dreamer.

"One day, darling," he continued, "I'll write my magnum opus and, believe me, it won't contain one shred of gossip!" He continued to repeat this over the next almost 40 years that I knew him. In fact, a month before he died we spoke on the phone and, despite being seriously incapacitated by a stroke, he vowed he would be back typing out the manuscript for his long-awaited book as soon as he replaced the receiver.

Needless to say, we left Olivier's together that night.

Joe told me later, "I called Olivier the next day to thank him for inviting me. I told him, Olivier you may have changed my life forever!"

"How so?" Olivier had apparently asked him already anticipating the answer. After all, he had been responsible for setting us up.

"Introducing me to Caroline, I've haven't felt this way about a girl in years, I'm so grateful!"

"That, mon ami, was very obvious to everyone!" Olivier had chuckled, "Good luck!"

As we headed towards my apartment in a cab, Joe suddenly asked,

"Would you do something with me?"

I half expected an invitation to his place and bristled slightly that he would put me on the spot so soon.

"If you're going to invite me to your apartment, the answer's definitely no!" I said more emphatically than I felt. For some reason, the thought of returning to my second-floor walk-up that night to be faced by loaded questions from the ever-inquisitive trio of Ming, Rupert and Manny did not seem that inviting.

Joe laughed. "No, no! Not that. I hope you don't think. Heavens no! What I wanted you to do, if you don't mind a late night, is come downtown with me while I file my column."

As a budding journalist, this idea naturally thrilled me.

"Of course!" I replied, little imagining that, by accepting his invitation, I had started a routine that would continue for the next four years.

The office of the *World-Telegram & Sun* was housed in a dank building downtown on Houston and Canal Streets. Electric light bulbs swung on wires suspended from the ceiling of the newsroom. Flies buzzed around them, typewriters clattered noisily in the background and the night editor, peering out from under his green eyeshade, barked out his orders to the hovering journalists waiting around on desk duty. For a young journalist like me, this was heady stuff. This, I decided, was where I wanted to spend the rest of my life. Phones ringing, news breaking, excitement mounting, a surge of adrenalin immediately pumped through me.

Joe sat down at his typewriter, pulled out his notes and started typing about the parties he had attended that night. He looked up at me every so often, worried that I might be bored.

"You don't regret coming?" he asked.

"Are you joking?" I laughed, "This is pure, unadulterated heaven to me!" And I meant it. I could have sat there all night absorbing the atmosphere, observing the frantic goings-on, listening to the breaking news stories.

At around 3am, tired but exhilarated, Joe dropped me off at my apartment. I sneaked in hoping not to wake the others and collapsed on the sofa, unwilling, for once, to share my bed with Manny. Something had happened that night and, although it was probably obvious to all, I hadn't yet figured it out.

In less than a week Joe had convinced me to move out of 59th Street and into his studio above Carnegie Hall. It was a huge double-height room with a minstrel's gallery. On the second floor, off the balcony, was the small bedroom. There was a lot of light from the floor-to-ceiling windows on two sides of the room and views facing east towards the river and uptown towards 72nd street. On the ground floor, on either side, as you entered the studio, was a galley kitchen and a small bathroom. In the main room and up on the balcony there were copious bookshelves, stuffed with books stacked in complete disorder.

Our neighbours in some of the other studios included the Italian impresario Gian Carlo Menotti, the famous NY street photographer Bill Cunningham, fashion designer Gloria Vanderbilt, the actor Marlon Brando, the photographer Richard Avedon, the jazz pianist Bobby Short and one floor above us was the Actor's Studio run by Lee and Paula Strasberg.

"There are enough characters and stories in this building to write an epic novel." Joe said to me as Cecil, the elevator operator, helped us move my bags across the hall to studio, 906, ". Isn't that right, Cecil?"

"Perhaps the Princess will do it some day!" Cecil replied, beaming at me.

From that moment on I became Cecil's "princess". He watched out for me, carried my bags for me, hailed cabs for me and escorted me to my door whenever I was alone. He was a gentle giant from Jamaica, adored by all the residents of 881 Seventh Avenue, my new home. He became my good friend and confidante. One day I asked him why he insisted on calling me "Princess" and not Caroline.

"You got class!" He announced, "You're kind, you're pretty, you're intelligent. You're not like the rest of the ladies in this town! You just got class."

It's hard for me even now to contemplate on the tragic event that befell my good friend and confidante, Cecil. Many years later, in 1989, I returned to New York and immediately went to pay a visit to Cecil. Joe had long moved out of Studio 906 so I asked Jimmy, the other elevator operator who was on duty that day about Cecil's whereabouts. He shook his head sadly. He told me that some years back Cecil had been tried and convicted for second-degree murder and had been in prison for almost a decade. I was shocked.

"But, Jimmy, he could never hurt a fly! You know that as well as I do! " I protested.

Jimmy nodded. "I know it, Miss Caroline!"

I was very upset by the idea of my gentle champion, Cecil, languishing in some U.S. jail, perhaps never to be free again. I desperately wanted to send him a message from his "Princess" or, better still, visit him but Jimmy told me no one knew where he was being held.

"Hasn't he even told you when he will be let out?" I asked.

"Nope. Nothing." Jimmy stared down at his feet. "He was my friend. More than twenty years he was my best friend, Miss Caroline. And he's gone."

I didn't push Jimmy further. It was obvious he was distressed. I tried to change the subject.

"Remember, Jimmy, the first day I arrived in Studio 906 with Joe?" I touched his arm. "Do you know what I thought? I thought living in Carnegie Hall, this is going to be heaven."

Jimmy nodded again. "Mr Joe was a fine man," he smiled. "And Miss Campbell too – a fine woman."

The memories were suddenly very clear. I realized I had been gone for over twenty-two years and yet it all seemed so recent. I could hear Joe's voice as he swung open the door to Studio 906 and ushered me in.

"Jeannie Campbell lives above us, you'll love her. She's completely mad. I'm the godfather of her daughter Kate."

I certainly knew Jeannie by reputation. She was the granddaughter of Lord Beaverbrook, founder of the Express Newspapers. She was a journalist and, before arriving in the States, I had devoured her weekly columns in the *Evening Standard* on political life in Washington and New York.

There were two particular things about Jeannie that had intrigued me. The first was that she had been married to one of my idols, the bad boy of American literature, Norman Mailer by whom she had a daughter, Kate, Joe's goddaughter. The second thing that fascinated me about her was that rumours abounded across the Atlantic, fuelled I'm sure, in part, by Jeannie herself, that she had been carrying on a longstanding affair with Jack Kennedy. In 1964 for anyone to admit publicly to such a thing about someone as sacred as Jack Kennedy was almost tantamount to treachery. A decade later, of course, all that would change dramatically.

On the top floor of 881 Seventh Avenue, lived the frail-looking one-time actor, eighty-year old Miss Lylah Tiffany, with her rheumy eyes, her wide-brimmed black hat and her pet chichuaua, Toots. Miss Tiffany and Toots, I soon found out, were two of New York's most endearing characters. Nobody could remember a time when they hadn't seen Miss Tiffany in her wide-brimmed hat playing her accordion at night on the sidewalk outside Carnegie Hall with the increasingly infirm and emaciated Toots curled up asleep beside her. Every night for forty years, come rain, sleet or snow, Miss Tiffany was there. The little money she made, she told me, she kept in cash under her mattress. But when she took me upstairs to inspect her "little money", as she referred to her lifetime savings, it amounted to no less than $11,000, a small fortune in those days. (Equivalent today of around $105,000)

"Don't trust the banks," she sighed, trying to stuff a thin wisp of wiry grey hair back under her wide-brimmed hat, "they steal your money!"

Whether that was meant as a warning or as a belief based on personal experience I never found out.

About a year after my first encounter with Miss Tiffany, Toots died at the venerable age of 13. Or, as Miss Tiffany put it, "He was 91 but I thought he'd outlive me!" She was inconsolable and, to those of us residents worried about her welfare, we became increasingly concerned that she wouldn't survive without him.

Several days later, Joe, Cecil and I hatched a plot and, when she returned home in the early hours she found a chihuahua puppy in a basket waiting for her outside her door. It was love at first sight. As she bent down to pick him up, the puppy leapt into her arms, dislodging her wide-brimmed black hat and messing her wispy grey hair. But Miss Tiffany didn't seem to notice. Tears were flowing down her cheeks.

"Toots! Toots! It's my Toots!" she kept repeating, over and over. Cecil picked up her accordion, I picked up her plastic bag with her evening's takings, Joe unlocked her door to let her in and then we left the two of them alone.

The next night Joe and I visited her in her regular spot on the steps of Carnegie Hall. "Toots" was curled up beside her and she was playing her heart out.

"What have you named him, Miss Tiffany?" I asked, stroking the sleeping dog.

Miss Tiffany stopped playing abruptly.

"What do you mean?"

"Caroline just wondered if you'd thought of a name for him yet," Joe explained.

"Name?" she looked nonplussed, "why should I think of a name? He's Toots. He's always been Toots. You know that. Why do you ask?"

Later she told me she believed in reincarnation and that there was no doubt in her mind as soon as she saw the new puppy that he was the reincarnation of her beloved Toots.

Two years later I helped Miss Tiffany pack her plastic bags. She was finally leaving the studio that had been her home for so many years. She was being taken off to an actor's retirement home in the Adirondacks. As she sat on the sidewalk, bundled up among her packages waiting for the taxi to take her away, her wide-brimmed hat askew and her accordion on her lap, she shed a few tears. I instantly noticed Toots was not curled up beside her.

"Where's Toots?" I asked alarmed.

Miss Tiffany hunched her frail shoulders and wept.

"I had to give him away," she whispered, "they don't want him where I'm going. Cecil's finding a home for him."

I gave her a hug.

"He'll be fine," I said unconvincingly, "Cecil will make sure he's well looked after. Please don't worry about him, Miss Tiffany."

"I can't help it," she sniffed, "he was all I had. He means everything to me."

The taxi came and Cecil and I helped Miss Tiffany into the front seat, taking great care not to dislodge her wide-brimmed hat. She insisted all her plastic bags were placed behind her on the back seat where she could keep an eye on them. I tried to imagine the taxi driver's expression if he just happened to peek into one of those bulging shopping bags and see Miss Tiffany's "little money"!

I clasped her hand through the window as the taxi started to draw away.

"Wait a minute," she said. Despite her weak voice, the command was strident and the taxi driver abruptly applied the brakes.

"What is it, Miss Tiffany?" I asked.

"Tell Joe, don't forget to write about me," she said.

I promised I wouldn't forget. And, as her taxi pulled out of sight, Cecil gave me one of his big bear hugs. I think we were both sad to see her go, knowing that, without Toots, without her nightly station outside Carnegie Hall and faced with life in an old people's home, she would probably not last long. Her life would simply ebb away.

Despite being owned by a bachelor, studio 906 was surprisingly well-kept. Cecil's aunt, Lillian, who lived in New Jersey, came once a week to sweep up, dust, polish and gossip about the antics of her extended family. Lillian was very happy to meet me that first day.

"Mr Joe needs a woman," she confided. "He been alone too long. You can see it. It's not right – a man alone, you know. You make him plenty happy, girl. Mr Joe, he be a good man. He deserve a good woman! And Cecil tells me you be a good woman!"

"I don't know about that, Lillian!" I laughed.

"You're young. You're healthy. You be that woman!" she replied emphatically, leaving no room for argument.

At that moment the door swung open and Mr Joe arrived.

"I've got Jeannie and the tree!" He announced. "Where are we going to put it, Lillian?"

Jeannie Campbell was not as I expected a wife of Norman Mailer or a lover of JFK to be. For some foolish reason, I expected both men to go for trophy women, blonde, curvaceous and long-limbed. And Jeannie was none of these. Mailer referred to her as "a lion of the species" in his novel, *An American Dream* that he was busy writing at the time.

"She was a handsome woman," he wrote. "She was big. She had a huge mass of black hair and striking green eyes…She had a large Irish nose and a wide mouth…But her complexion was her claim to beauty. For her skin was cream white. And her cheeks were coloured with a fine rose. Centuries of Irish mist had produced that complexion."

To me, Jeannie was undoubtedly an attractive woman with a commanding presence but she was certainly not beauty queen material. It was a warm Spring day in New York and she was dressed very conventionally in Scottish tweeds, with a pastel lambswool twin set and a row of pearls and what I refer to as "sensible" shoes, English leather brogues with laces.

"Jeannie, this is Caroline! Caroline this is Jeannie!"

"Yes, the one you never stop talking about!" Jeannie smiled and then drew me to her ample bosom and kissed me. "You must be special to have got our Joe," she said with a smile. "Make sure you look after him!"

She abruptly let go of me and swivelled around. "Now where are we going to put this rubber tree, Lillian?"

"Couldn't you leave it upstairs, Miss Jeannie, and I'll water it every week?" Lillian suggested hopefully.

A fine idea I thought, considering the size of the tree waiting outside in the hall.

"Oh, no, I can't possibly do that. I promised it to Joe," Jeannie said. "I'll take it back when I return."

That appeared to be the end of the discussion. So the four of us proceeded to grab the tree at various points and drag, push and haul it into the studio, spilling gravel, earth and dry leaves as we went. Lillian was muttering away under her breath about the mess we were making as we struggled to pull the tree over her newly polished hardwood floor. Eventually, we managed to resurrect all 30 feet of it, up against the balcony, securing it with a rope.

"There, you see!" Jeannie exclaimed, proudly standing back and admiring it, "I told you it would look great here, Joe. Now you can climb up to bed at night instead of using the stairs. It'll be a good exercise for you!"

She said her goodbyes, kissed us all, including Lillian and left in a typical rush.

"That's Jeannie for you," was Joe's explanation, after she slammed the door shut. "So what do you think of the woman who has no navel?"

"I beg your pardon?" I asked, not quite grasping the question.

Lillian blushed, "Mr Joe, please!"

"No navel, it's true!" he continued, "She had it surgically removed, or covered up. She thought it was an ugly thing! You ask her next time you see her."

I contemplated the idea of a woman with no navel. It sounded suitably surrealistic for Jeannie but I couldn't imagine what she would look like in a bikini.

"It's a bit bizarre, isn't it?" I asked.

"Well, it certainly jump-starts an interesting discussion at dinner parties!" Joe laughed.

"When will she be back?" I asked.

"With Jeannie, who knows?" Joe replied, "Next week, next year. She's got a new man in her life, so maybe never!"

Lillian said, "My, my! Miss Jeannie, no navel, I do declare! Wait till I tells my husband that!" And then, placing her hands on her aproned hips, laughed uncontrollably.

Life with Joe, I found out very swiftly, was anything but boring. The phone never stopped ringing, the invitations never stopped arriving and people would drop in on any excuse just for a chat. For a few weeks, I had the definite feeling that many were passing by simply to give me the once-over. Joe had acquired scores of female friends over the years and they had become quite possessive of him. His was a good shoulder to cry on when their husbands played away from home. Or, if their husbands were too tied up with work, Joe had been happy to escort them to dances, cocktail gatherings, film premieres, gallery openings and first nights at the theatre. And he was a useful extra man for dinner parties. All this, they realized, would abruptly change now that I had appeared on the scene. They needed some reassurance from Joe that he would still be available for the occasional date and I needed to reassure them I was no threat. Joe was very skillful about handling both their hurt feelings and my sense of being an unwelcome intruder. In the end, they totally accepted me. And it wasn't long before they started giving me advice as to how to get by in New York.

"Sharpen your edges a bit, little one," Julie Gabor, the mother of Magda, Zza Zza and Eva, told me one night, "you're much too, how shall I say it - sweet? If you vant to be success in New York you gotta become more stronger, you know, more selfish and more demanding. Stay as you are, darlink, and you'll die, for sure, I should know."

I guessed, of all people, Julie Gabor should certainly know what she was talking about. After all, she had successfully educated her three blonde daughters to appreciate what she considered the "finer" things of life – ageing millionaires, 24-carat diamonds and multi-million dollar trust funds made out in their favour, but not necessarily in that order.

At a ladies' lunch party the actress Mamie Van Doren told me, "God, darling, you look so young. Make yourself look a bit older otherwise Joe will be had up for statutory rape. And none of us would want that now, would we?"

In the end, though, I think most of Joe's friends, both male and female, were happy for Joe that he'd finally found someone he could live with and, more to the point, someone who could actually live with him.

In fact, it even surprised Joe how easily he slid into "married" life with me, as he called it. He had been a bachelor for 45 years. So to invite me to live in his studio was a life-changing decision for him.

"I had absolutely no misgivings," he told me a month or so after I moved in. "It seemed like the most natural thing in the world to me. I never hesitated for a moment. Nor have I regretted it."

I never found my new lifestyle with Joe easy, since it required going out to at least three or four parties every single night. While I got used to attending these parties over the years, the truth was I was an introvert at heart.

"Look on the bright side, darling," he constantly reminded me. "It certainly has its advantages."

I had to admit that was true. Firstly, I was able to make important new contacts that were helpful to my work as a radio producer. And secondly, it enabled the two of us to take all-expenses-paid junkets to places such as Jamaica for the opening of a new resort in Montego Bay, to Aruba for the opening of the casino at the Sheraton Hotel, and to Palm Beach for the opening of *The Nutcracker Suite*. One night we could be playing charades with Gloria Steinem, Gay Talese, Clay Felker, Elaine Dundy and Tom Wolfe and another we could be attending the opening night of Margot Fonteyn and Rudolf Nureyev in *Romeo and Juliet* at Lincoln Center.

One of the first events Joe and I attended together was the opening in March 1964 of the new Gallery of Modern Art, owned by my friend, Huntington Hartford who I had met at the Red Lion Pub in Mayfair at Ming's farewell party. "Hunt" introduced us to Salvador Dali, whose enormous 1954 painting of the Crucifixion dominated the great entrance hall.

One weekend we flew down to Washington at the invitation of Perle Mesta to attend an event she was organizing, the 50th Anniversary Tribute to her best friend, Ethel Merman. A decade earlier Perle herself, the original Democratic "hostess with the mostess", had been immortalized in the successful Broadway musical, *Call Me Madam*.

"And, best of all," Joe told me, "if there is nothing else for us to do, we can always go downstairs (Carnegie Hall) and get free seats in the stalls or standing room at the back."

That too was true. I knew I couldn't complain. In just a few short months we had listened to artists such as Arthur Rubenstein, Aretha Franklin, Nina Simone and Ray Charles – all for free.

We were also invited to every first night, every movie premiere, every gallery opening and every concert and ballet performance, including the Beatles at Shea Stadium, Rene Magritte at the Museum of Modern Art and Laurence Olivier on

Broadway. Other than the endless society parties, I knew I had very little to complain about.

Six months after I met Joe I gave up the futile attempt of trying to combine my 1010 WINS schedule with his nightly routine. Although his contacts had become increasingly useful to my work and I was managing to get some "awesome guests", as my boss, Sandy Lesberg, described them, I found I just couldn't take the pace anymore. Among the guests, I had managed to invite on the show were pin-up girl Jayne Mansfield, Republican Mayoral candidate John Lindsay, composer Burt Bacharach, actors Gig Young and Tony Randall, New York Senator Jacob K Javits and the legendary theatre critic Clive Barnes.

But the pace was furious, too furious for my constitution. I started taking amphetamines to keep me alert and functioning. Our combined nightly routines gave Joe and me little alternative other than trying to sleep during the day. For Joe that was fine but, for me, that was impossible. The phone rang all the time and people constantly dropped by to leave an invitation, a request or simply to gossip. They had little understanding of the needs of us "night owls" and I found myself perpetually weary from lack of sleep.

I was sad to say to have to say goodbye to Sandy and Betty. But I was happy in the years to come to follow his hugely successful career in both radio and publishing. By the time he died in 2022, aged 97, Sandy Lesberg had fronted a radio show on WOR for twenty years and gone on to write 40 books of memoirs of his time in London, Paris, Amsterdam and Vienna, and subjects as varied as 18th Century art, crime, and cooking.

"Who was that?" I asked one night, after Joe had been talking on the phone for over an hour.

"Oh, don't worry, darling, that was just Rita being Rita!" Joe smiled indulgently, getting back into bed, and cuddling up to me. "Honestly, you don't need to worry about her," he whispered in my ear, "I've known her for years. She's got alimony problems with her husband, Tom Guinzburg. She just wanted my advice."

"How am I supposed to handle all these neurotic women?" I asked. "They seem to look on me as a threat."

"Not Rita. She's dying to meet you." Joe said.

"Not sure I feel the same way about her," I laughed.

"She's invited us for dinner tomorrow night." Joe said.

And so I met, the actress, Rita Gam. Joe and I were late, of course. We were always late to everything. We had attended two parties before showing up at her door. On catching my first glimpse of her, my first thought was. *Oh, Rita, those piercing blue eyes, that jet black hair, that flawless complexion, those perfect scarlet lips and those enviably high cheekbones, I would die for any one of those.*

Any woman would die for any one of those. And even her voice was distinctive - low, seductive, the kind of voice I had spent years trying to cultivate. It put me at ease straightaway.

"Darling, I'm so happy Joe has found you," she gushed as she embraced me at the door. "We are going to be very good friends, you and I."

"I'm sure," I mumbled, although I wasn't that certain.

This elegant woman who escorted us into her grand Park Avenue duplex was not in my league, I thought. She was a product of the 1950s Hollywood studios. I was a flower child, very much a product of the 60s.

I followed her into the opulent apartment she had once shared with her husband, Tom, the ownership of which was still being contested in their divorce settlement. Thick, lush drapes hung from the windows, expensive paintings covered the walls and, at one end of the room, the floor to ceiling bookshelves were dominated by books published by Tom, who also the editor of The Paris Review.

Photographs of Rita in her hey-day, in various film and theatre roles, adorned every available surface. Rita with Ray Milland in *The Thief*. Rita with Gregory Peck in *Night People*. Rita with Jack Palance in *Sign of Pagan*. Rita with Grace Kelly. Rita with Marlon Brando. Rita with Broderick Crawford. Rita with Norman Mailer. Rita with Andy Warhol. And, of course, Rita with the film director Sidney Lumet.

"Sidney was Rita's first husband," Joe said, as I replaced the photo on top of the walnut writing desk.

"Darling, I could tell you some stories about him!" Rita purred as she indicated to me to sit down. "But then Gloria has probably told you them already."

"Gloria", I surmised, was Gloria Vanderbilt, Lumet's second wife, who happened to be our neighbor in the Carnegie Hall studios where she lived with the black cabaret pianist, Bobby Short.

"Not yet, she hasn't!" I replied, "Perhaps she doesn't know me well enough!"

Rita proudly showed us her latest award, the Silver Bear, from the jury of the International Film Festival in Berlin for her role as Estelle Rigault in Ted Danielewski's *No Exit*, a film based on Jean Paul Sartre's play.

She talked about her career as a celebrity journalist and that she hoped to produce a documentary one day about the film business around the world. She talked about her imminent divorce, her children, her potentially lucrative alimony settlement which, apart from custody of the two children, had to include possession of the Park Avenue apartment, a summer home in Long Island and, of course, her stake in Viking Press.

"Do you know how Tom started in publishing?" Joe asked to change the subject, seeing that I was slightly overwhelmed by Rita's persistent banter.

"No idea," I said, "I thought he inherited Viking from his father."

"He did," Joe replied. "But his father only took him into the business because, at the age of 8 or 9, Tom read *The Story of Ferdinand the Bull*. He loved it so much that he pleaded with his father to publish it. His father very reluctantly agreed and it went on to sell over 4 million copies on its first print run!"

"So his Dad said, Tom, I think you're a natural to join the business!" Rita finished the story.

We didn't eat until about 11pm when Rita finally took a break from talking. We ate our meals on our laps. Rita continued to dominate the conversation. I didn't pay much attention. I let her and Joe get on with it. The reasons for her divorce, the alimony for her, the tuition fees for her kids and the details about the eventual settlement were really of little interest to me.

"Darling, it was so lovely to talk to you and get to know you," Rita said, embracing me again at the door when we eventually left after midnight.

"I hardly said a word," I whispered to Joe as the elevator door closed behind us. "She did all the talking. So she didn't really get to know me at all."

"That's Rita for you!" Joe laughed.

And he was right. That was Rita. I knew her from 1964 till her death in 2016. Our lives crossed many times and in several different countries. But Rita was always the same. She was always Rita. I still wonder, even after those 52 years of friendship, whether she ever really got to know me.

Chapter 8
An Evening with Frank Sinatra

Another fellow "night owl" in the Carnegie Hall studios was the jazz pianist, Bobby Short. Bobby was the highly successful resident cabaret performer at Manhattan's elegant Café Carlyle. Often, on the way home at night, Joe and I would drop by the Carlyle to enjoy Bobby's unique talent on the piano.

One afternoon, soon after I moved in with Joe, Bobby called him to say, "Joe darling, Frank Sinatra's in town. Gloria and I are planning a dinner for him next week. I hope you and Caroline can come."

The "Gloria" he referred to was his very close friend, the designer, Gloria Vanderbilt Cooper. Independent and headstrong, Gloria, had recently defied the wrath of her wealthy family and shocked New York society when she decided to move in with Bobby, the gay black pianist.

The dinner party numbered around twenty people. And, even though we literally lived just down the corridor, Joe and I, predictably, arrived late. Dinner had already begun. Bobby got up to welcome us. He was dressed, not in his usual impeccable pin-striped suit but in a flowing white beaded caftan. He drew me to an empty chair next to Bill Paley, the founder of CBS Television.

On my other side was Peter Duchin, the popular resident pianist at the St.Regis Hotel's Maisonette Club. Peter's wife Cheray Zauderer was seated across from us. Frank Sinatra sat a little further up, on my side of the table, between Gloria and Bill Paley's beautiful wife, Babe. There were several other people there, some of whom I recognized, such as society beauty Fiona Thyssen and publicist Earl Blackwell, and others I did not. When we arrived the conversation and the wine were both in full flow.

Mouthing excuses, I edged into my seat. Bill Paley was very gracious. We had already had a nodding acquaintance at various functions before but this was the first time I was able to have a conversation with him.

I told him one of my best friends, Rupert Hitzig, worked for him.

"Talented young man he is, he'll go far!" Bill predicted. And, although neither of us could have possibly known it then, he was right.

Our conversation then veered towards the one person in New York that always managed to shock, fascinate and amuse me, Truman Capote. It was no secret that Truman was infatuated with Bill's wife, the very beautiful Babe Paley, a woman Truman referred to as one of his "swans". There was a time when Truman was so often in her company and in her homes in New York and Long Island that the Paley marriage could have been accurately described as a "ménage a trois".

"Aren't you just a little bit jealous?" I teased after a couple of minutes warm-up.

"Of Truman?" he asked incredulously, "Why? He keeps my wife amused, entertained and flattered while I'm hard at work. What more could a man want?" He laughed.

I could see his point. "You mean all gossip and no sex?"

He laughed again, "You got it! Hey, you're a bright kid. When you need a job come and see me!" He raised his wine glass and winked.

By the end of the night, toasts were being made, each one more slurred and more cringing than the last. Most were in praise of the evening's "special" guest, Frank Sinatra, telling him what a great man he was, what a privilege it was to be in his company and how fortunate we all were to know him.

Personally, I had never seen the attraction of Frank Sinatra, neither as a man nor as a singer. It seems there was a huge difference in his appeal for those born before and those born after the war. To the Sixties generation not only was he not of our decade, he didn't even seem part of our century. To us, brought up on the Beatles, the Doors and the Rolling Stones, Frank Sinatra was irrelevant. He was history, a musical relic from another era. I found it hard to understand the adulation he enjoyed among my parents' generation. To me, he was physically ugly, his language was vulgar, his manners coarse and he was already infamous for treating women with lecherous contempt and men with physical and verbal abuse.

And this night, at Bobby Short's dinner, I was about to witness Frank Sinatra at his undeniable worst. When the toasts were over he raised his arms, stumbled to his feet and reached for his glass to respond. The toast he made was not quite what everyone was expecting. Carefully surveying the room, eyeballing each woman in turn, he said, "I am privileged to be here. Thank you Bobby for inviting all these beautiful hookers. I want you all to know that," he paused for dramatic effect and then, very slowly and deliberately pointing to each of the "hookers" around the table one by one, he said, "I have fucked every single one of them," until his finger arrived at me, hesitating briefly, he added, "except her, who is she?"

A chill of complete horror pervaded the room. No one dared look anyone else in the eye. Wives, mothers and daughters froze. Husbands, fathers and sons glared. On both sides of me, I felt Peter Duchin and Bill Paley shift uncomfortably. Everyone looked deep into their wine glasses, not daring to say a word.

I think the immediate reaction of all of us must have been had we heard right? Had Frank Sinatra just said what we thought he had said? Everyone looked at the drunken singer desperately hoping he was going to laugh, say it was a joke, or apologize for his bad taste. But no, he was still standing there, innocently swallowing the contents of his glass, studying the expressions around him, thrilled at the mayhem he had just caused. One by one heads started to look up, each person looked at their escort. Doubts and questions must have been flooding their minds. *Could what he said have been true? Was it just possible? When? Where? How did it happen? How dare he? How dare she?* I shuddered to think what the conversations would be like later behind closed doors.

This was my first and, considering the circumstances, fortunately, my last close encounter with Frank Sinatra and it clearly illustrated to me what an odious, obnoxious and belligerent character he was. He had broken every code in the book and he still stood there, conceited, gloating and self-satisfied as he watched everyone else in the room squirm. Drunk or not, there were no excuses to be made. And, besides, there was no doubt he was enjoying himself immensely. If nothing else, it clearly demonstrated he had no class at all. If he was determined to make such a compromising statement he should have made it in his own home, not at the home of someone he called his "friend". By announcing this at someone else's dinner party he had committed an unspeakable offence. Poor Bobby Short looked more shell-shocked than anybody.

I decided there and then that I despised Frank Sinatra and I silently vowed to sully his name in public whenever and wherever I had the opportunity. I was thrilled, decades later, when I met the diminutive blonde author, Kitty Kelley, and she handed me a copy of *His Way*, her devastating unauthorized biography on him. And I noted with glee that, despite threats against her life, despite moves to injunct the book, Sinatra and his mafia friends were unable to prove successfully to a court that the lurid details it contained about his links with organized crime and many of the disreputable activities he had indulged in throughout his career were not the truth, the whole truth and nothing but the truth.

The book was published intact in 1986 and gave the public an insight into the more unsavoury aspects of his life and character. By this time his bad behaviour was well-known, his filthy language was legendary and his uncouth bullying treatment of women was publicly acknowledged. But, despite all this, the public still continued to adulate him. In their eyes he could do no wrong.

Perversely it was Kitty Kelley, not Sinatra, who was considered by many to be the villain. She had dared to write the unpalatable truth about an American icon. It was Kitty Kelley, not Sinatra, who was vilified and shunned following its publication. And it was Kitty Kelley, not Sinatra, who suffered most from the after-effects. I tried to analyze why that should be. It confirmed something I already knew about the American public, that it is willing to forgive everything, sordid language, criminal activities and even physical abuse of women as long as the person is a much-loved celebrity. And Frank Sinatra was just such a celebrity.

Chapter 9
Tiptoeing Through the Tulips

Once I gave in my notice to Sandy Lesberg, I had more time on my hands. I started to develop real friendships, rather than the many passing acquaintances I was making with Joe. And, while I accompanied Joe to most of the nightly events he had to cover for the newspaper, I often opted to spend time with my best friend, Sarah Dalton, another aspiring English writer who, along with her brother, David, one of the founders of Rolling Stone magazine, were both making names for themselves within New York's pop culture scene. Sarah mingled with artists like Andy Warhol, Claes Oldenberg and Jasper Johns, while David's circle of friends included Little Richard, Janis Joplin, Jimi Hendrix and Jim Morrison.

Although I genuinely disliked most nightclubs, the Scene on 8th Avenue and West 46th Street, came to be one of my favourite watering holes in New York. Steve Paul, the enterprising 23-year-old owner, was determined to make his basement club the most important music venue in the city. Steve lived like a pauper most nights, sleeping rough on friends' couches even though money appeared to be plentiful. He was constantly flying off to Seattle, Los Angeles or London to find new bands, offer to be their manager and invite them to play at the Scene.

Steve was known for his magic touch. With very few exceptions every artist who played at the Scene became famous. Many musicians, hoping to be discovered, wanted Steve's touch to rub off on them. Even widely known artists and bands, such as the Velvet Underground, the Progressive Blues Experiment, Janis Joplin, Jimi Hendrix, Rick Derringer, Duane Allman, Frank Zappa and the exceptional "white" blues guitarist Johnny Winter, all accepted Steve's invitation to play at the Scene. Despite strong competition from other music venues over the years, the Scene grew in reputation, popularity and strength.

One of Steve's earliest, and most unlikely, discoveries at the Scene was Herbert Kaury, alias Vernon Castle, alias Emmett Swink, alias Danny Dover, alias Rollie Dell and, now the alias we knew him by, Larry Love "The Singing Canary". But even Steve, with his innate sense of success, did not immediately recognize Larry

Love's unique appeal. Sarah had already heard Love in some smaller clubs in Greenwich Village and had begged me and David to go and listen to him with her.

"You've got to check him out," she giggled, "You won't believe your eyes and your ears! "

She was right about that.

So, once again, Sarah, David and I descended on the Scene, this time with Larry Love in tow. During a break in the evening's entertainment, Sarah asked him if he would get up and sing a solo for us. In fact, encouraged by Sarah, Larry had brought his ukulele with him in the vain hope he might be invited to play at the Scene. He looked pleadingly at Steve who shrugged his shoulders.

"Go on, Steve," Sarah begged, "please let him!" David and I joined in, eager to experience this weird singing phenomenon once again. Steve, who had a soft spot for the two decorative English girls who frequented his club, didn't need much convincing.

"OK, I guess. Why not? What the hell?" Steve ushered Larry towards the microphone. "What's your name again?" he asked.

"Tiny Tim!" Larry answered, without hesitating.

"Excuse me?" Steve looked surprised, "I thought you said -"

"Tiny Tim!" Larry repeated quietly but firmly.

Looking nonplussed, Steve tapped the microphone. "All you folks here tonight, please welcome Tiny Tim!" he announced.

The tall, gangly figure of Herbert Kaury's latest incarnation rose from his seat, tossed his long curly chestnut tresses away from his face and picked up his ukulele.

"Excuse me, Miss Sarah. Excuse me, Miss Caroline," he whispered politely as he left the table and walked to the front. Then, in a falsetto voice that would later become his trademark all over the world, he sang, "Tiptoe Through the Tulips."

When he finished he looked towards Sarah and me. "That was for my very special friends, Miss Sarah and Miss Caroline, thank you both," he announced to the astonished crowd, who stood rooted to the spot, not quite sure what to make of the performance they'd just witnessed.

And thus, Herbert Kaury's latest alias, Tiny Tim, was born. I was speechless, little guessing that within three years *"Tiptoe Through the Tulips"* would echo across the world earning the singer a platinum disc.

The effect of this extraordinary entertainer on the audience that night was indescribable. Probably for the first time in its, so far, brief but explosive history, the Scene was completely hushed, whether out of sheer disbelief, amazement or respect I shall never know. But, by the time the song was over, Steve Paul, the music entrepreneur, certainly knew. From the audience's reaction Steve immediately sensed Tiny Tim was going to be a big, big star. And from that night on, Steve became his manager and Tiny Tim became a regular at the Club.

And as the Scene's reputation grew, so did Tiny Tim's. People from all over New York would come to listen to him, in amazement, in amusement or in shock. Why they came in such numbers didn't matter to either Steve or Tiny Tim. All that mattered was that they came. From swank uptown restaurants and clubs, such as Le Club owned and run by Oleg and Igor Cassini, or the smart El Morocco nightclub frequented by New York's top "400", or the fashionable Four Seasons to downtown Greenwich Village bars, nightspots and cafes, people from all backgrounds and from all social levels made the nightly pilgrimage to the windowless cellar on West 46th to listen enthralled to the weird and wonderful phenomenon that was Tiny Tim.

Most were turned away disappointed. The basement venue was so small it was unable to accommodate the large numbers of eager fans lining up on the sidewalk outside. Recently Sarah and I reminisced over those early days.

"You, David and I were the lucky ones," she said. "We were so privileged. Steve would always let us in. But most people were turned away at the door."

One evening, following a somewhat dreary uptown dinner party, I even managed to drag a reluctant Joe down there with our friends New York Senator Jacob Javits and his wife, the irrepressible Marion, and out-of-towners Governor Henry Bellmon of Oklahoma, British actor Bill Travers and Irish writer Conor Cruise O'Brien. Despite all their initial protests, they were later forced to admit that a live performance by Tiny Tim was an experience not to be missed.

Steve soon realized Tiny Tim was an asset to the Club in many other ways. He enjoyed meeting people and talking about his life, his religious beliefs and his long and rocky career as an entertainer. He had endless tales about the successes and failures of each of his previous incarnations. He had stories about his Polish family's struggle for survival. And he had hilarious anecdotes about his own hygiene and beauty programmes, which involved, among other things, a daily manicure, splattering cologne over his face, brushing his teeth with goat's milk and taking a shower several times a day. If Tiny Tim looked like a beatnik straight out of a Jack Kerouac novel, he certainly never smelt like one. Most nights he reeked of Elizabeth Arden's Blue Grass but, occasionally, he'd try something a little more adventurous such as Jean Patou, which always reminded me of my Jugoslav grandmother.

The sheer novelty of a performer like Tiny Tim had struck a chord with New Yorkers. Here was a clean living individual (he didn't drink, he didn't smoke, he didn't take drugs and I doubt if he even had sex) with old-fashioned values, jealously guarded principles and quaint codes of behaviour. He was quiet-spoken, polite, unassuming and gentle. To jaded New Yorkers, used to the brash, spoilt and, often, uncouth conduct of their pop stars, Tiny Tim was, like the old-fashioned songs he sang, a breath of fresh air from a bygone era.

Finally the Press got to hear about this phenomenon. And, by 1968, just three years after first his performance at the Scene, Tiny Tim was whisked off to appear before millions of Americans on Johnny Carson's Tonight Show. This was immediately followed by offers of recording contracts, club bookings and concert spots around the world. At the age of 45, or thereabouts, Tiny Tim, as Steve Paul had accurately predicted, had finally made the big time.

Sadly, the very success of the Scene led to its premature demise at the height of its fame. Sarah informed me, "Teddy, the maitre d' had his legs broken. The mob wanted a piece of the action."

So, after years of sleeping on friends' couches, Steve Paul, the entrepreneur with the magic touch, retreated to his new home, Rita Hayworth's vast estate in Connecticut.

He told Sarah twenty years later that, "In those days you didn't need money. You didn't need anything. I slept on peoples' couches. Today, it's different. It's into the bunkers."

Smiling he swept his arms around the palatial living room boasting walk-in fireplaces on either end, "And now, twenty years later, I find I need all this!"

Chapter 10
Blinded By the White

Someone else who was about to make the "big time" in 1965 was actress, Sharon Tate. Following her success in the much-hyped TV version of Jacqueline Suzann's explosive novel, *Valley of the Dolls*, Sharon had just completed filming on her first feature film, *Eye of the Devil* with David Niven and Deborah Kerr.

Prior to the film's release, Joe and I were invited to meet Sharon at the home of our neighbour, publicist Earl "Mr. Celebrity" Blackwell. Earl was known as the undisputed king of New York society. For the past two decades, in his book the *Celebrity Register*, he had defined who was a true American celebrity. Earl lived on our doorstep, on the southeast corner of 57th Street and 6th Avenue, right opposite Carnegie Hall. Entering Earl's luxurious Etruscan-style penthouse home, complete with a Mediterranean roof garden was like stepping out of modern-day New York into an 18th-century Italian villa, complete with terracotta tiles, stone fountains, stucco moldings, mosaic floors and trompe l'oeil frescoes.

As Joe and I walked into Earl's apartment that night there were, it seemed, around twenty men milling around just one very beautiful girl, Sharon Tate. The men were press agents, lawyers and financiers. All had a vested interest in making Sharon a major star. As one of them told me somewhat crudely, "We put a lot of money in that girl. Now it's pay-back time!"

In my very English way I retorted, "That's not a very nice thing to say."

I guess I still had a lot to learn about the way Hollywood worked. My only brush with moviedom so far had been an audition with the director, Joshua Logan. Sarah and I had hoped to secure minor roles in his movie version of *Camelot*. Josh had been the consummate gentleman. When deciding to reject us, he rose from behind his huge teak desk, shook our hands and said, "I'm very sorry but I can't give either of you a role. You'll both outshine my leading lady, Vanessa Redgrave. It wouldn't do, would it, to surround her with more beautiful girls than her!"

So I was not used to these Hollywood thugs, these unrepentant "money men" exacting their pound of flesh. I hadn't even met Sharon yet but I already felt sorry for her. When Joe and I were introduced to her I could sense from her expression that she was fairly relieved to see another girl enter the room. Although she looked as fragile and sweet as she always did on television, like some brittle porcelain doll, it was obvious the pressures of non-stop appearances, photo ops and publicity interviews were already beginning to take their toll on her.

"It's a big step for me," she told us. "I fly to LA tomorrow and then they tell me my life's going to be crazy after that. As if it isn't already!"

"Aren't you looking forward to it?" I asked.

"I don't know," she replied, wrinkling her nose, "I really don't. One moment I think it's all thrilling and I can't believe it's happening to me and the next, well…" Her voice trailed off.

"It won't be that bad," I said, trying to sound reassuring. "They're not all vultures out there. In fact, I've heard that some of them can be quite human!" I told her about my recent meeting with Josh Logan.

Sharon laughed. "I hope you're right but most of them aren't like that, sadly. They're hideous, really they are. They'll probably chew me up and spit me out, like they do with everyone else."

"I'm sure you can handle them, darling," Joe said, patting Sharon sympathetically on the back as one of the press agents appeared from nowhere, grabbed her arm and whisked her off to introduce her to yet another waiting journalist.

As Sharon left us, she turned and whispered in my ear, "I just hope I'll remember what it was like to be me."

"You will," I reassured her, "I'm sure you will."

As we left Earl's apartment, I went over to Sharon to say goodbye and wish her luck.

"I'll need it, lots of it," she smiled. "Thanks for coming. Perhaps we'll meet up again when I get back to New York and I'll tell you how it's been."

"It's a date, "I said. "Good luck. "

There could be no way any of us that night could have anticipated the gruesome fate that awaited her. And, when that appalling tragedy did occur just four years later, it was hard for me not to reflect on our very brief conversation and wonder if Sharon had had any power at all over those "money men", who were determined to eat her alive, whether she could have somehow prevented the appalling misfortune that befell her. I just hoped she had found even some brief happiness with her husband, the bad-boy director, Roman Polanski.

Joe and I were in Earl's apartment again some weeks later chatting to him when his telephone rang. He answered it and carried on a short conversation.

"That was Cary Grant," Earl said as he replaced the receiver. "I've invited him over. He's at the Plaza." Earl summoned Chang, his Chinese chauffeur, to the room.

"Now," he addressed Chang, speaking very slowly, "I would like you to go to the Plaza Hotel and pick up Mister Cary Grant. He will be waiting for you. OK?"

The chauffeur shrugged his shoulders. It was obvious he didn't understand a word except, perhaps, the name of the Plaza Hotel.

"Cary Grant, you know," Earl went on.

Again the bewildered Chang shrugged his shoulders.

"Cary Grant" Earl emphasized, "the famous movie star? You must know him!" Earl was beginning to lose his patience.

The chauffeur's face remained impassive.

Frustrated, Earl wrote down Cary Grant's name in capitals on a piece of paper and handed it to him.

"Well, it doesn't matter," he said, nudging the driver towards the door. "Just go to the Plaza Hotel. Mr Grant will be waiting for you in the lobby. I'm sure when you see him you'll recognize him. OK?"

"OK!" Chang beamed, grabbed the note and left.

Half an hour later the apartment door opened and Cary Grant walked in. I was eager to know whether Chang had, in fact, recognized him immediately or not.

"We're dying to know, what happened when Chang picked you up." I said, "Earl had a major struggle getting him to understand it was you who needed a lift. He didn't get it at all."

"Oh, it was fine," Grant laughed, "I was standing in the lobby waiting for him anyway. And, as soon as he saw me he flung his arms into the air, grinned from ear to ear and said, "Oh, it's you! Why didn't they tell it was you?" Then he asked me to autograph the piece of paper for him!"

On another occasion Earl accompanied Joe and me to dinner with Joan Crawford in her sumptuous Park Avenue apartment. Joan had just completed filming on *I Saw What You Did*, a thriller where she played a murderous old woman, Amy Nelson, plagued by teenage pranksters. I was curious to meet Joan since I considered that, although she had an unequalled tendency to be melodramatic, she was, after all, one of the great actresses of her generation. But I wasn't prepared at all for the weird evening ahead of us.

It was obvious from the start that dinner with Joan was to be no ordinary affair. The three of us were ushered into the living room by a uniformed maid. Joan was sitting bolt upright on a white sofa covered with plastic. She was dressed in an impeccable white V-neck cardigan over a neat white pencil skirt. As I quickly glanced around I realized the whole room was white. There was even a white ceramic bowl containing white tulips placed on top of the white grand piano. And everything, including photographs, paintings and furniture, was covered in transparent plastic. This, I learned later from Earl, was how she always entertained. She didn't want any of her guests to make a mess. Surprisingly, for someone so hygiene-conscious, she was smoking. She was inhaling a cigarette encased in a long, white holder. I extended my hand, as Joe introduced us but, evidently, fearing the transfer of germs, she chose to ignore it so I was forced to withdraw it swiftly, hoping no one had noticed.

"Charming," the trademark bright red lips parted briefly into a smile as she surveyed me up and down. "Won't you sit down, dear. Caroline is it?"

She patted the plastic covered seat beside her. "Earl tells me you're from London?"

The smile, I decided, was not genuine. It was the smile of someone long accustomed to adapting her mood and character for the benefit of the camera or an audience.

"I adore London," she went on, taking a sip of neat vodka, "I love your long theatrical tradition but, my dear, the theatres are so…." She paused to think for a suitable adjective, "so ancient. Most of them should be torn down or replaced, wouldn't you say? I mean they're falling apart! It's a disgrace!"

"I like them that way," I replied frostily, "it gives them character."

I thought I better change the subject swiftly. I shifted uncomfortably on the plastic covered sofa and asked somewhat foolishly, "Are you redecorating here?"

Joan arched a perfectly plucked eyebrow. "Now why would I want to do that, dear? I like it just the way it is!"

Silly me. I had fallen right into it and I hadn't seen it coming.

"I just thought because of the…the…" I stuttered, picking up the plastic sheeting and waving it limply in front of me.

I immediately regretted pursuing the subject. I felt my cheeks burning. I looked across at Joe for moral support but he and Earl were smiling, seeming to enjoy every minute of my discomfort. Right then I could have killed them both for not warning me. I decided I had no alternative but to prolong the joke, even at my own expense.

"I think you're absolutely right," I said to Joan, trying to keep a straight face, "I've always loved white. And what a brilliant idea you have to keep it clean. One day when I get my own house I think I'll do the same."

To my surprise and relief that seemed to do the trick. Joan was completely taken in and she went on to expound the visual, spiritual and emotional virtues of the colour white.

"Visually white is unassuming, inoffensive and harmonious," she explained. "Spiritually it's uplifting, uncomplicated and pure. And emotionally it's quiet, gentle and balancing."

I wondered if she was quoting from her favourite filmscript, from a Hollywood clairvoyant or from her personal interior designer.

"Yes," I agreed, and added a little cheekily, "I read that somewhere too!"

Joan gave me a withering look. This, I thought, was not a good start to a dinner party.

Earl butted in, trying to salvage the situation. "We went to the opening of *The Glass Menagerie* the other night, Joan dear. Did you see it yet?"

He was referring to the twentieth anniversary production of Tennessee Williams's play, starring Maureen Stapleton. Joan waved her arm disparagingly,

"Earl, dear, you know me - and you should know how I feel about him and his plays!" She pronounced the word "him" with evident disgust.

I had no idea what she was on about. The way she spoke the words sounded petulant and dismissive as though she either hated Tennessee Williams personally or his plays professionally or, indeed, both. Pity, I thought, since, unlike many contemporary playwrights, he wrote particularly strong female roles, most of which were totally "off-the-wall" and would have suited Joan's melodramatic talents admirably.

"It was a wonderful production," I said defensively. "I love almost all his plays and Maureen Stapleton was excellent as Amanda."

"No doubt," Joan replied icily, removing the cigarette from its holder and stubbing it out fiercely in the ashtray. I sensed then that Joan didn't like any form of competition, that a compliment about another actress's work was immediately translated into a threat to her own acting abilities.

The maid came in at that moment and announced that dinner was ready. If I was expecting to be ushered into a white dining room I was about to be disappointed. Joan beckoned her in. The maid disappeared for a minute and then reappeared pushing a trolley in front of her. It dawned on me then we were going to eat off our laps. This, perhaps, helped to explain the plastic on the chairs. The maid unfolded huge white napkins and draped them over our knees before handing round plates of homemade sandwiches. I half expected the television to be turned on so we could enjoy a TV dinner but, looking around, I saw there was no television set in the room. The laboured conversation would have to continue.

Joe came to the rescue. "Earl tells me you don't entertain too often?"

Joan sighed theatrically, "It's difficult in my business. I have too little time to myself. And the children need me when I'm at home."

I wondered where the children were. I hadn't heard a sound of anything that even resembled a child.

"Are your children here?" I asked.

"Oh, yes, but I always make sure they're in bed by 6pm. I need some time alone, you understand and, when I have guests, I don't want us to be disturbed."

I wanted to tell her I would have much preferred being momentarily "disturbed" by her children than by the persistent discomfort of her plastic seating arrangement that, on this hot summer night, was becoming increasingly clammy on the thighs despite the fact that I appeared to be seated directly beneath the full blast of the apartment's air conditioning.

For once I was very relieved when Joe announced we had to proceed to another party We made a hasty getaway, leaving Joan perched on her plastic-covered sofa, inhaling another cigarette and pouring herself another vodka. I think I'd had so much pent up embarrassment during the evening that, once in the elevator, I started giggling hysterically.

"The woman is completely insane!" I blurted out, clutching my sides. "How can she live like that?"

"Same condition as Howard Hughes," Earl explained, "simply terrified of germs!"

"You must admit it was worth it, though," Joe pointed out, "you'll be able to dine out on that yarn for a while."

Poor kids, that's all I could think of.

"Just imagine what it must be like having a mother like her! Perfectly tailored clothes. Perfectly manicured nails. Perfectly mascaraed eyes. Perfectly pencilled eyebrows! Perfectly painted lips! And an ego to match. Can you think of anything worse?"

I could have added the lack of warmth, the lack of affection and, above all, the lack of humour - how could any child bear that? It certainly didn't surprise me almost a decade later when her adopted daughter, Christina, published a "kiss and tell" book about life with *Mommie Dearest*, Joan Crawford. I doubted if there was room in Joan's house for two stubborn, strong-headed and willful women.

A few weeks later, I was sitting at our local Health Food Bar directly below Earl's apartment on 57th & 6th. It was lunchtime. As usual the place was packed. People were standing behind the bar stools waiting for them to be vacated. As I was sipping my juice, I heard voices behind me, chattering excitedly. I recognized the language. It was Serbo-Croat. I turned around to see a middle-aged couple, obviously very much in love, hugging and stroking each other, kissing and gazing into each other's eyes.

I told them I was about to leave and one of them could have my seat. But first, I asked, "Are you from Jugoslavia?"

The woman answered, "Yes, my husband has just arrived in this country! I hadn't seen him in 15 years!"

I told them my mother was from Dubrovnik.

And the woman replied, "The person who smuggled my husband out of Jugoslavia was from Dubrovnik."

She then asked me what my mother's name was. I replied, "Daska Ivanovic."

The woman looked intrigued. "Does she have anyone in her family called Vane Ivanovic?"

I said, "That's my Uncle, my mother's older brother!"

The woman threw her arms around me. "Your Uncle saved my husband!"

I couldn't believe it. We looked at each other, totally incredulous. The man smiled, then, somewhat awkwardly, bent over and hugged me too.

"Please thank him for me!" he whispered, "I have waited all these years. I never thought I would see my wife again."

I had heard family rumours that my Uncle Vane had managed to smuggle many people out of Communist Jugoslavia following the end of World War II. But here, in 1965, at the unlikely venue of a health-food counter on 57th Street, I had the proof.

My father, Geoffrey Kennedy.

My grandmother, Milica with Vladimir, Daska & Vane.

My motherm Daska

My sisters, Tessa & Marina

My Mother with Alexander, Marina, Tessa and me.

My Stepmother, Daphie and Christopher.

Stepfather Billy McLean (right).

Casa Ivanovic in Formentor.

Family Portrait in Mallorca 1952.

Front View of La Guarda.

My friend, Caterine Milinaire.

Julie Gabor with Magda, Zza Zza and Eva.

My friend, Rita Gam.

My neighbours, Norman Mailer & Jeannie Campbell.

Caroline Kennedy

Bobby Short and friends.

Our elevatorman, Cecil, by Bill Cunningham.

Gloria Vanderbilt & Truman Capote.

Jimi Hendrix and Johnny Winter playing at the Scene.

Tiny Tim playing at the Scene.

Earl Blackwell with Carol Channing.

Joan Crawford.

Sharon Tate.

Caroline Kennedy

Edie Sedgwick and Baby Jane Holzer

My friend Baby Jane Holzer & Andy Warhol

My friend, Sarah Dalton and artist Jasper Johns

Chapter 11
Andy Edie & Baby Jane

I realized very soon after I had moved in with Joe, that I was woefully ill-equipped, in the fashion department, to compete with all the "First Night" ladies in the audience. How could I possibly hope to be as well-dressed as the likes of Carolina Herrera, Babe Paley, C Z Guest, Gloria Vanderbilt and others who were all in an unspoken competition to turn the most heads as they sashayed down the aisles and who would inevitably make it onto the front page of *Women's Wear Daily* or into the columns of Joseph X Dever or Suzy Knickerbocker the following day. These ladies were there simply not to see but to be seen.

But this was the early 60s and, by now, a new generation of style princesses with an anarchic sense of fashion, were the ones turning heads at first nights and movie premieres. These included, top models Marisa Berenson and Peggy Moffitt, society darling Amanda Burden, and "the first of the free spirits" Christina Paolozzi. But the Queen of them all, of course, was Andy Warhol's muse, Edie Sedgwick. Instead of wearing an elaborate ballgown, Edie would sashay down the aisle, dressed only in tights and a simple top, or a mini skirt and a brightly-coloured sweater or gold harem pants with a bra top. Eyebrows would arch and gasps of horror would follow her. Edie was delighted with this reception every time. She and Andy liked to shock. And, just like the previous generation of society beauties, they too liked to be noticed, photographed and written about.

So, by the end of 1964, thanks to my friend, Sarah, I had met some of New York's most prized artists, Larry Rivers, Claes Oldenburg, Robert Rauschenberg, Jackson Pollock, Roy Lichtenstein and Jasper Johns. But the artist I was really intrigued by was Andy Warhol. To me Warhol, though naturally shy on a personal level, epitomized everything that was brash, cocky and arrogant in the art world of New York in the early Sixties.

In a few years, the master of self-promotion had made an unparalleled transformation from minor commercial artist to living icon and, despite his lack of social skills, he appeared to thrive on his newfound celebrity status. He and his coterie of female acolytes, Baby Jane Holzer, Viva, Ingrid Superstar, Ultra Violet and Edie

Sedgwick, could be seen, almost every night, at art openings, movie premieres and first nights. And, despite their outrageous fashions and their willingness to shock they were written about, photographed, filmed and adored by journalists and society matrons alike. And, like everyone else, I too became fascinated by them.

I was particularly captivated by two of Warhol's stars, Baby Jane Holzer and Edie Sedgwick, both of whom I got to know quite well. The two were very different in appearance. The one, an impeccably dressed, upper crust, leonine blonde and the other a leotard-clad, crop-haired super waif.

But, unlike the other girls who formed part of Warhol's entourage, Baby Jane and Edie did have something in common. They both came from privileged backgrounds, the former from a wealthy real estate family on the East coast, the latter from a wealthy ranching family out West. To Warhol, a self-made man, this added immensely to their fascination. For, even at the end of his life, despite the monumental success he achieved and the financial security that accompanied it, Warhol remained impressed by "old" money and flattered by the adulation from what he perceived as Manhattan's "elite".

The glaring difference between Baby Jane and Edie was that whereas the former "dabbled" in Warhol's underground whilst maintaining an upper-middle-class lifestyle, complete with a respectable husband, black tie dinners and fashionable lunch parties, Edie totally rejected her West Coast family background, distanced herself from the life it offered and devoted herself entirely to the Warhol Factory.

Ironically, as Andy Warhol's popularity grew so Edie's assumed bohemian existence became increasingly upper middle-class again as they were invited into the homes of the rich, famous and powerful. But while Baby Jane preserved her detached, sophisticated and impeccable image, Edie adopted an increasingly androgynous look and, whether by design or accident, ended up as a mirror image of Warhol.

I remember Joe whispering to me one night as Edie passed us, clinging to Andy's arm, "Don't you think Edie's getting to look more like Andy than Andy does himself?" I had to admit it was true. They had begun to look remarkably similar.

As the excitement of being part of the Factory gradually wore thin, Baby Jane began to detach herself from the booze, the drugs, the crazed parties and the bizarreness that its lifestyle demanded. Edie, on the other hand, embraced it all, the sex, the amphetamines, the bouts of depression, the persistent bulimia and, finally, in a desperate bid to be noticed by Hollywood, even breast implants.

Sadly for Edie, this bid for mainstream recognition was destined to fail. By that time, she had burned herself out. The drugs, the sex and the eating disorders had taken their toll. Her frail body gave up the unequal struggle.

In the end, Baby Jane, with her innate instinct for self-preservation, became a rare thing - one of the very few Warhol survivors. But Edie had so identified with him that, like several other of his superstars who died a premature death from drugs, alcohol or suicide, she ultimately became his most celebrated victim. And while Joe and I became quite close to Baby Jane over the four years I was with him in New York, Edie always remained something of an enigma.

One evening Joe and I sat briefly with Edie in a darkened corner of the Scene. On the surface she appeared as she always did, serene, vulnerable and beautiful. But I couldn't help thinking she reminded me of a caged bird, flapping its wings in a desperate but hopeless struggle to release itself.

We started talking about books and our favourite authors. We found out we had something in common. We both admired Truman Capote. In fact, we remembered the two of us had first met briefly the previous December at the New York Armory where Truman had given the first public reading of his eagerly-anticipated, unpublished non-fiction novel, *In Cold Blood*, describing the tragic, ruthless murder of the entire Clutter family at their farm in rural Kansas.

Fever had been mounting in New York for a few weeks before the event since the rumour had gone out that, although Truman was supposed to be reading from *Breakfast at Tiffany's*, he would in fact be reading passages from the much-heralded and long-awaited, *In Cold Blood*.

It turned out to be a thrilling, yet deeply disturbing, night as both author and audience were only too aware that the young murderers, Dick Hickock and Perry Smith, were due to be executed pending the outcome of their third appeal to the Supreme Court. (Indeed, the following month, January 1965, the Supreme Court rejected their latest appeal and they were executed on the 14th April the same year).

"Wasn't that an amazing night?" Edie shouted to make herself heard above the pounding music. "It's a great book. One of his best. Do you dig his short stories? We do. Andy loves The Innocents, because it's gothic. But my favourites are Children on Their Birthdays and Miriam."

Joe and I discussed her choices later that night. Somehow they were very revealing. We couldn't help imagining that Edie identified with the menacing ghostlike quality of Miriam and the aloof, somewhat ethereal beauty of the doomed Lily Jane Bobbit. Joe told Edie that he and I both intended to be authors one day and maybe, when she was a big star in Hollywood, we'd write about her.

For a brief second during our conversation I sensed the little bird wanted to break free but, without realizing it, Edie was trapped in a deadly web. She desperately wanted the fame, the stardom and the notoriety that being Andy's consort offered but, at the same time, she failed to see it was dragging her deeper and deeper into a self-destructive abyss from which she was unlikely ever to recover.

A few weeks later, I visited the Warhol Factory to interview Andy for a special edition of the *Sandy Lesberg Nighttime Programme*. If I had expected to find the place a hive of activity, I was sorely disappointed. A couple of early-risers had just spilled out of bed and were stumbling around bleary-eyed, cigarettes dangling from their lips, cups of cold black coffee in their hands. Most were still curled up dead to the world, on every available surface, sofas, chairs, beds, tables and floors. This was 2pm and the Factory was still sound asleep.

Evidence of the previous night's party remained in the congealed leftovers of take-out meals, bulging trash bags, empty spirit bottles, discarded clothing, the tell-tale signs of cigarette papers and overflowing ashtrays dotted about the rooms. In the corner of one room, a continuous film played silently on screen. I recognized the dark, brooding looks of one of the Factory's most famous actors, Ed Hood in *My Hustler*. The afternoon sun pierced the flimsy blinds reflecting rainbow prisms on the silver metallic wallpaper. I looked around for the famous shock of white hair but Andy Warhol was nowhere to be seen.

I chided myself for not accepting Baby Jane's earlier invitation to visit the Factory with her. Nor had I gone inside with Edie, when I dropped her and her friend off late one night in a taxi on my way home. Edie had told me everyone would still be up but, foolishly, I had decided 3am was too late for a chat, a joint and a cup of coffee. Looking around me now, I realized that, like nocturnal animals, the Factory's principal residents were up all night and asleep all day.

I felt foolish. I had arranged to interview Andy Warhol and he wasn't even there. Someone, who introduced himself as Greg, volunteered to peer under a few sheets and blankets to see if any of the dormant bodies belonged to Andy. I thanked him but told him not to bother, that I'd come back another time. I said I was curious, however, to see the art rooms, if he was willing to show them to me.

These rooms were where the silkscreens were created from Andy's designs. These rooms were the nerve center of the Warhol Factory. These rooms were where the Factory's non-residents came to work on a normal 9-5 basis. This was where the money was made to keep the whole operation, the books, the artwork, the films, the newsletters, the underground movement and the publicity machine going.

To enter these rooms was like entering a different world. Suddenly I became immersed in lights, colour, noise, music and shelf upon shelf containing the celebrated lithographs, screen-prints and designs. Here were the artists who executed Andy's ideas. And they were all hard at work, oblivious perhaps, of the sleeping bodies next-door. This, indeed, was a factory undeniably designed by a commercial artist for commercial success. I thanked Greg and left. I came away never having actually interviewed Andy Warhol but, somehow, knowing him little better than I did when I arrived.

Chapter 12
In the Company of Writers

"Come on, little one, pack your bags, we're off!" Joe stood over the bed, gently shaking me awake.

"Off? Where to?" I grunted, turning over to see what the heavy lump was at the end of the bed. It was Joe's battered old suitcase, already packed, and waiting to be locked.

"The Caribbean!" he replied nonchalantly, "Hurry, otherwise we'll miss the plane!"

"What is this?" I asked, half asleep, "a joke?"

"No, a little holiday. We've been invited to the opening of the Casino at the Sheraton Hotel in Aruba. I bet you'll be out of bed in a second when you see the guest list!" He dangled a piece of paper tantalizingly above my head, which I feebly attempted to snatch out of his hand.

"You can do better than that!" he laughed, walking out of the bedroom. "Come, get it. I'll fix you some coffee."

I pulled back the sheet, swivelled my legs over the side of the mattress and tested the cold hardwood floor with my toes. Stumbling out onto the minstrel's gallery, I played with the idea of shinning down Jeannie's rubber tree, which I could have sworn had grown and swelled a good few feet since its arrival. It seemed to have a mind of its own and, attracted by the light from the huge picture windows on two sides of the room, its tentacle-like branches appeared to be spreading to all corners of the studio.

When I reached the bottom of the staircase Joe handed me a cup of steaming coffee.

"If you hurry up and pack," he said, "we'll have time to have breakfast in the deli before we leave."

By "the deli" he meant our neighbourhood Horn and Hardart's, the cut-price, over-the-counter, fast food eatery that served as our breakfast club. It was clean, cheap and convenient.

"So who's going with us?" I asked,

"Your friend, Caterine, for one." Joe replied. I was relieved to hear that. Caterine would be a good companion on a trip like this and, after all, it was she who had been instrumental in arranging the blind date between Joe and me in the first place. Since then we had all spent many memorable weekends together with our mutual friend, the sculptress Barbara Mortimer and her husband Stanley, in their idyllic Litchfield, Connecticut retreat.

"Who else? Where's that piece of paper?" I asked impatiently.

Joe picked it up and read off some of the names. I shrugged my shoulders. Typical New York socialites, I wasn't that interested.

Then he hesitated, "Here's the good part," he teased.

"Let's see it!" I made a grab for the paper but he pulled away. "Come on, I'm not in the mood for teasing."

I made a second grab, spilling the coffee down my dressing gown. This time Joe gave in.

I devoured the list quickly. It was peppered from top to bottom with society names but then there, staring me in the face, were the names of some of my favourite authors: "JOHN STEINBECK", "TRUMAN CAPOTE", "JAMES MICHENER", "TOM WOLFE" and "GORE VIDAL". Other equally impressive names were there too, some of whom I'd already met. Charles Addams, creator of the Addams Family, Art Buchwald, satirist and columnist for the Herald Tribune, Burt Bacharach the composer and, someone who I hadn't yet met, Al Capp, creator of the L'il Abner cartoons.

For a moment I stood rooted to the spot. In all my life I have never been "celebrity-struck", nor, like some people I know, ever thrilled at the prospect of meeting famous people. I have never, in fact, been a name-dropper or a social climber. But all this was about to change. The idea that I was soon to meet some of my favourite authors convinced me it wouldn't take much for me to become shamefully "author-struck".

"Aren't you impressed?" Joe asked.

"Impressed? I'm dumbstruck." I replied. And I meant it.

I didn't need any more encouragement from Joe. My packing was probably completed in less than ten minutes, plenty of time to eat breakfast around the corner and contemplate how I would pluck up the courage to ask the great John Steinbeck for an interview.

"Why didn't you tell me about this trip before?" I asked Joe while munching on a chocolate fudge brownie.

"I thought it would be a nice surprise for you." Joe smiled. "Besides we have nothing better to do this weekend."

"Do you think I could get to interview some of the writers?" I asked eagerly.

The mere thought of interviewing the incomparable John Steinbeck suddenly filled my stomach with butterflies. What would I ask him? Had I read all his books? Could I remember them sufficiently to conduct an intelligent discussion about them? And what could I say to James Michener, a man who, I was acutely aware, took seven painstaking years to research each of his books on Hawaii, Japan and Spain. The adrenalin rush had faded. I felt faint. I pushed aside the plate leaving my fudge brownie, for the first time ever, half eaten.

Joe smiled at me in a fatherly way.

"God, I'm an idiot!" I announced aloud.

Joe kissed me on the forehead and got up to pay the bill.

"Come on, let's get to the airport before we miss our flight!'"

The plane had been chartered by Sheraton hotels. Everything was free and the people on board were definitely in party mood. Although not everyone on the guest list had showed up (Truman Capote and Gore Vidal were noticeably absent), the plane appeared almost full. While Joe wrote his column ready to file on our arrival, Caterine and I meandered up and down the aisle stopping to chat with friends or being introduced to new ones.

"Caroline, I'd like you to meet a good friend of mine, Al Capp." Earl Blackwell grabbed my arm as I passed his aisle seat. "Al, I don't think you've met Caroline Kennedy yet."

I stretched out my hand across Earl. Al Capp held onto it far longer than was necessary.

"Charming," he smiled.

Earl had obviously noticed.

"Don't worry about him, darling girl, he's a well-known lecher but he's completely harmless."

Caterine was beckoning me to join her further up the plane. I withdrew my hand with some difficulty from Al's forceful grasp, made my fumbled excuses and made my way up to the front of the plane.

On the way down the aisle, I noticed John Steinbeck, drink in hand, eyes closed, deep in thought. I felt a sudden urge to touch him on the shoulder, wake him from his reverie, introduce myself and ask him for an interview. But, being a professional wimp, I quickened my pace as I passed him lest he should open his eyes and notice me staring at him open-mouthed, like the dumbstruck fan that I was.

Caterine, meanwhile, had been chatting to the notorious Venezuelan playboy millionaire, Reynaldo Herrera. I had met Reynaldo some summers before. His niece, Mercedes, was a neighbour of my family in Formentor, Mallorca. Ever the gentleman, Reynaldo, despite his advanced age and his dependence on an ebony and silver cane, rose from his seat to greet me. He kissed my hand.

"Two beautiful unattached girls," he drooled, "I must be in heaven! Come here, little Carolina, let me give you a big hug."

I drew closer and he enveloped me in his arms, squeezing me against his chest.

"You hear my heart, mi amor?" he whispered in my ear, "that's how you. How you say it? You turn me on."

That evening Joe wanted some time alone to interview some of the other guests so Caterine and I arranged to meet up with Reynaldo Herrera, who turned out to be a generous benefactor. After treating us to a champagne dinner he thrust $1000 dollars into each of our respective palms and sent us off to the hotel Casino.

"Here, sweet ladies," he smiled erotically, "have some fun with this. If you lose you come back and find me. There's much, much more! My room number is 507, remember that!"

There was no doubting the inference of his last remark but, purposely ignoring it, Caterine and I set off for the gambling tables. We both chose blackjack because, being comparative innocents, that was the only game we knew how to play. Needless to say, by the end of the night we left the table empty-handed but neither of us had ever enjoyed losing money so much. It didn't belong to us so we didn't care and we could afford to be profligate, taking foolish risks and placing large bets on dubious cards.

We didn't, however, take Reynaldo up on his offer for more money. Neither of us felt tempted to go tapping on his bedroom door in the middle of the night. I strongly suspected that the price we might have to pay was, at worst, an hour or more in his bed struggling to avoid any physical contact with him and, at best, an awkward, fumbling grope in his darkened room, neither of which appealed to either of us.

On the last day, it occurred to me I hadn't yet plucked up the courage to interview John Steinbeck, my main reason for coming to Aruba. Subconsciously I suppose, I had been putting off approaching him in case he rejected me.

When, on the last evening, I did eventually find Steinbeck on his own, I introduced myself and asked if I could sit down beside him. Gentleman that he was, he appeared genuinely flattered by my attention. Sadly, though, our talk only lasted about five minutes before his friends, including Al Capp approached inviting him to join them for dinner.

"Won't you join us for dinner, Caroline?" Al asked, "We'd love it, wouldn't we, John?"

Steinbeck smiled at me, "Yes, And perhaps Joe can join us too."

Reluctantly I replied, "Thanks, but I think Joe and I have other plans."

I was only half-lying, I had managed to arrange an interview with James Michener after dinner.

Though my moment with John Steinbeck had been brief, sadly too brief even to write up, the interview I had with James Michener, later that night, lasted an hour, at least, and it was eventually published a year later.

"It's not easy to be a writer these days," Michener explained, "I am trying to duplicate the great English travel writers, the literary travellers."

He quoted several examples including Isabella Bird's Travels, Lady Calderon de la Barca's "Mexico" and D.H. Lawrence's "Sardinia. I told him those books had been devoured by me in my late teens when my love of early travel books had become a passion.

I asked him the reason for his undeniable infatuation for the South Pacific.

"You'll find out when you get there!" he replied, "You will go. I can tell by your enthusiasm you're a fellow wanderer, a natural traveler."

"One day I'll definitely go there!" I said.

An hour later, Michener's third wife, Japanese-born Mari Yoriko Sabusawa, turned his attention to his watch. He dutifully got up, shook my hand and whispered,

"Keep working hard. It's worth it, believe me. Maybe one day I'll see your name on the cover of a book and I'll be able to say I encouraged her when she was just starting out. That will give me great satisfaction. Go ahead, Caroline, just do it!"

Chapter 13
The First of the Free Spirits

From 1963 onwards Manhattan's social events were considered incomplete without the presence of Christina Paolozzi, the daughter of an impoverished Italian Count and a prominent American heiress. Christina, referred to in the society pages as "The first of the Sixties free spirits", provided an invigorating breath of fresh air to those New Yorkers who had managed to shake themselves loose from the moralistic shackles of the 1950's.

To the majority of them, however, who remained judgmental and bound by strict codes of behavior, Christina managed to provide insult after insult. Her initial shock was to conduct a very public affair with a married man. And he was not just any married man. The man in question was Yul Brynner, the bald-headed Russian actor who was then at the height of his fame, following his successes in *The Magnificent Seven* and *The King and I* for which he received an Academy Award.

Christina's carefree attitude, her naïve immorality and her sense of fun were contagious. I had never met anyone quite like her. Her warmth, her spontaneity, her rebellious streak and her generosity of spirit had a lasting impact on me and on all those who knew her. Christina loved life and she loved living it to the full. We discovered an immediate and enduring kinship that survived both our marriages and living on different continents but was finally cut short by her premature death from a brain tumor in 1988.

Many nights Christina and I drove around town, either on our own or with a group of friends, to see what mischief we could get up to. We would start in downtown Greenwich Village, dropping into places such as the Peppermint Lounge, Ondine's, Max's Kansas City and the Scene, checking out the music, the atmosphere and the people. When, finally worn out, we would end up either in her Park Avenue apartment or in the Carnegie Hall studio.

One summer night Joe had an old friend in town. Mark Birley was the owner Annabel's, the most popular nightclub in London. Joe suggested we show Mark a different side of New York, something a world away from fashionable Berkeley Square – a visit to the famous Apollo Theatre in Harlem. Used to the stuffy atmosphere of London's social scene, Mark was thrilled at the idea. Although Harlem at night was considered dangerous territory for anyone other than its own residents and, thus, out of bounds to most white New Yorkers, neither Christina nor I gave it a second thought. There was a cab strike so the four of us piled into an uptown bus and watched out of the window, fascinated, as the architecture, the mood and the character of New York changed in front of our eyes. There was nothing subtle about these changes. The well-maintained buildings of Fifth Avenue soon gave way to drabness, decay and dereliction the further uptown we went. Wretched poverty and a sense of futility, despair and hopelessness were etched into the faces of the people in the street.

The crowd gathering outside the Apollo when we arrived that night looked at us suspiciously. This was understandable since we were the only white people there. No doubt they immediately recognized us for what we, undeniably, were - four upper-middle-class whites out looking for some action.

Inside the place was literally jumping. Martha and the Vandellas were playing live onstage. The audience were clapping, dancing and singing along with them. The lights, the atmosphere, the colours, the fashions, the music, the noise and the sheer exuberance, in stark contrast to the streets of Harlem outside, were exhilarating. Mark, in his very British way, was enchanted by the whole scene. I realized how different it must have seemed to him compared to the staid, somewhat prissy atmosphere of his own club in London.

As we danced to Martha and the Vandellas that night, Christina and I had no idea that this would not be our last visit together to Harlem - the next one under very different, far more serious, circumstances.

Not long after our visit to the Apollo, Christina did something that astounded all her friends, even me. She announced she had fallen in love. Not with someone any of us knew and not, as we would have imagined, with a handsome playboy jetting her off in his private plane to the polo fields of Argentina. Nor with a famous movie star sweeping her off to life in a Beverly Hills mansion. Nor, even, to a romantic, but impoverished, European nobleman like her father. No, she told us, she had fallen in love with a young intern trauma surgeon, Howard Bellin.

"Howard who?" Joe asked.

"You might not have heard of him now," Christina replied tartly, "but give him ten years and he'll be more well-known than me."

In her choice of Howard, Christina was, for the first time, showing a different, more sober, side to her personality. Perhaps the timing was right for her and life in the fast lane was beginning to pall. To us, as onlookers, their opposing characters could have clashed abysmally but, as it was, they both appeared to benefit from each other, blossoming in opposite ways. Howard became more outgoing and less obsessed by his work. And, while not losing any of her sense of fun, Christina managed to stifle some of her natural exuberance to settle into life as a young surgeon's wife.

Joe, for one, didn't think the marriage would last. "Christina's far too headstrong," he predicted. "She'll opt out within a couple of years, you'll see."

I was a romantic. The idea of a failed marriage, particularly one involving my best friend, upset me.

"I think you're wrong." I protested. "Christina has met her match this time. You haven't seen them together like I have. Howard's absolutely right for her and she knows it. She adores him."

"We'll see!" It was obvious that Joe, like many of our friends, needed convincing.

Most could not believe that the ubiquitous blonde with the piercing blue-green eyes, the girl who loved to be everywhere at the same time, the enchanting rebel who loved to shock, would ever settle down to a normal family life. How wrong they all were. And how happy I was when, some summers later in London, Howard and Christina proudly introduced me to their two sons, Marco and Andy. I could see then that, despite the normal ups and downs endemic to all long-term relationships, despite the numerous public affairs flaunted in the media, theirs remained, without doubt, a strong marriage.

One evening, during the feverishly hot summer of 1965 Christina called me, "Caroline darling, you've gotta help me out!"

"What is it?" I asked, half expecting her to answer, as she often did, that we should all go downtown for an evening's fun and games.

"There's a local hospital workers' strike, haven't you read about it?" she continued breathlessly, "You must come and help Howard at his hospital. They desperately need auxiliaries!"

"But…" I stammered. I was about to tell her that I fainted at the sight of blood.

"No, you've got to help, Caroline, I'm asking all my friends. Please come!"

I realized there was little point in prevaricating. "OK, OK, I'll do it."

There was a sigh of relief at the other end of the phone.

"Which hospital should I go to and at what time?" I asked.

"The Hospital Center," she replied.

"Where's that?" I asked.

"Harlem, 120th Street!" she replied, "near the East River."

"Harlem? You've got to be kidding me!"

"I'll pick you up at six. OK?"

"In the morning?"

"No, the evening. We've gotta do the night shift you and I. That's when Howard's on duty!"

"All night? Christina, honestly I really don't think."

But I should have learnt by now that it was a waste of breath trying to say no to Christina. Her charm won out every time. I folded immediately, realizing there was no use fighting it.

"Caroline?"

"OK, yes, that's fine. I'll be ready!"

"Thanks, I love you. I won't forget it."

"You might not forget it but you may regret it!" I laughed. "See you tomorrow at 6pm."

I put the phone down. I looked over at Joe. "You won't believe that!" I said, "That was Christina wearing her Florence Nightingale hat. She wants me to be a nursing auxiliary at Harlem Hospital Center tomorrow night!"

"And you said yes?"

"I guess I did," I replied.

Due to the ongoing transit strike in New York, Christina had ordered a chauffeured car to pick me up. I felt as if we were going off on one of our nightly jaunts to the discos. But, instead, we were heading uptown to a very rundown general hospital right in the heart of Harlem. I was not sure the hospital workers, who were probably on a picket line outside the main gate, would appreciate our altruistic reasons for being there.

As we made our way uptown, Christina gave me some idea about what I was about to experience.

"There are shootings every night, particularly at this time of year," she said, referring to the hot summer months when tempers frayed easily. "And stabbings too. Howard usually stitches them up and then they insist on going home. They're normally back the following week, Howard says, with some other injury."

I was beginning to feel sick already. I wasn't cut out to be a nursing assistant – that much was obvious.

"Have you done this sort of thing before?" I asked her.

"Only over the last couple of days - during this strike," she replied. "But I am already planning your reward."

"What reward, what are you talking about?" I was offended that she thought I needed to be recompensed for a doing her a favour.

"I didn't mean that. But Howard and I are planning to give a dinner party for Leslie Uggams when she opens at the Cocacabana. We thought it might be nice if we invited all our 'nursing auxiliaries' to come along."

We arrived at the hospital and, as I suspected, a handful of striking staff with placards were stationed outside. I felt like scab labour. We couldn't very well pass ourselves off as patients up in Harlem. So, with heads held high, we catapulted ourselves out of the chauffeured limo and made a dash for the door of the Emergency Department.

The scene inside was utter bedlam. Young mothers with howling children, lone adults in slings and plasters wailing loudly, youths with various injuries picking a fight among themselves as they waited to be seen by a doctor. The floor looked like it hadn't been swept for a week. There were bloody swabs everywhere, soiled dressings and discarded food wrappers, drinks cartons and cigarette butts. I took one look and started to panic.

"What shall I do? Where shall I start?" I shouted to Christina above the racket.

"Let's go and see Howard first," she said, taking me firmly by the arm and whisking me away, "just to let him know we're here. He'll tell us what to do!"

She led me towards the operating theatre where Howard, unrecognizable in blue cap, mask, surgical gown and gloves, had just completed an operation.

I stood silently outside the room thinking *'what the hell am I doing here?'* I watched, transfixed, as Christina donned her own gown and mask, scrubbed her hands, eased on a pair of rubber gloves and went to stand beside Howard. She nudged one of the auxiliary nurses.

"Thanks, Jane, you can go now!" she whispered. "I can take over. The car's waiting for you outside."

Howard looked at Christina. I could see from the wrinkles forming around his eyes that he was smiling. Above her mask her distinctive pale blue-green eyes stared back at him. That look, I think, was the defining moment when I knew for certain their marriage was going to last. Christina had finally come of age.

Howard, peeling off his gloves, walked towards the basin to scrub his hands. Christina and another nurse started wheeling the trolley out of the room. Howard approached me at the door. He removed his mask and beamed at me.

"Thanks for coming, Caroline," he said. "Isn't Christina great for arranging all this. I don't know what I would have done without her and all of you."

"She's very persuasive," I smiled. "So now that I'm here, tell me what can I do to help".

"Why don't you stay out in reception and, after the house doctor has triaged the patients, bring them into theatre for me. You'll need to get a gown and mask. The receptionist will show you where."

He started to walk back into operating room. As he reached for the door, he turned back. "Oh, and if they're any real emergencies alert me straightaway. OK?"

I was alone, or so it seemed. All kinds of people, in all states of distress and conditions, poured in through the doors of the Emergency Department. Getting them to line up at the Receptionist's desk was a major battle. They finally formed a queue of sorts, after jostling, shoving and pushing their way as close to the front as they could. As is always the case, the stronger ones got to the top while the weaker, and probably the needier, ones were shunted behind. It didn't take long for the bullies to work out I had no idea what I was doing and they took full advantage of it.

Within half an hour the door burst open and a man, with his throat, apparently slashed from ear to ear, was being dragged in on the arms of another man. The man carrying him shouted for help but all I could see was the blood bubbling and frothing from his companion's neck. I felt my own blood drain from my head. My brain started to feel dizzy and, before I knew it, I had passed out on the linoleum floor.

The next thing I was aware of was Christina propping me up on her lap, attempting to pour brandy down my throat.

"Hang on" I whispered faintly, "I'm a teetotaller, remember? What happened?" I tried vainly to remember the scene.

"You fainted."

I nodded weakly. "Yes, I'm sorry. I did try to tell you I tend to do that at the sight of blood!" I smiled. "Too late now, I suppose."

Memories started to come back to me. "What happened to that guy? The one with his throat cut?"

"Howard's sewing him up right now."

"Who slashed him? What's the story?" Feeling better I sat up, eager to hear her explanation.

"Well, apparently, the guy who brought him in did it. They're best friends but they got drunk and had some fight over a girl. Howard says he'll be OK."

"How romantic!" I joked, "I wish two men would fight over me!"

Christina made good on her promise. Despite the fact I had been totally useless at the hospital, she still insisted I join her and Howard for the Leslie Uggams evening at the Cococabana. Our nightly jaunts downtown were now less frequent as Christina and Howard settled into married life.

Later that year, Christina was offered a syndicated fashion column through the North American Newspaper Alliance (NANA). She was thrilled at the prospect but doubted she could handle it on her own.

"Grammar and spelling, Caroline," she giggled, "are not my greatest talents, as you know!"

"You're not kidding!" I replied. "Your spelling is atrocious!"

"Then should we write it together, the two of us?" she asked. "Would you do it with me?"

I didn't know much about fashion so I asked if we could meet the editor who had offered her the job and discuss, perhaps, the idea of writing on several other topics besides fashion.

"Social and celebrity interviews, for instance," I suggested, "since both of us have the opportunity to meet a whole cast of characters who come through New York. Would he go for that idea, do you think?"

So, by the end of 1965, I finally had my first article published and syndicated across North America. Surprisingly, it was not Joe but Christina and my godmother, Olga Horstig, who I had to thank for the launch of my career as a paid journalist.

By early December the excitement had been mounting in New York following the announcement that, for the very first time, the sensuous French movie star, Brigitte Bardot would be visiting the city to publicize her latest movie, *Viva Maria*. And I was thrilled to receive a phone call from my godmother, Olga Horstig, offering me the much-coveted opportunity to meet and talk to Bardot behind the scenes. Olga was a top movie agent in Paris, her roster of clients including, Dirk Bogarde, Alain Delon, Michelle Morgan, Anthony Perkins and Charlotte Rampling. Olga and Brigitte had met decades earlier, during the filming of Roger Vadim's *And God Created Woman*. Brigitte had been 16 at the time and, from then on, regarded Olga as her substitute mother, calling her Mama Olga and trusting her with her most intimate secrets. By 1965 Bardot was a huge international star but had never visited the US due to her fear of flying.

Some said that Bardot didn't need to appear in person to make an impact on people. Her photographs and her movies were enough to catapult her to the very top. But, whilst most stars travelled the world to make films and to publicize them prior to distribution, Bardot stayed mainly in France, content to make European movies. Occasionally she would come to England but always travelled there by sea. I had already met her there once with Olga when she was evicted from the Dorchester Hotel for wearing a particularly modest outfit for her, a trouser suit. I remembered then the newspapers had had a field day.

"What's the matter?" she had growled in her strong French accent, "I'm not even showing my, how do you say, nude skin. And the Eenglish make a big fuss. What ees this place? Who are zese people?"

But now, in December 1965, she had made a brave decision, to fly to New York for the promotion of her first American movie, a western entitled, *Viva Maria*, co-starring Jeanne Moreau.

As soon as they arrived in New York, Olga invited me to the Plaza suite to interview Brigitte. This was a unique opportunity not offered to any other New York journalist. Brigitte was not giving any interviews, except one formal press conference followed by a television appearance. Olga told me I would be the only newspaper journalist allowed backstage with her. When word of this privilege got out I was inundated by offers to publish my article but I had promised it to the North American Newspaper Alliance (NANA) and they agreed to syndicate it all over North America.

Joe was so proud of me when he saw the article printed in several newspapers. To tell the truth, I was pretty proud of myself too. With the arrogance and optimism of youth, I knew nothing could stop me now. As a journalist, I thought, I was on my way.

My second and third articles, interviews with James Michener the previous year and with Tom Courtenay following the New York premiere of *Dr. Zhivago* were also published through NANA. With these three articles under my belt and a series of Christina's fashion columns in print, she and I were approached by the *New York Post* to write a daily column together. The suggestion was we would each write three a week. I couldn't quite believe my luck that another top job was about to land in my lap, without making any effort.

Strangely, among my mother's effects when she died in 2003, I found a letter I had written to her at that very time. It read:

"Something very thrilling has also cropped up and that is that Christina and I may have a daily column in the *New York Post* (an afternoon newspaper). Imagine that! We'll each write three a week. I hope to know by the end of the week whether it'll come off or not. I am so excited about it but it really seems too good to be true. Keep your fingers crossed.....Joe had no idea till three days ago that we were negotiating it. He is very excited about it too! Meanwhile, I think we shall have an 80% Christmas as Joe and I are jetting off to Palm Beach for the weekend. He has to cover the opening of *The Nutcracker Suite*. Don't you envy me?"

By the end of the following year, I had come to a conclusion. Much as I loved Joe, our exhilirating life in New York and the thrilling prospect of becoming a regular columnist, there was something gnawing at me. I recognized it immediately. It was the feeling I'd got before I came to New York. I was getting itchy feet again. I realized if I remained where I was, I would stagnate. My life was a constant buzz, yes. Because of Joe, I had could meet "anyone who was anyone" in New York, yes. I had just carved out a career, a career that I desperately wanted, yes. But there was something missing. Somehow it had all been too easy. I knew I could simply embrace it, exploit it and happily remain where I was forever. But my urge to travel had become too great to resist. Something had to change. I knew that.

Since my early teens, I had been devouring books by authors like Gertrude Bell, Isabella Bird, Margaret Mead and Freya Stark and I yearned to follow in their footsteps. Like Gertrude Bell, I wanted to feel equally comfortable with all kinds of people. Like Isabella Bird, I wanted to be a female trailblazer in remote and distant lands. Like Margaret Mead I wanted to immerse and assimilate myself into other cultures. And, like Freya Stark, I wanted to trek through uncharted territories searching for ancient cities. My head teemed with plans for adventures to remote and exotic places.

This interest was kindled in part by listening to inspiring, and often hair-raising, stories about my stepfather, Billy's, escapades in Sinkiang, Kandahar, Ethiopia, Albania, the Congo and Yemen. Place names that sounded so intriguing and so alluring that I couldn't wait to see them for myself. A road trip from Paris to Athens, the previous year, with Sarah, had added to my desire to see more of the world. I realized I loved being on the move, discovering new places, meeting new people, and learning about new cultures. I was already familiar with Europe but there were so many other places, so many far-distant places, the other side of the world that were beckoning to me. And I couldn't resist.

Joe was very understanding. "I knew this day would come, little one," he said. "And I never wanted to clip your wings. You've given me four precious years and I will cherish them. And, you know, if things don't work out, you can always come back. I will always welcome you home."

His words made me cry. I felt so guilty. He had offered me a life so rich in opportunities, so fascinating in experiences and I understood how fortunate I had been to meet him.

On one of our last evenings together, we had dinner in Greenwich Village with Francis Bacon, Tennessee Williams and Salvador Dali. And I remember asking myself, *am I completely crazy to leave all this? Will I ever get such an opportunity again? Who wouldn't have given everything they had to have an intimate dinner with these three remarkable men*? And here I was, making the decision to step away from it all and admit to myself that my urge to travel was stronger than my desire to meet even icons such as these. Yes, I decided, I probably was crazy.

But I had made up my mind and nothing would change it.

Leaving New York also meant I had to say goodbye to my girlfriends, Ming, Sarah, Christina, Caterine and Baby Jane. I knew I owed them a lot too. All of them had, in some way, helped me truly experience my New York period to the full. They had not only been my friends and my confidantes but also my accomplices, accompanying me to numerous pop concerts, plays, movies, art exhibitions, fashion shows, discos, nightclubs and poetry readings, occasionally sedately but very often causing mayhem. I would miss them too.

I always considered Joe Dever my guardian angel. Decades would pass and I would still feel him hovering over my shoulder, helping me make the right choices. And still, to this day, I feel tremendous gratitude that Joe Dever was part of my life. We remained very close friends up until he died following a stroke in 1997.

Chapter 14
A Stint at the BBC

In the Spring of 1967, at the age of 23, my room in Eaton Square awaited me. My family was preparing for my homecoming. And I had accepted a job at BBC News to start on June 5. I probably should have told everyone, my parents, my siblings and my new boss, that this situation was only going to be temporary. The BBC, I had decided, would simply be a stepping-stone, a place to hone some skills before embarking on my travels.

With a new job came a new boyfriend, John Wells, who was a founder member of the highly successful satirical news magazine, *Private Eye*. So, although I initially missed my coterie of friends in New York, I couldn't be sad for long. I was now surrounded by comedians, satirists and impersonators, friends and colleagues of John, including John Bird, John Fortune, Peter Cook, Dudley Moore and Barry Humphries.

At the end of May, John and I flew to Jordan as guests of the Crown Prince. We were taken to Petra, "the rose-red city, half as old as time" that had been photographed in 1925 by my great-grandfather, Sir Alexander Kennedy, who published a book on its antiquities entitled, *Petra - Its History and Monuments*.

Coincidentally, my first day at work was Monday, June 5 1967, the first day of the Six-Day War, the third war between Israel and a coalition of Arab States. I found it hard to believe that John and I had just returned from Jordan and had even been swimming in the Gulf of Aqaba a day before the guns went off there but had noticed nothing out of the ordinary. It seemed unreal. In fact, had I not needed to turn up for work that Monday, we probably would have ended up staying longer in Jordan and would have been caught up in the brief but deadly war. Again, my guardian angel was protecting me.

In the hopes that I was going to settle down in London, my mother had bought a flat for me at 15 Draycott Place, just off King's Road. And, from there, every day I drove my grey Sunbeam Alpine convertible to the BBC News at Alexandra Palace in North London. My neighbours above me were Henry Woolf and Susan Williamson, actors with the Royal Shakespeare Company. On a brief visit back to

London in 1964, I had seen them appear alongside Patrick McGee and Glenda Jackson in Peter Brook's groundbreaking production of *Marat-Sade*. When I moved into Draycott Place, they were all in rehearsals for *As You Like It*.

About a month after I started in the BBC newsroom, on June 29, I was standing by the ticker tape machine waiting to tear off the latest news and bring it to the news desk, when I noticed shocking photos of the movie star, Jayne Mansfield, who had been killed instantly when her car hit a trailer truck at night near Louisiana. Her children, who had been sleeping in the back seat, thankfully survived. As I gathered up the gruesome tape, a vivid memory returned.

In 1964, I had arranged an interview with Jayne and her young lover, the Dutch author and self-described libertine, Jan Cremer, for *The Sandy Lesberg Nighttime Program*. Cremer had recently become a cult figure in New York, creating enormous shock waves with his autobiography, *I, Jan Cremer* that set out in minute detail his very intimate relationships with many women and with Jayne Mansfield, in particular. When I met him he was also rumoured to be having an affair with one of Warhol's muses, Nico, from the Velvet Underground.

As 1967 drew to a close, my plans were materializing for my first solo journey to the Far East. I had booked myself the following April on the Trans-Siberian Railway that ran from Moscow in the west, across Siberia to Nakhodka in the Far East. All that was left to do was to book train tickets from Liverpool Street Station to Harwich, the ferry from Harwich to Rotterdam and another train ticket from Rotterdam, though East Berlin, West Berlin, Warsaw to Moscow. I also needed some financing. So I approached Heinemann and was offered an advance for a travel book of my solo journey around the world.

I had letters from the Associated Press war correspondent, Bob Tuckman, and NBC cameraman, Tom Streithorst, both of whom I knew from New York, offering a roof over my head when I arrived in Saigon and I had I a loose agreement with Lee Howard, the editor of the *Daily Mirror*, that he would pay for and print any article I wrote from Vietnam.

When word spread that I was planning to go to Hanoi and Saigon, panic started to set in within my family. When my parents couldn't dissuade me, I received a call from my grandmother, Milica, in Monaco. I expected her to use all her skills to talk me out of it. But I was to be pleasantly surprised.

"Now listen to me, Caroline, you are going to travel the wordl."

My grandmother could never pronounce "world" properly. It used to make me giggle. Even when she was trying to be stern, which was not often, she would always make the situation funny by delightfully mispronouncing her words.

"It's world, Baba. It's pronounced WORLD, with the D at the end."

"Never mind that! What I want to say is I have sent you a ticket. You are coming to stay with me next weekend. I have something I want to tell you."

On Saturday morning I arrived in Nice. There was my grandmother and her driver smiling at me when I exited Customs. I hugged her. The familiar scent of Jean Patou wafted over me as she held me in her arms.

"What did you want to tell me?" I asked.

She laughed. "It can wait till we get back to the apartment. Just tell me, how is your mother?"

We chatted all the way back to Monaco. In her top floor apartment overlooking the harbour, she settled herself down on the plush sofa. Her black silk coat billowed around her. Her wispy silver hair was tied back in a bun. Her heart-shaped face, as usual, was perfectly made-up. Her hands, plump and dotted by liver spots with well-manicured fingernails. Her brooch of yellow diamonds, her matching earrings and her gold and diamond Cartier watch were all so familiar to me.

She plumped up the silk cushions behind her back. We were surrounded by photos of our family on every available surface. They, too, I realized would become part of this conversation. Mostly in black and white, some in faded colour, these photos illustrated memories of the past decades of her life. Her early days in Dubrovnik, Zagreb and Belgrade. Summer holidays in Formentor. Winters in the Scottish Highlands. Serbian Orthodox Christmases at her suite in the Dorchester Hotel. Launches of the family tankers in Tokyo, Hamburg and Athens. Cruises to Ithaca, Sardinia and Ravenna on her yacht, the Daska. Backgrounds as varied and cosmopolitan as her life - New York, London, Rome, Cap Ferrat, Corfu, the Dominican Republic, Indo-China. Cousins, aunts, uncles, nieces, nephews, grandchildren, sisters, brothers. A cornucopia of vignettes from all our lives silently staring back at me from the safety of their solid silver frames. This was her dynasty. This was the family she had created and nurtured, spreading her widow's wealth to all, even to the most distant relatives back in Jugoslavia. Within her wide circle of friends and relations, scattered around the world, her generosity had become the stuff of legends.

She patted the seat beside her. I sat down in the same place I had sat just a few months before, beside Princess Grace during an after-dinner game of charades. Since her wedding to Prince Rainier eleven years earlier, Grace considered my grandmother her surrogate mother and confidante. She often dropped by to relax and chat when the confinement, isolation and formality of Palace life got her down.

"Sit down," my grandmother commanded, "and listen to me!"

I had never known any family member disobey her orders. Self-taught and multi-lingual Milica had married one of Jugoslavia's richest men. After his death she had taken up residence in Monte Carlo to offset taxes and was immediately courted by Prince Pierre, the father of Prince Rainier.

Wherever she went Milica Banac was always considered very much the "grande dame", the powerful matriarch of a sprawling multinational family. People tended to jump to attention when she entered the room as though she was royalty. Funny and loving to those who knew her but slightly intimidating to those who didn't, she was impishly imperious, exceedingly generous and gloriously wacky. And now she had demanded my presence before I set off around the "wordl" so that she could give me some "advises".

I sat down beside her. She took my hand in hers and looked me directly in the eye. "How long will you be away?" she asked.

"Not sure, Baba. Maybe two years." I replied.

She leant over and kissed me on the forehead. "Well," she said, "you travel for as long as you like. Travel is good. You learn a lot. That's how I learnt during my life."

"I intend to," I replied.

"Be free. You take as many boyfriends as you want. Don't listen to your mother. You can have lots of babies. But you mustn't let them interfere with your travel plans!"

I was about to interrupt but she waved her hand for me to keep quiet.

"You send them to me here in Monte-Carlo. I will look after them. I won't tell your mother."

I looked at her. She was joking, surely? But, no, I saw she was deadly serious.

"But I'm not planning to have babies on this trip," I spluttered.

"But you may," she smiled conspiratorially, raising her finger to lips, "and if you do, it needn't ruin your adventure. I will look after them until you get back."

I don't know how many babies she expected me to give birth to in the course of two years. But it was good to know I had an ally should anything unforeseen happen. I kissed her.

"Thank you, Baba, that's very kind. I will remember that."

"It's a secret from your mother, remember? She wouldn't approve." She attempted a wink.

"Our secret," I agreed.

The next day I returned to London, mission accomplished. My secret with Baba was safe. I knew I could rely on her if any "baby mishap" occurred during my travels.

On my return, my stepfather, well known as an intrepid wanderer, pressed some rare gold coins into my hands, saying, "If you get into trouble these will help.

They're better than any currency and will get you home should you run out of money!"

"Thanks," I said, looking at the five shiny coins in wonder. They looked unique, probably worth at least a couple of thousand to a collector. I turned towards my room.

"Oh, and another thing," he said, "don't tell your mother this…"

Why was everyone trying to keep my mother out of the conversation, I wondered.

He added, "I've got a few friends in Qatar and Abu Dhabi who could help you out financially." And then added, "If you needed it, of course. I'll give you their contact details, just in case."

"Thanks," I said, "but I doubt…." I did not fancy asking a Middle Eastern potentate or anyone else for money if I was stranded. I was on my way to Vietnam. I had a contract from Heinemann's and I was going to write a book.

"They'd probably even ask to marry you!" he chuckled as I disappeared down the hall. "They always ask me about my beautiful stepdaughters!"

I placed the five coins in the zipped compartment of my luggage and forgot about them.

"Are you in or out tonight?" my mother asked.

"Out!" I replied, "and I better get ready." I put away the items she had bought me for my travels – a hairbrush (up to the day she died, she always complained I never brushed my hair), a sweater for Siberia, a sarong for Vietnam and a long list of her friends and diplomats who she wanted me to look up during my travels.

"Always register at the British Embassy everywhere you go," she had advised. "You never know when you might need their help."

I said, "Yes, of course, Mummy," not, for one minute, thinking I would check in with the local British Ambassadors or any of her friends who might be under instruction from her to make sure I didn't associate with the "wrong type of people."

I was going to the Carlton Tower Hotel to have dinner with David Niven Jr who was planning to introduce me to his friend, the UPI photojournalist, Sean Flynn.

"You're both heading for Vietnam," David had told me a week or so earlier when I had met him at a dinner party, "Sean's an old hand in Vietnam, he's on his third assignment, so I'd like to get you two to meet before you both set off. He can give you some tips."

Sean Flynn turned out to be every bit as handsome and charming as his famous father, the movie star, Errol Flynn.

And as an "old hand" in Vietnam, Sean had many hair-raising stories to tell.

"I've been injured a few times too," he laughed, rolling up his trousers revealing a deep scar on his knee.

"And he has grenade fragments on his arms and chest," David said. "Are you sure you want to go there, Caroline? It's dangerous!"

"Certainly not for the faint-hearted!" Sean smiled at me. "But I can see you're determined. So how can I help?"

I told him about my plans to write a story for *The Daily Mirror* about young Vietnamese girls and their babies who had been abandoned by their US soldier boyfriends. He listened and jotted down a few names and phone numbers.

"And this is my number," he added. "If I'm not there, leave a message and I'll get back to you."

I tucked the piece of paper away in my bag.

"This will probably be my last good meal in a long time," Sean said with a delicious smile at me after ordering a sirloin steak. "I'm off tomorrow morning – early!"

"Lucky you, " I replied, "I'm not leaving until April and then I'm going by train through Rotterdam, West Berlin, East Berlin, Warsaw, Moscow and Siberia. Then after a couple of weeks in Japan, I will stop off in Hong Kong to get my visa for Saigon."

We arranged a date to meet up in Saigon at the end of May and hugged each other goodbye.

"You're sure you'll be there?" Sean whispered, "I'll be waiting for you!"

"Of course!" I responded, "I'm counting on you to show me the ropes."

Neither of us could have foreseen that, by the time of our planned rendezvous in Saigon just a couple of months later, Sean would be reported missing, presumed dead, having possibly driven his motorcycle over a landmine near the border with Cambodia.

Anticipation was mounting. Bob, my boss at the BBC, gave a small farewell party and handed me two packages containing 36 rolls of film as a gift. Gilles Milinaire, brother of my New York friend Caterine, moved into my flat in Draycott Place having agreed to rent it for the two years I would be away. I said my goodbyes to every member of my family.

And then, finally, the big day arrived. I was on my way. The adventure was about to begin.

Chapter 15
11,000 Miles & 8 Time Zones

"Are you sure you're safe? I've been so worried about you." After a disturbing number of clicks, my mother's voice echoed down the line.

"I haven't been able to sleep since...since.."

"That's why I called you." I joked. "I just knew you'd be worried sick!"

I recalled the agonized look on her face when she and my older sisters hugged me goodbye at Liverpool Street Station.

"We thought we'd never see you again," she sniffed.

Ever dramatic, despite the bad connection, I could hear my mother was crying now.

"I might even die before you come home!" she continued.

"Of course, you won't!" I laughed. "I said I'd call you at the first opportunity. And here I am!"

It was Saturday 20th April 1968. I was ten days away from my twenty-fourth birthday. I had just arrived in Moscow and I was about to set out on the biggest adventure of my life, alone on a 8,000-mile journey from London to Nakhodka by train and then on to Japan, Hong Kong and Vietnam. I was not about to be deterred by my mother's fears, even if I felt a little guilty by her very real concerns for my welfare.

"But it's been a week already. And it's dangerous there. I read they're building up the troops on the border," she continued in a conscious effort to make me give up my plan and encourage me to return to the safety of home.

My mother was now sobbing loudly into the phone.

"I read it in the papers," she cried. "You must be careful. You're all alone. There may be a war between Russia and China!"

"Then I'll make a quick escape to Hanoi to join my friend, Sean!!" I retorted. "Honestly, Mummy, it's OK, I'll be fine. I'm in Moscow, safe in the Hotel

Metropol. I'm going to see Lenin's tomb tomorrow. It's his birthday so there'll be marches and stuff. And then, in the evening, I'm going to the Bolshoi. Your favourite ballerina is dancing, Maya Plisetskaya."

"But you don't know anyone there!" my mother persisted. "What if you're kidnapped? I don't have any friends who can help you."

"Then you can sound the alarm as it would cause an international incident!" I retorted lightheartedly. Then, more gently, "Of course I won't be kidnapped. And in two days I'll be safely on the Trans-Siberian."

"But that's exactly where the troops are heading. Through Siberia and up to the Chinese border."

I decided to change the subject. This conversation was heading nowhere. I knew what she wanted. She wanted me to come home. Not in two years. Not in a year. Immediately.

"Do you want me to tell you about the journey here?" I asked.

She composed herself. "Yes, do tell. How was it?"

"Well, it was quite an adventure. The ferry from Harwich to Rotterdam was uneventful, other than I thought I lost my luggage. Then some nice Customs Officer came to my rescue and managed to locate it for me on a train bound for Paris. Then from Rotterdam to East Berlin I found myself in a compartment with a young Polish man, Ryszard. He was on his way to Munich to teach English. He was really sweet."

My mother's voice suddenly softened. "Oh, you liked him then?"

"No! Not like that, Mummy! He was just very nice. And we had hours to talk. So he told me his life story. And I told him mine. Strangers on a train, and all that." And then I joked, "I think he knows more about me than you do!"

"I should hope not!" My mother sounded offended.

"Of course not. But you know how it is with strangers? If you find yourself sitting beside someone you assume you may never see again, you tend to tell them your deepest secrets, don't you?"

"I don't know. I've never found myself in that position," Mummy replied. That was probably true, I thought. I doubt my mother had ever been on a train, or indeed, any other form of public transport on her own.

"Word got out that Ryszard and I were literate. And soon we had a queue of people begging us to fill in their money declarations and customs forms for them. They were counting every single ruble and cent in their purses. Then we forged their signatures!"

I could hear my mother gasping.

"Don't worry, it was OK, thank heavens. But I admit, I was quite worried about it. I had no idea what the penalty would be for forging signatures on East German Customs Declarations forms."

A series of clicks interrupted our conversation again.

"What's that sound?" my mother asked.

"They're probably eavesdropping!" I joked.

"Don't say that!" my mother sounded alarmed.

"I was only joking," I replied, "sort of!"

"It's no joke," she said. "We're in the Cold War, darling! Anything can happen!"

"You worry far too much," I replied.

My mother sighed. "So will you see this Ryszard again?" she asked, changing the subject.

"Well, we exchanged addresses and phone numbers so we might meet up when we both get back to London. He'll be away two years too. But I must tell you about when I got to the border of Poland and Russia. Now that was scary!"

I could feel my mother starting to panic.

"Why? What happened?"

"We had a long wait at the border. It was pitch dark when we pulled in to the station. About 10pm. We were told we could all get out and stretch our legs because the train wouldn't leave until after midnight. So I got off the train and walked up and down the platform a few times. It was really cold so I went into the ticket office to warm up. There were lots more people in there. Some of them were beginning to file out onto the platform with their children and luggage eager to board the train. I sat down and took out my book. But I kept looking up at the clock above the ticket office to make sure I got back out onto the platform in good time. There was no way I wanted to be stranded on the border in the middle of the night."

I paused, letting it all sink in.

"I'm already worried for you." I could almost hear the panic in my mother's voice.

"You don't need to be." I reassured her. "I'm here in Moscow, speaking to you, aren't I?"

"So what happened next?" My mother's voice sounded barely relieved.

"Well, about 11.30 I looked up from my book again to check the clock and I suddenly realized I was all alone in the ticket office. I heard a tremendous commotion coming from outside and my heart sank. I thought the train was leaving without me. I cursed the ticket master as I dashed out onto the platform and got a real shock - there was no train. For a few seconds, I panicked. There was no one on the platform. I was about to dash back inside and find the guard but then I heard voices coming from above me and I looked up. And there, suspended on heavy metal cables, was my train, with all the passengers looking out of the lighted windows."

"What happened?" My mother now sounded frantic.

"I had to laugh. Partly in relief. And partly because all those people with their faces pressed against the lighted windows looked so comical. Apparently, the rail gauge is different between Poland and Russia so they had to literally lift the train off the rails and change the wheels to fit the Russian track! They then swung it over and placed it on the other side of the station. I had to cross the bridge in complete darkness. The only light was from the windows of the train. It was all very surreal!"

The operator abruptly interrupted.

"Достаточно. Необходимо больше рублей." (Is enough. More rubles needed).

"Mummy, I've got to go. I don't have any more rubles."

My mother, panicked, "She's "cutting us off?"

"Yes," I said, "Goodbye. I'll call again. Give everyone my love!"

There was a loud click.

"I love you," I said.

But it was too late. I replaced the receiver and walked out of the phone booth and into the spacious lobby of Moscow's oldest hotel.

"Built Before the Revolution" the poster beside me announced proudly. "The Most Luxury Hotel in All of Russia– Come Stay With Us at the Hotel Metropol."

"Luxury" it was not. Like most Soviet buildings, I discovered, it was basic. And it was functional. It had an expansive lobby with a rudimentary reception desk, a few cumbersome armchairs and a very wide central staircase running up to the spacious landings above. On each floor at the top of the staircase was a heavy wooden desk manned by an unsmiling policeman or woman. Or maybe they were from the Russian Intelligence (GRU) placed there to spy on guests, I never found out. But I did notice the policewoman on my floor grabbed my room key from me whenever I left and assiduously wrote down all my comings and goings so I surmised she must have handed that information to someone.

The following day, Sunday, April 21st, I set out to join the birthday celebrations for Lenin in Red Square. I joined the long line of schoolchildren and citizens who were slowly snaking their way towards the tomb that held the embalmed corpse of Vladimir Ilyich Lenin.

I hadn't really anticipated the genuine devotion, or forced devotion, the Soviet people felt for their former leader who, by 1968, had already been dead 44 years. And, until then, I thought only the British enjoyed the masochistic sport of queuing. But I was surprised how patient they all appeared to be. Even the children lacked exuberance and tolerated hours stoically waiting in line for a glimpse of Lenin's embalmed corpse.

"It seems the Soviet people really like to queue for hours," I remarked to my Intourist guide, a young Muscovite called Pavel.

"We learn from an early age," he replied. "We queue for bread, for meat, for milk, for butter every day for our families. But mostly we queue for Lenin!"

I noticed part of the queue in front of me snaking off towards another building.

"Where are they going?" I asked.

"Ah, that is the Necropolis. They pay their respects to Comrade Josef Stalin and to Comrade Yuri Gagarin first," he replied. "But mostly to Comrade Gagarin!" he added, his blue eyes twinkling.

The world's first cosmonaut had died in a mysterious plane crash just one month earlier.

"How did he die?" I asked.

"They say he was flying over forest shooting deer," Pavel whispered in my ear, making sure no one was listening. "They say his plane went out of control."

"Really?" I whispered back. "Do you believe that?"

Pavel grinned and shrugged his shoulders.

"In Soviet Union, who knows what to believe?" he replied. I was surprised at his not exactly toeing the party line.

"Maybe just…maybe, he was…" Pavel gestured as though he was drinking. "We never know. But, mostly, we just wonder!" he added.

He reached into the breast pocket of his scruffy grey canvas Intourist uniform and withdrew a packet of cigarettes. He offered me one. I shook my head.

"Don't smoke, thanks," I said.

He shrugged his shoulders and lit up a cigarette. Before he replaced the packet in his pocket he showed it to me.

"Laika," he said, "first dog to orbit earth. 1957."

I took the packet from him.

"I remember," I replied. "Sweet dog. What happened to her?"

Pavel shrugged again.

"Still up there, maybe!" he joked. "She never come back."

The mausoleum housed in a solid red marble building in Red Square contrasted with the gaudiness of St Basil's Cathedral whose multi-coloured onion domes were clearly visible above me.

The impeccably preserved corpse of Lenin, dressed in clean clothes for his birthday, lay undisturbed in his glass-sided sarcophagus, eyes closed, one hand clenched, the other open, oblivious to the scores of people shuffling past him to pay their respects.

There was probably only one other body in the world that could lay claim to such expensive, elaborate and constantly updated embalming techniques, I thought, and that was the body of Eva Peron.

The next morning the real adventure began. Pavel had ordered an Intourist taxi for me at 6am to take me to the Yaroslavl Station to catch the Trans-Siberian train, that would take me from Moscow, across the vast steppes of Soviet Russia, the seemingly endless tundra of Siberia, through the high Urals and around the world's deepest freshwater Lake of Baikal to Nakhodka on the East coast, a journey of nearly 6000 miles. Crossing over countless rivers, including the massive Volga, the train would pass through villages and towns with names such as Ekaterinburg (a name now synonymous with the tragic ending of Russia's last Tzar, Nicholas II and his family), Omsk, Novosibirsk, Tomsk, Irkutsk, Ulan Ude and Khabarovsk.

In the taxi, I admit I was scared. I was totally in the hands of this Intourist taxi driver who could have been taking me anywhere. But, fortunately, there was nothing to be worried about and I arrived at the station unharmed.

The platform was a confusion of people and sounds. Food vendors, soldiers, families, hawkers selling their home-made wares and even a band of ragtag musicians playing a mournful song. The taxi driver, carrying my suitcase, skillfully jostled his way through the throng, beckoning me to follow.

"The soldiers are on their way to the border with China," he explained in broken English as I watched the young men in shabby uniforms and long grey coats embrace their weeping wives, mothers and children.

Like me, I thought, they are journeying into the unknown. All I knew of Siberia was from the movie, *Dr. Zhivago*. And, of course, news stories I had read about the gulags, about slave labour sent to work in the coal mines and about exiled criminals and political foes being "sent to Siberia" as a lifetime punishment for bad behaviour, infringement of the law or political dissent.

But these young soldiers were different. They were being sent as cannon fodder, possibly to die in the local flare-up between two emerging super-powers – China and the Soviet Union, that shared a common border stretching over 2500 miles and where disputes and conflicts were rarely absent.

The taxi driver found my carriage and beckoned me to follow him. We clambered on board. I am not sure whether my heart was pounding from fear or excitement. I had been anticipating this trip for a year while working for the BBC News. My colleagues there had even had a whip around before I left to raise some funds for me. And my boss had "stolen" two large cartons of 35mm film so that I could record my trip and, perhaps, send some of the photos back to the BBC for publication.

"After all," Bob, my boss, had explained, "it's not every day one of our colleagues travels the length and breadth of the Soviet Union at the height of the Cold War and during one of the biggest build-ups of Soviet troops along the Chinese border. We need photos, Caroline. Lots of them."

And now here I was boarding the famous Trans-Siberian train, sadly not the one Agatha Christie wrote about, nor the one featured in so many films and documentaries, but the unglamorous one, the slow one, the one whose top speed was just 20 MPH, the one that was designated "hard" class without any of the opulent trappings, expensive European fixtures and understated elegance of the "soft" class.

"Hard" class meant I would have to share a cramped compartment with three men, two bunks on each side. My ticket was checked. I had been assigned to a lower bunk. I was grateful for that, at least.

"The upper, how do you say, bed?" the taxi driver asked.

"Bunk," I said.

"Ah, yes. Bunk. It will be tied back against wall during day. So you share yours during day with man above."

"Not an ideal arrangement," I laughed. "What if I want to lie down during the day?"

The driver shrugged his shoulders. I could see he was eager to leave. A whistle sounded above the general noise of boarding passengers, somber music, shouting and last-minute sales of food through the windows of the train.

"You OK?" he asked. "I leave now."

He shook my hand and left me in the carriage with my three compartment-mates who had already become firm friends over a bottle of vodka. I turned around and they eyed me with a mixture of curiosity and feigned disinterest. Who was this young foreigner with long blonde hair, dressed in a floor-length Biba coat and knee-length boots? What was she doing on their train? Where was she going?

I smiled at them. I got out my notebook from my pocket. My mother had written down what I should say to people when I met them.

"Zdravo, zovem se Caroline. Ja sam engleski i putujem u Nakhodku"

(Hello, my name is Caroline. I am English and I am travelling to Nakhodka.)

This was to become my standard phrase over the next two weeks.

I also found out that "hard" class meant only one toilet for around 30 people. It turned out to be a lurid green metal box room at one end of the carriage, with an elevated bowl over a hole in the floor where, if I cared to look down, I could see the stony ground and the metal sparks flashing beneath me. There was a small cast iron basin with cold water, a broken mirror and a fan that didn't work. A bucket sat in one corner and I wondered whether it was for slopping out or washing oneself.

When I got hungry or was simply feeling adventurous, I discovered that "hard" class also necessitated a long walk to the dining car at the rear of the train. This, in itself, was not a past-time for the faint of heart. It involved passing through several carriages that contained the chaotic communal sleeping quarters of the train where most of the soldiers and the poorer Soviets and their families were forced to sleep, three bunks deep on either side and where numerous pungent bodily aromas mingled and lingered without a breath of fresh air to dispel them.

It also involved strong muscles to force and hold open the thick spring doors between the carriages. And it required a good balance and some nimble footwork to avoid stepping on intoxicated bodies lying on the floor and to negotiate a path from one carriage to the next across the moving metal divide. People, suffering from lack of air in their stuffy, airless quarters, would congregate either side of the carriage doors breathing in the brief and exhilarating rush of icy air whenever the doors were opened.

My first meal on the train was eggs. In fact, every subsequent meal I had on the train was eggs - scrambled, fried, boiled and poached. I didn't test the meat dishes as I didn't know how fresh it would be by the end of the journey. And the idea of having a bad case of diarrhea, considering the primitive condition of the toilet and the queues that lined up outside it, did not appeal.

As we crossed the vast swathe of central Soviet Union, the train stopped at tiny, insignificant stations every twenty minutes or so. At every stop, we all piled out religiously, desperate to breathe some cold, clean air, stretch our legs and to buy local bread, potato and cabbage soup or grilled kebabs wrapped in flatbreads from the local hawkers. Some people, I noticed, even preferred to use the toilet on the station or relieve themselves behind a tree or telegraph post rather than use the increasingly unhygienic facilities on the train. As the state of the toilets on the train became harder to stomach, I even resorted to this method, much to the amusement of the soldiers and the children. Fortunately, I had my ankle-length Biba coat that obscured my deeds and, having been warned by Pavel about the lack of toilet paper on the train, I had stocked up on my own supply before leaving Moscow.

Few, if any, people boarded or disembarked at these smaller stations. I had hoped that one of my sleeping compartment comrades would not be going the whole distance and would free up much-needed space. But, I found out that, like me, they were on the train for the full journey.

For most of the trip, I read copiously. I had brought about twelve books with me, including *The Naked Ape, The Magic Toyshop* and *The Confessions of Nat Turner* and although they added to the weight of my luggage, I was very glad that I had them with me. I also wrote in my journal as one day blended into the next, with no highlights, no lowlights, just consistent monotony. I spent a lot of time, looking out through the misted windows of my compartment, daydreaming about the days when the Trans-Siberian boasted a gym, comfortable beds with fresh linen sheets, a piano room and maid service.

And while I scribbled away under the fogged-up window, or withdrew into the darker recess of my bunk and read under the small reading lamp, the three men in my room smoked tobacco, ate raw onions and drank a home-made brew of schnapps 24 hours a day.

Needless to say, after a few days, the small cabin became almost insufferable with the combined odours of onions, human sweat, stale clothes, cigarettes and halitosis. And I was probably just as much to blame as the men because by then, the state of the lavatories meant that showers were out of the question and, although I religiously applied deodorant under my arms and brushed my teeth twice a day, I could not have been in a very hygienic state by the time the second week of the trip came around.

One night I had to resort to ringing the bell for help, as the man above me was so drunk he fell out of his bunk on top of me, whether by accident or design I never did find out. The attendant certainly had no doubts. The man must have realized he had met his match as soon as the attendant entered the cabin. She was an immense, hairy female with a black moustache beaded with sweat. She dispatched him with ease, simply scooping him up in her large dimpled arms and tossing him back onto his upper bunk as though she was throwing a child's ragdoll. She then admonished him in what I assumed was an avalanche of Russian swear words, wiped the perspiration from her moustache, wagged her finger at him one more time, shouted some Soviet blasphemies and slammed the compartment door behind her.

The chastened man couldn't bring himself to look me in the eye after that. He would stare into the dregs of his schnapps, puff on his cigarette and ignore me whenever I entered or exited the compartment. The other two appeared equally embarrassed, maybe because they hadn't come to my rescue and had just sat and watched to see how the little drama was going to end.

At least I now knew I had a protector on the train as it had become increasingly obvious as the days passed and my trips to and from the dining car revealed that I was, as I had suspected, the only foreigner on board. I tried to use a few words of my mother's mother tongue, Serbo-Croat, to start a conversation but since my vocabulary was limited to "good morning, darling", "I love you, darling," and "you are beautiful", my efforts were limited and met with some rolling eyeballs, surprise and a certain amount of derision.

During these long, dreary days, I admit I had occasional moments of regret, thinking back wistfully on my New York days with Joe and imagining what my friends, Sarah, Caterine and Christina were up to. Were they all missing me? Or were their lives so busy they didn't even notice my long absence? But these moments of regret didn't last long. I was on my way to Vietnam and every slow mile the train passed got me that much closer.

Occasionally the train would crawl into a big city, such as Irkutsk, immediately identifiable by the huge manufacturing buildings and smoke-belching chimneys of the local metal, fuel and aviation industries. At every station, the compulsory posters of Lenin, bearded chin protruding, arm outstretched, lined the platform. Vendors and hawkers shouted their wares, some even attempting to muscle their way onto the train in order to beat their competitors. More soldiers bade sad goodbyes to their crying children who clung to their fathers' long army coats and then, humping their knapsacks, they turned and jostled their way reluctantly to the communal sleepers at the rear of the train to begin their journey to the Chinese border and to an unknown fate.

Even in late April, as we continued to creep our way across the endless steppes, the days remained despairingly gloomy and the ground was still covered in several inches of snow. The landscapes were bleak with only an occasional thicket of trees, very few birds and animals, vast great spaces without a single dwelling and with only the massive railway linking the little villages across the vast rolling steppes. And all along the route, the snow was blackened from the soot and flying cinders from the coal-fired engine.

But as we approached the Urals these persistently overcast days began to lighten. The monotonous, treeless landscape gradually began to take on a new character. The flat tundra slowly gave way to the sporadic foothills of this ancient mountain range that stretches more than 1500 miles south from the frozen Arctic, its snowclad peaks beginning to emerge in a haze on the distant horizon. Thorny bushes dotting the landscape heralded ever steeper hills, covered in thick clumps of towering pine trees, now shaking off the last snows of the Arctic winter from their branches.

Slowly we snaked our way around the southern shore of Lake Baikal, close to the Mongolian border. After the dreary featureless flatness of the snow-covered steppes, I was eager to see this particular lake, known as possibly the oldest and largest freshwater lake in the world. Only, once again, I was to be vastly disappointed. Instead of an area of natural beauty, I was horrified to find that the lake had been polluted by the toxic effluent from the local paper industry. I guess

I shouldn't have been all that surprised. The Soviet Union had never been known for its protection of the environment. I had already seen in other parts of the country that neglect and damage were commonplace. But somehow I hadn't expected such devastation in this remote place surrounding Siberia's most famous lake.

Without any concern about the destruction it was causing, the two-year-old Baykalsk Pulp and Paper mill had been spewing all its effluent, including chlorine and bleached paper residue, directly into the lake, resulting in poisoned water, swathes of rotting algae and the devastating loss of fish, including the sturgeon, the Arctic grayling and the unique omul, Lake Baikal's endemic species. As I surveyed the damage from my window, I remembered that Pavel had told me that "Baikal" meant "nature" in Mongolian. Right now that irony didn't escape me. Nature Lake, what a tragedy.

I still had about 1250 miles to go before I reached Khabarovsk in the Soviet Far East, a University town where I planned to stay a couple of nights in a hotel, have a hot bath and, having been starved of any conversation for so long, find some English or French-speaking students to talk to.

The twice-daily trip to the restaurant car, no longer an adventure, was becoming more of a necessary chore. On top of that, I was getting bored with a diet of just eggs. So, for the last few days before reaching Khabarovsk I decided to risk buying the local food available at all the small stations we passed through. My daily diet from then on consisted of a slice of rough, flourless bread, steamed dumplings filled with limp, overcooked cabbage and a non-descript cake that was more like a rough, rock-hard scone. Rather than bring the food into the train and adding to the less than fragrant aromas in the compartment, I would gobble it all down while walking up and down the platform getting my daily exercise.

When the train finally pulled into Khabarovsk late at night, I was packed and ready to leave before the stationmaster could even blow his whistle. I nodded to my room-mates and, with an enormous sigh of relief, shut the door of the cabin for one last time.

Somehow in the middle of the scrum of people, soldiers and suitcases spilling out onto the platform, my Intourist guide, Natasha, found me. I guess with my long blond locks and my Biba clothes, I was not too difficult to spot and for that I was grateful. A hot bath beckoned. As the days had passed on the journey, the image of a steaming hot bath had grown out of all proportion to a point of obsession. Just imagining the joy of eliminating the grime, the soot, the smells and the thick grease that felt like it was clinging to every pore of my body had been plaguing my thoughts for days.

Natasha shook my hand, beamed and said, "Welcome to our beautiful city, Miss Kennedy!"

Whether Khabarovsk was beautiful or not, I thought, just because I was so grateful to have arrived there it would forever rival Paris, Dubrovnik or Venice in my mind.

In the taxi on the way to the hotel, Natasha told me she was studying to be an interpreter for Intourist.

"Education is free in our country," she explained proudly. "And we have 80 universities. I went to the one in Moscow. 37,000 students, 9000 of them resident in the University."

She was obviously trying to impress me and it worked. I asked her if she belonged to the Komsomol (the All Union Leninist Young Communist League), a political youth organization with a membership, I was told, of 23 million.

"Yes, " she replied, "I am a local editor of one of the Komsomol newspapers. Our motto is *'Everyone is a Friend of Everyone'* and you must go out of your way to help people and to help less developed areas. I was lucky to live in Moscow, the cradle of communism. I would like to travel abroad but my responsibility as a member of Komsomol is toward my country. So I have moved to Siberia. Many of our members are coming here because we believe it is part of our country with a great future. We want to teach the people here how to cultivate their land."

She asked me if we could be pen-pals and if I would write to her about my experiences in Siberia. I agreed. But secretly doubted I would follow through as I imagined any letter I wrote would be intercepted before she received it.

An hour later, Natasha dropped me off at my hotel. On the third floor, the water in the bath trickled out of the tap. I realized it would take hours to fill. I threw myself onto the bed, revelling in the clean sheets, picked up the phone and called my family.

I am too embarrassed to describe here the filthy scum rim that adhered to the interior of the bath after I had wallowed in it for an hour in the steaming water and scrubbed my body from head to toe.

The following morning I asked the receptionist the way to the University and set out, under a welcome blue sky, carrying all my books and most of my winter clothes, including two Biba trouser suits, my knee-length boots and my ankle-length coat. I planned to donate them to the first girl I met who spoke English.

With my new-found freedom, I strolled at a snail's pace, enjoying the Spring weather and photographing everything of interest along the way. Despite enough warnings, any thoughts of spies, secret police and GRU Intelligence officers couldn't have been further from my mind. Khabarovsk, I was delighted to discover, was indeed a beautiful city. It could have rivalled any European city with old Colonial-style houses painted in pastel colours, busy sidewalk cafes, wrought-iron street lamps and wide boulevards lined with blossoming trees and shrubs. It's true that a few ugly Soviet-style buildings were dotted in between the grand houses but the overall impression was of a much gentler city dominated by the turquoise and golden spires of the Russian Orthodox Church, glinting in the morning sun, towering majestically over the rooftops.

I reached the Pacific National University and asked for the English teacher. I soon had a gathering of students around me. They escorted me to the English class. I explained to the teacher what I was doing and said I would wait until her class ended and then I would like to talk to the students.

But she was intrigued enough to ask me to address the class. And, when I started unloading the twelve US and UK books, from my shoulder bag, there was a mad rush to grab them.

As one student explained to me, "We are learning English. But we are not allowed any American or English books. And we won't be able to travel. We learn English just to teach other students English."

The clothes too disappeared in a second. Suddenly we were all best friends. Linking arms, they walked me outside onto the grounds of the University and we sat under a tree while they catapulted me with questions, all demanding answers.

What did I think would happen in Vietnam following the Tet Offensive?

How did I see the space race ending?

Would the Soviet Union and the West ever be friends?

And, of course, the greatest academic conundrum of them all, who did I prefer the Beatles or the Rolling Stones?

And as we queued for lunch in the canteen the questions kept coming. I took group photographs of all of us and realized this could be a university anywhere in the world with curious young students desperate to learn. Only this was the Soviet Union. And the reality was that these girls, this generation of students, would miss out on travelling the world. They would never have the freedoms I had. Like their parents before them, they could only dream about having them. They wouldn't even be able to choose where they wanted to work after university. They would be assigned a teaching position in a school somewhere, perhaps far away from their families and friends, and they would have no choice but to accept it. And they would probably end up sharing a small room with several other teachers in a bleak tower block on the outskirts of some remote Soviet city. And they would simply make do. That would be their life.

I realized with sadness that our brief encounter was probably the closest any of them would ever get to feeling free, the very rare opportunity to talk with a foreigner without being interrogated or punished for the infringement. With any luck, one day their children would have more freedoms but not these young girls, so keen to learn but deprived of so much that we take for granted.

I hugged them all at the end of the day and made my way back to the hotel. That night there was a knock on my door. I got out of bed and there were two men standing there. My heart started palpitating. They looked unsmiling. One held the door open and the other walked in.

"We hear you take photos. Photos not allowed. We must see your film. Give me camera and all film."

My heart sank.

"We just look," he said, more menacing than reassuring. Dutifully, I handed him my camera. He opened it and removed the film.

"More film?" he asked.

I pointed to my suitcase.

He bent down and opened it. He found lots of used rolls of film waiting to be printed and the two large unopened cartons my boss at the BBC had given me.

Methodically he went through every single roll, deliberately pulling out the film, holding them up against the light to try to make out the images while, at the same time, knowing he was destroying them. Every single one ruined. Even the unused ones.

So much for illustrating my book, I thought. And there I had been all this while thinking the Soviet Union was not as bad as I had been led to believe, that all the talk about espionage, suspicion of foreigners and fearmongering was all nonsense. This was a brutal lesson in reality.

When he was satisfied, he thrust the spools of ruined film into my hands and left. His silent comrade closed the door behind them.

I fought back my tears. The most precious photos were the ones I had just taken with the students that day, my new friends, the ones whose addresses I had written down with a sincere promise to send them all the photos of our day together. Now I would be letting them down.

But then an uncomfortable thought occurred to me. *Had one of them alerted the authorities, had one of them actually squealed on me?* It was possible. But it was too unsettling to contemplate. *If yes, which one of them was to blame? Or was it the teacher? The teacher who had been delighted to welcome me into her class and asked me to address her students? Or was it none of them? Was it someone who was skulking in the background, who had followed me all the way from the hotel to the University?* For my own peace of mind, I decided that the latter was the more likely answer.

Needless to say, I was quite grateful the next morning when Natasha arrived early to take me back to the train station. This was to be the last lap of my gargantuan trip across the Soviet Union and Siberia, the last 500 miles to the port town of Nakhodka, just northeast of Vladivostok.

At the station, my eyes immediately landed on two young men who definitely looked European, not Russian. Desperate for conversation, I made a beeline for them, introduced myself and the three of us clambered aboard together.

Martijn and Thom were Dutch. They were travelling for a year before starting four years of university back in The Hague. Like me, they had worked out the cheapest way to get to the Far East was by the Trans-Siberian. Like me, they had also travelled "hard" class. And, like me, they had finally given up on using the toilet on the train and had resorted to relieving themselves behind the trees at the local platforms. They had arrived in Khabarovsk two weeks ahead of me and had illegally rented a small boat with an outboard motor and chugged slowly up the Amur River, stopping in the little communities along the way to buy food, set up their tent and overnight under the stars.

With the sunshine of the Soviet Far East warming the outside temperature, no longer did I have to spend my time blowing on my fingers to keep them warm, pulling my woolen hat down over my ears to prevent a severe case of otalgia or demisting the windows with my scarf so I could strain my eyes against the glare of snow for a rare glimpse of wildlife. Now the three of us could actually look out and see the tall pines thinning out and receding behind us. And we could watch the peaks of the Ural Mountain range disappear into the highland mist, as we crossed back over the Amur River and descended south-east towards the lowlands and the shores of the port town of Nakhodka on the Sea of Japan.

Tokyo beckoned for the three of us as we spent the evening playing cards and sharing our plans for the next few months. Martijn and Thom were hoping to spend three months travelling all over Japan and then, if they still had some money left, sail south to Thailand. My plans were to spend a month in Japan, then sail to Hong Kong, get my visas for Laos and Vietnam and then fly to Saigon to meet up with Sean Flynn.

As I gazed out of my hotel window overlooking Nakhodka Bay the following morning I couldn't help thinking that this was the beginning of the rest of my life. *Would I regret my decision to come halfway around the world by myself? What would the future hold for me? Would I ever write that book? Would I show bravery or cowardice in the face of the many dangers that would face me in Vietnam? Or would I simply die an unnecessary and premature death in a foreign land, one more casualty, one more statistic, un-mourned by anyone other than my close family and friends?*

"Ready?" Martijn asked, knocking on my door. "We're leaving now."

"Time to leave Siberia!" Thom laughed, putting his arm around me. "Shall we celebrate?"

"Definitely! "I said, as I slammed the door of my hotel room behind me. "Yokohama, here we come!"

We laughed, picked up our suitcases, ran down the stairs two at a time and went to look for the bus that would take us to the ferry.

We had all forgotten, of course, that we would have to go through Customs at the ferry terminal. We lined up for over thirty minutes until we got to the head of the queue. Martijn and Thom got waved through. But I was stopped. My heart beat a bit faster. Perhaps word had got out about my photographs. Maybe I would be forced to have another inspection of my suitcase.

Well, in retrospect, if it had only been that, I would have been lucky. It turned out the Customs officers in Nakhodka were very thorough. They went through everything, including my shoulder bag, reading my letters, opening my lipstick and testing my foundation and mascara. Then they came to my box of Tampax. That presented an enormous problem. The customs officers had obviously never come across Tampax before. They tore open the box, pulled out the tubes, opened them up, removed the tampons, looked through each tube as if they were looking through a telescope and shrugged their shoulders, nonplussed. Meanwhile, everyone else had passed through Customs and was waiting, watching this spectacle.

Baffled, the two officers went off to find another, more senior, officer, an officer with a peaked cap and gold stripes on his lapel, an officer who probably should have known what Tampax was. They showed him the tampons and he, too, shrugged his shoulders and shook his head. They then strolled over to me, whispering among themselves.

"Что это" (What is this?), the senior officer with the gold stripes asked.

I grabbed the empty box from my suitcase, removed the instructions and began to give a fairly graphic demonstration of what tampons were used for, much to the shock of my audience. Out of the corner of my eye, I could see Martijn and Thom giggling hysterically.

The three Customs officers shuffled uncomfortably, their combined cockiness momentarily demolished. Unsure where to look or what to do, they began trying to shove all the tampons back into their little tubes. Finally, realizing that what comes out of a tube doesn't always go back in, they dumped all the tampons, the tubes and the torn paper back into the box and handed it to me. I, in turn, handed it back to them.

"This is my gift to the women of Siberia!" I announced defiantly and, feeling momentarily triumphant, started repacking my case, knowing that all eyes in the room were focused on me at that moment.

Relieved that the ordeal was over, I joined Martijn and Thom, who gave me a hug and a thumbs up. Then the three of us boarded the ferry boat for Japan, put all memories of Siberia behind us and looked forward to our next respective adventures.

Chapter 16
A Twist of Fate

After the persistent drab grey of Siberia, the riotous colours that greeted my Dutch friends and me in Tokyo made us feel alive again. Just getting off the train and walking down Shibuya Street for the first time, mingling with the students dressed in the latest fashions, the girls with Vidal Sassoon hairstyles, the men with mops like George, Paul, John or Ringo, was reminiscent for me, of walking down King's Road in Chelsea on a Saturday afternoon. But these students had taken British fashion to the extreme and had made it their own. The styles were similar but the colours were more vibrant, yellows, oranges, reds, greens and purples.

Neon lights blazed above our heads, music pulsed loudly from every shop and café doorway, garish billboards, advertising everything from whiskey to television sets, assaulted our attention - the complete embrace of Western subculture was dramatic, something totally unexpected to any of us. Despite being over 10,000 miles away from London, I suddenly felt at home. I had expected to feel as alien in Tokyo as I had done in Siberia but it wasn't the case. Even my long blond hair didn't make me feel out of place or different. American movies were playing in the Toho Cinemas, *Valley of the Dolls* and *Cool Hand Luke* alongside local Japanese productions, *Zatoichi the Outlaw* and *Son of Godzilla*.

We had arrived in the middle of Japan's "economic miracle" and proof of it was on display everywhere we looked. Businesses appeared to be booming. The middle class appeared to be thriving. Even the young people appeared to have money and were able to sit, chat and dance for hours in the local dives, street cafes and bars. Everywhere there were beckoning signs, flashing neon arrows inviting people to come in, taste the local delicacies, drink the local cocktails or dance the latest craze. After three weeks of austerity travelling across the Soviet Union this undisguised display of commercialism couldn't have offered more of a contrast. I was tempted to try everything.

We also arrived at a time of massive student unrest. Over 3000 students and young political activists had already been arrested and several killed for rebelling against high tuition costs, substandard working conditions and what they perceived as their government's complicity in the Vietnam War. These riots had resulted in the closures of hundreds of schools and Universities across the country as students everywhere staged long-term sit-ins, barricaded themselves inside their campuses, set up kangaroo courts to denounce members of their faculties while, at the same time, holding out against armed riot police who were ready to arrest and kill.

It was the time, too, of women's protests. Traditionally Japanese women had accepted their twin roles of being tied to their homes and child-rearing but, suddenly, in the 1960s, all that was changing fast. Women were burgeoning in the workforce, becoming radicalized, joining demonstrations, voicing their demands and testing their strength in numbers.

As in the UK, a sense of youthful anarchy pervaded the atmosphere. Age-old customs were being discarded. Respect for long-held views was being reevaluated. New young voices were being heard. And Japan's ancient traditions were either being discarded altogether or being reinvented with a focus on youth.

"It seems to be a world-wide phenomenon," I remarked to Martijn and Thom, as we sipped our drinks at a sidewalk café and watched a group of young people beside us, holding a transistor aloft and enthusiastically singing along with Manfred Mann's *"Mighty Quinn"*.

"It's not quite what I was expecting," I added. "How about you?"

"Throwing off the shackles of the past," Martijn said. "I guess just a few years later than in Europe."

"It must have a lot to do with the anti-Vietnam war movement." I said.

"Are you sure you still want to go there?" Thom asked. "I'll be really worried thinking about you there!"

"You and my mother!" I laughed. "Of course, I want to go."

"Why don't you give up the idea and come with us? You can write about the Western cultural invasion here." Thom said.

I shook my head.

"This is goodbye then," Thom raised his glass of Suntory whiskey to me.

They left the next morning, after big hugs and promises to reunite one day and, for the first time, I suddenly felt very alone and vulnerable. Looking in my journal I saw I had a few names to look up in Tokyo, but the one that caught my attention was a name supplied by my New York friend, Caterine Milinaire. The name was Kaji Kawazoe. Caterine described Kaji and her husband as the very trendy owners of the Baby Doll Boutique and the popular Chianti Restaurant.

I picked up the phone beside my bed and dialed the number. Someone picked it up the other end.

"Kon'nichiwa, koreha daredesuka?"

"Is that Kaji?" I asked.

"Hai, sore wa watashidesu. Kore wa daredesu ka?"

"My name's Caroline. I'm a writer. I was given your name by a mutual friend, Caterine Milinaire."

"Oh, Caterine, she my very good friend!" Kaji replied.

"Yes, she told me," I said, relieved that I wouldn't have to explain myself in Japanese. "Well, I just arrived in Tokyo and I don't know anyone and she said for me to call you – because you know everyone!"

Kaji giggled on the other end of the phone.

"She right. I know lots of people. I have big party tonight. You must come. I give you the address, right?"

"I'll be there, thank you!" I said.

"You meet lots of people. Other writers, artists, designers, actors, photographers, friends. Many people."

I proceeded to write down the address for the party.

"See you at 8 then," Kaji said. "I will be wearing red wig and very short green dress. So you can recognize me!"

I thanked her and put the phone down.

Jackpot, I thought!

With her scarlet wig and emerald green mini, Kaji was easy to spot that night. She was obviously very popular. She was surrounded by a large group of people. I walked up and introduced myself and she hugged me. She then introduced me to the circle of people around her.

Caterine was right. Kaji did know everyone. Kaji was right too. I did meet many people that night. And, because I was a friend of hers, they immediately accepted me.

Firstly, an American businessman, Bill, and his English wife Annie. Bill took me aside.

"My publishing job brought us here to Tokyo about 3 months ago," Bill told me. "We were in London before that. And poor Annie's still adjusting. She's very homesick. It would be wonderful if you could come and stay with us."

I was thrilled. Bill approached his wife and put his arm around her shoulder,

"Caroline's going to stay with us for a while."

Annie's face brightened. She put her arm through mine.

"Are you sure?" I asked. "Is that OK with you, Annie?"

Annie said it was more than OK, she'd be delighted. And she confirmed she would come to my hotel the next morning after breakfast to pick me up.

Then I met a young fashion photographer, Daido Moriyama, who along with a poet and a few other photographers was about to launch a sub-culture photography magazine called "*Provoke*". He asked if he could take my photographs in his studio. Of course, I accepted.

I met a writer and an editor from Milan, Fabrizio and Matteo, who both worked for Rizzoli Publishing and who invited to take me to a sumo wrestling match at the famous Kuramae Kokugikan stadium the following week. Again, I accepted.

And then I met an actor, Masumi Okada, an extremely handsome flirt who invited me to drive out of town with him for a few days to his beach house in Kamakura. Of course, I accepted that invitation too.

Yet again, I felt my guardian angel was definitely sitting on my shoulder that night. I sat down beside Kaji and told her how serendipitous her party had been for me.

"I knew it," she said. "People here, very friendly!"

I had always known travelling alone made sense. And it was certainly confirmed to me that evening. People are far more likely to take you under their wing if you are alone. I realized too I had been right to turn down Martijn's and Thom's offer. Had I been with them that night, I realized I would have missed out on all this.

I was packed and ready in the lobby of my hotel when Annie arrived the next morning to pick me up. I felt guilty that I didn't even have a new book to give her. I explained that I had given them all away to the students in Khabarovsk. She didn't mind. She said she just wanted the company.

"It's taking me a long time to adjust to life here," she said. "I should be accustomed to it by now. But below the surface, it's just so different."

"Tell me about Kaji," I said, as we drove through the residential suburb of Hiroo toward her house.

"She's the only daughter of a multi-millionaire publisher, a very influential friend of the Prime Minister," Annie replied. "After University in the US, she wanted to be a dress designer. So he set her up with her own business. And, actually. she's really very creative and has a good business head on her shoulders. She's done very well."

"She certainly knows how to throw good parties," I said.

"She does. And she throws them every month. And they are always well-attended. You were lucky. Your timing was perfect." Annie said.

"How did you meet her?" I asked.

"Through Bill's work. Kaji's dad is also in publishing. So Bill met her father when we first arrived. And Kaji happened to be in her father's office at the time. She likes picking up waifs and strays. We had just arrived so she immediately invited us to her next party."

"We were both lucky then!" I said.

We arrived at their two-storey house, surrounded by freshly-clipped hedges and blooming scarlet and yellow hibiscus shrubs. Annie showed me my room, some of her own paintings, acrylics depicting landscapes surrounding her family home in Northumberland, hanging on the walls.

"Are you painting here?" I asked.

"Not yet," Annie replied. "I haven't even had the enthusiasm to unpack my easel and paints. Bill keeps telling me to give it a try. He said I'll feel much better once I start painting again."

"He may be right," I said.

"There's just so much to get used to here," Annie looked like she was about to cry. "It's all a bit overwhelming. It was hard enough to get used to London. I'm a country girl!"

"Let's have a cup of tea," I teased. "Isn't that what we Brits would do in these circumstances?"

Annie smiled. "Yes, you're right. You unpack and I'll put the kettle on. Only I don't have a kettle! So we'll have to make do with a saucepan of water! I'm going to enjoy having you here," she added as she disappeared behind the door.

"How did you meet Bill if you lived in the country?" I asked as we sipped our tea on the patio.

"I was in London, at a book launching party. I had done the illustrations for the book. He was there. And he persuaded me to stay on for a few days in London. So I did. And then he was very gentlemanly. He escorted me all the way back to Northumberland by train. So he was a hit with my parents!!"

By the second cup, I had managed to convince Annie to unpack her paints and canvasses. I accompanied her into the garage and helped her drag the large wooden crate containing all her art gear inside the house. With a hammer, chisel and some muscle we managed to rip the nails out and open the lid. Everything was carefully wrapped and labelled. Annie looked genuinely excited as she scooped up some of the packages and laid them out on the floor.

We set up the easel in a small unused room adjoining the living room. By the time Bill arrived home that night, we had transformed the little room into a perfect studio, even dragging in a table that wasn't needed in the kitchen for her paints and brushes, removing the heavy curtains to give more light and hanging some of her artworks on the walls.

"Oh, wow, that makes me so happy!" Bill beamed, hugging Annie. "Now, perhaps, you and Caroline can drive out into the countryside during the days. She can sightsee and you can paint some local landscapes."

Very early the next morning I experienced my first earthquake. I was lying in bed, awake, when the tremor occurred. The room shook violently for a couple of seconds, Annie's paintings all tilted and I heard a couple of things falling and shattering in another part of the house. Bill and Annie rushed into my room to see if I was OK.

"I would have hated to explain to your mother what had happened to you on your first night in our house," Bill joked.

I received three phone calls over the next couple of days. One from Daido suggesting a day for me to sit for photographs. The second from Fabrizio, saying that he and Matteo had bought the tickets for the sumo wrestling match and they would pick me up the following week. And the third call was from Masumi inviting me to the screening of a new Susumu Hani movie with a formal dinner afterward. It turns out all three of them had received my phone number from the all-too-willing matchmaker, Kaji, who was determined that I would not feel alone at any time during my stay in Tokyo.

Over dinner, I told Masumi about my date with Daido sitting for some photo portraits.

"I'm going to take you!" he announced, suddenly all very proprietorial.

"Are you jealous?" I laughed.

"No!" he pouted. "I just don't want you to go alone. Daido has a reputation, you know!"

"And you don't?" I teased. "It's alright. I just crossed Russia and Siberia alone. I can look after myself."

"I'm still going to take you," he said.

And that was that. He did take me to Daido's studio for both photographic sessions over the next couple of days. The photos were quite unusual - black and white, provocative, sexy but, somehow, old worldly. They were enticing enough for my future husband to borrow them from my files one day, keep hold of them and even hang on to them as part of his own collection after we divorced.

"Who was your last girlfriend?" I asked Masumi as he drove us out to his beach house one day.

"Dewi Sukarno," he answered, nonchalantly.

"The wife of the General?" I asked.

I'll Be There

"Yes!" he replied, "that's her!"

"While they were married?"

"A brief affair then," he said. "But then he died last year and that's when we rekindled it."

"Wasn't she much younger than him?"

"Yes. 38 years younger," he answered. "But she knew exactly what she was doing. She's a very headstrong lady, believe me. That's her attraction. She used to be like you. She knew what she wanted. She wanted to be a writer. She wanted to be an adventurer. She wanted to be a free spirit. Just like you."

"So what happened?"

"She decided that wandering writers don't make money. So she focused her talents on things that would make her rich," he said, "I'm not sure it made her all that happy though."

"I'd never give up this freedom for money," I said, childishly. "That's probably my major fault. I'm not nearly ambitious enough."

Masumi kissed me on the cheek. "That's what makes you special," he said. "She was never a true artist."

I didn't let Masumi come to the sumo wrestling with me. I told him he wasn't invited, which he wasn't. I wanted to enjoy the company of Fabrizio and Matteo without Masumi around to hold my hand.

"But I speak Italian," he insisted. "They may feel like speaking their own language after a few months in Tokyo."

"How many languages do you speak?" I asked.

"English, Danish, French, Italian and Japanese,' he replied.

"Not just a pretty face then?" I laughed. "But you're still not invited. It's their treat for me. And, besides, you've probably seen sumo wrestling several times already.

"That's why I would be helpful. I could explain everything to the three of you," he persisted.

"Sorry," I said, emphatically. "Whatever you say, it's not going to work!"

The two irrepressible Italians drew up at Annie's door to collect me the following evening in a taxi. Their Milanese exuberance was contagious. And we laughed and sang Elvis Presley's versions of famous Italian songs, "Surrender", "Santa Lucia" and "It's Now or Never" all the way to the famous stadium.

Too soon though it was time to leave Japan. My plan was to go to Hong Kong where I would apply for my visa to Saigon. Annie drove me to Yokohama where I boarded the President Wilson liner bound for Hong Kong's Victoria Harbour.

In the welcome solitude of my single cabin, the high-octane, high-volume cacophony that was the seething, pulsating, rebellious city of modern Tokyo slowly subsided. I could begin to concentrate on my journal and plan how the next few weeks or months might pan out. I placed a call to Bob Tuckman, war correspondent of the Associated Press in Saigon. I had met him in New York with Joe several times on his sabbaticals from Vietnam, and he had promised Joe he "would keep an eye on me" once I arrived in the country. I left a message to say I would probably be arriving in Saigon by the end of June.

But, once again, fate was to change my plans - this time, quite dramatically.

On the first night on board, I was invited to sit at the Captain's table. The other guests included three Filipinos, filmmaker, Henry Francia, his fiancee, poet Betsy Romualdez and businessman, Jimmy Jacinto. Henry and Betsy told me they had been living in New York for a couple of years but had decided to return to Manila for their wedding.

The following day Betsy, Henry and I met up on deck.

"You must come to Manila!" Betsy insisted, "You can stay with me and my family. I really want you to be there for our wedding."

It was a very attractive invitation and, although seriously tempted, I was still doggedly single-minded about going to Saigon.

We chatted endlessly that day and, by the end, Betsy and I had become firm friends. As we sat out on deck the second day, the ship's loudspeaker crackled loudly. We stopped talking and listened. The Captain's voice boomed out across the ship.

"With great regret, I have to inform you that Attorney General Robert Kennedy has been shot! That is all the information I have right now. I will make a further announcement when I know more!"

As the words sank in, all activity on the boat ceased. Excited voices fell silent. Games came to an abrupt halt. Parents grabbed their boisterous children and hushed them. Couples held hands. Strangers hugged each other, gasping and sobbing. Some stood there silent, disbelieving. Others collapsed into deck chairs wailing. Elsewhere, people hung their heads, crossed their hearts and prayed. Henry, Betsy and I looked at each other aghast, unspoken questions forming on our lips. *Surely this can't be true? Not another Kennedy murdered? Was Camelot now at its end? Had our hopes and dreams really been shattered yet again? How? Why? When? Where?*

Sharing this tragic moment only succeeded in cementing my friendship with Henry and Betsy. And, by the time we parted company in Hong Kong, I had promised them that if my visa to Vietnam was going to take a long time, I would definitely make a side trip to Manila to attend their wedding.

"You will be my bridesmaid," Betsy said emphatically as she hugged me goodbye.

Again I was alone. Alone in Hong Kong. I had two names to call. An old friend, Kim Fraser, from my holidays in Scotland. And Ian Black, formerly a journalist with the *Daily Express* and now a columnist for the *South China Morning Post*.

With no inkling that this phone call would provoke the most terrifying experience of my life, I dialled Ian's number.

Chapter 17
In Search of the Maharishi

"Och, Caroline, it's good to hear you! You've arrived then!" Ian sounded genuinely pleased to hear from me. "Wait right where you are and I'll send a car to pick you up. You'll be staying with me, of course!"

I hadn't seen Ian for a while and it felt good to hear his lilting Scottish accent again. And it was fun that evening to wander around Hong Kong with him, chatting about the direction our lives had taken since we last met briefly in London. It was breathtaking riding the cable car up to the highest point of the island, gazing out at the picturesque junks in the harbour at sunset, watching the seething mass of humanity below us, rushing this way and that in their eagerness to get home for their evening meal.

That night I went to bed exhausted but exhilarated and made plans to visit the consulates of Vietnam and Laos the next day. How could I know that the innocent perceptions of Hong Kong I had acquired that night looking out over what seemed on the surface to be an enchanting city would end up changing so swiftly and so perilously?

After filling in my visa forms in the morning at the respective consulates, I followed Ian down to his office. It had been some time since I had sat in the newsroom of the *World-Telegram & Sun* with Joe and I realized now how much I missed the buzz, the clatter, the camaraderie and the thrill of the scoop.

All talk that morning was of the Maharishi Mahesh Yogi, the guru who had inspired not only the Beatles but many other lost young souls of my generation seeking spiritual answers to their lives. He was due to arrive on a Cathay Pacific flight from Los Angeles and was scheduled to hold a Press conference that afternoon at the Overseas Press Club on the top floor of the Hong Kong Hilton.

Ian was cursing. It had just dawned on him that he couldn't attend. His whole afternoon, he told me, would be taken up discussing the recent spate of serial rapes with the local police chief, Murray Todd.

"Ach, it's too bad" Ian said, shaking his head despondently, "I really wanted to go. Tell you what though, Caroline, why don't you go instead of me? You could write the story. Will you do that for me?"

Would I do it for him? Was he mad?

"You know you don't even have to ask that question, Ian," I laughed, "I'll be there in a flash!."

Here I was with an opportunity, out of the blue, to meet the strange, enigmatic Maharishi, the man responsible for influencing the lives of so many young people of my generation. How could I possibly refuse?

So at 3pm that afternoon I found myself on top of the Hilton Hotel, notebook and pencil in hand. And, as I arrived, in my long flowing robes, with beads dangling around my neck and my hair tumbling halfway down my back, flashbulbs began to pop incessantly.

"Excuse me, Maharishi, how does it feel to be in Hong Kong?" one reporter beside me asked.

I looked behind me. I saw nobody.

"Is this your first trip to Hong Kong, Maharishi?" another reporter piped up.

Where is he? I wondered, *I can't see him. Who on earth are they talking to?*

"Will you be staying here long? " a third reporter chipped in.

I was nonplussed.

"Will the Beatles be following you here?"

"How do you spell your name, Maharishi?"

The questions were coming thick and fast. I looked around. The Maharishi must surely be somewhere nearby.

But no, I was alone. To my amusement, it suddenly dawned on me that these Chinese photographers and journalists had not been very well briefed by their editors and had actually mistaken me for the ubiquitous Maharishi! Feebly, I tried to explain to them their error, that the real Maharishi had not yet arrived but they were so determined I was the guru that it proved futile trying to explain otherwise.

An English voice at my shoulder whispered, "Play up to it. I just heard the guy's not coming. He's missed his flight. You're the story now!"

And so it was. The next day in most of the Hong Kong papers, under a headline about the elusive Maharishi who never showed up, was a story about the hippie girl from London who took his place.

And thus a very real nightmare began. It started innocently enough with a phone call.

I was sitting in Ian's flat, munching my breakfast and silently giggling at my photograph and unexpected write-up in the morning papers. Ian had left early, hot on the trail again of Hong Kong's latest scourge, the serial rapist.

I picked up the receiver.

"Yes?"

An Indian voice asked, "Is this Miss Caroline Kennedy?"

Foolishly I answered, "Yes" but then instantly regretted it. *Who was this man? How did he know where I was staying? Who gave him this telephone number? Why was he looking for me? What did he want?*

He went on. "My name is Professor Khan, Nadir Khan. I read the story in the paper today. I too was at the Hilton Hotel yesterday. I wanted to introduce myself to you then but you were busy. Have you been following the Maharishi's teachings for a long time?"

"No, no I, I was just," I stammered. I was about to tell him how I happened to be there, that it was all an innocent misunderstanding but Professor Khan butted in.

"I think you have. I think you are interested in meditating. I, too, have been studying these things for a long time. It's part of my research in comparative religions for the University of Bombay, you see. Would you mind if I interviewed you?"

By this time, I had slightly recovered my composure. Thinking quickly I surmised that in order to have obtained my phone number this Professor Khan, whoever he was, must have already spoken to Ian at the newspaper, which meant that either Ian knew him or, at least, had approved his credentials.

"Well, I really don't really practice meditation," I said, "I'm probably not the right person to speak to. "

There was a mutter of disappointment down the line.

"But," I added, "I am still fascinated by the whole Maharishi phenomenon."

"I thought so." The Professor sounded somewhat relieved. "Perhaps we can meet to discuss this. These interviews I am doing will form part of my thesis, so I would be grateful if you would consider it."

"Well, I'm not sure I have anything relevant to say." I stuttered truthfully.

Undaunted Khan continued, "Where would you like to meet?"

"I don't know Hong Kong too well. In fact, I only just arrived the day before yesterday." I paused, and then added imprudently, "But I do know how to get to the Hilton Hotel."

"So how about the coffee shop downstairs?"

I remembered the coffee shop. Its windows looked right out onto a busy main street. *Surely,* I reassured myself, *it couldn't be too risky to meet there?*

"OK, I'll be there." I said. "What time?"

"2 pm. Will that be alright?" he asked.

"2 o'clock. Fine. I'll see you there. But how will I know you?"

"Don't worry, Miss Kennedy, I'll know you! I saw you yesterday, remember?"

The phone went dead. Professor Khan had replaced the receiver before I had a chance to consider how foolish and impetuous I was being and change my mind.

I toyed with the idea of phoning Ian to check out my mysterious caller. But I restrained myself, arguing that he would certainly not have given out his home number to just anyone, particularly when he was currently investigating a pretty grisly story. In fact, even before he had left me alone that morning he had impressed on me to double-lock the apartment door after him and warned me not to open it to anyone.

"You can never be too careful in this business," he had told me gravely as he left. Dutifully I had bolted the door behind him and gone back to my coffee and newspaper.

And so it happened, that afternoon I found myself at the Hilton Hotel Coffee Shop, an hour later than our scheduled appointment. I was hoping that, by the time I arrived, Nadir Khan would have given up on me and decided to leave. I looked around. The place was packed. People, tourists and locals, in couples and in groups, mostly chatting gaily, paid scant attention to me, other than checking out my hippie garb or wondering, perhaps, to themselves whether it was my face that had stared back at them from the pages of their morning paper. But no one came over to claim me. No one appeared to show the slightest interest so I sat down, ordered a cold drink, took out my book and waited. But not for long.

I was aware of someone, rather large, hovering over me. *How did he suddenly appear?* I wondered. *Where had he come from?* I had purposely had one eye on my book and the other anxiously surveying the entrance. I hadn't seen him enter. Confused, I looked up and saw a wide smile displaying flashing immaculate white teeth.

"Miss Kennedy?" He extended his hand toward me. His eyes were hidden behind a magnificent pair of mirrored sunglasses. All I could see were two disconcertingly distorted images of myself.

"Yes, that's me." I put my book away and stretched out my hand to reach his.

"Nadir Khan. Would you join me at my table? "

So he had been there all along, I thought. He must have been watching me. It was all a little disturbing. I picked up my book and dutifully followed him to his table in the corner.

"Please," he said, gesturing to me to sit down.

He helped me with my chair and then slumped down opposite me, took out a handkerchief and mopped his damp brow.

"Hot, even for me!" he smiled. Then, reaching into his top pocket he withdrew a rumpled business card and handed it to me. I looked at it. It read, "Nadir Khan, Professor in Religious Studies, University of Bombay".

From the letters following his name, Professor Khan appeared to have several academic qualifications, none of which I recognized. But, instead of finding this fact alarming, I reassured myself that Indian doctorates would probably have very different abbreviations from English ones. I watched myself through his sunglasses forcing a smile at him. Although uncomfortable with not being able to see directly into his eyes, I was feeling a little more secure.

"Can I order you something?" he asked.

"Thank you. Tea would be fine."

The Professor beckoned the waiter and ordered us both some black tea. He then proceeded to ask a lot of questions. Attempting to put me at ease, he started with questions about my family, my schooling and my aspirations in life.

"Do you have any family here in Hong Kong?" he asked, smiling broadly.

"No, none," I replied, "they're all in England. I'm on my way to Laos and Vietnam. I'm just stopping here to pick up my visas."

"So you don't know anyone here?" He slurped his tea noisily, his mirrored eyes waiting for my response.

"I have an old friend, he works for the *South China Morning Post*, Ian Black, you probably know him?"

The Professor nodded then, taking out his notepaper and pen, abruptly changed the subject.

"Do you get comfort from meditating?"

"Look, Mr. Khan," I said, "I'm sorry but I told you on the phone, I've never meditated in my life. My personal opinion is that the Maharishi is a big fake but still fascinating for that. And I don't rate any of the other so-called gurus very highly either."

Professor Khan appeared somewhat upset by these remarks but made a point of jotting them down nevertheless.

"But I thought you must be a disciple of his?" he stammered, perhaps mad at himself for having selected this most unwilling of converts.

"I'm sorry," I repeated, "but I did try to warn you over the phone. I was only at that press conference because I was asked to cover it by Ian who was out chasing some story."

"But why your photo in the newspaper then?"

I laughed. "Never heard the newspaper expression 'slow news day'? They had to fill the allotted space with something, I just happened to be there."

Eventually, he put his pen and paper down, apologizing. "I'm sorry, you've been very patient. But, perhaps, if you can be patient a little longer I can tell you now about an extraordinary woman I interviewed recently? I think you'd be very interested to meet her."

I looked at my watch.

"Oh, do you have time?" he asked, suddenly concerned.

I nodded reluctantly. I wasn't quite sure where all this was heading. I had plans to visit Ian at his office towards the end of the day and then we were going to go out for dinner. So I still had plenty of time.

The Professor went on to describe the woman in almost euphoric terms.

"She's only a native Chinese but, it is my belief, she is far superior to the Maharishi. This lady has a way of helping people relax, breathe properly and reduce the stress in their lives. She's well respected here in Hong Kong. But she really should be more famous than she is. If only the world could know about her. You're a journalist, if you met her, perhaps you could write about her work, help to get her recognized?"

"Perhaps. But I shan't be here for long." I was skeptical. "As soon as I get my visa I'm off to Vietnam. So there's not much point as I won't be back in England for at least a couple of years."

Professor Khan persisted. "But let me, at least, introduce you to her. You can make up your own mind then."

I thought about it. There couldn't be any harm, I supposed. "OK. I'll meet her."

He could probably determine by the tone of my voice that I didn't sound very enthusiastic. Despite this, the Professor grinned and shook my hand vigorously.

"Good, good, Miss Kennedy. A wise decision. You won't regret it. She lives in Kowloon. You can take the Star Ferry. It leaves every ten minutes, you know. Perhaps we can meet in the lobby of the Peninsula Hotel at 3 pm tomorrow? I'll make the arrangements with her."

"3 o'clock in the Peninsula lobby." I confirmed. "I'll see you there."

In the meantime, I thought, I'll find out more about this curious Nadir Khan.

I actually had no intention of keeping the appointment. I told Ian about it over dinner. He didn't appear too alarmed. On the contrary, he was rather intrigued by the strange Indian Professor and his new Chinese "guru".

"What the hell?" I said. "I might as well go. Meeting this woman in the Peninsula Hotel can't hurt, can it? And besides," I reflected, "I think I actually quite liked him".

It was true. On the whole, after my initial doubts, Nadir Khan had struck me as being unassertive, polite and well-mannered. There was no doubt in my mind that he was what he said he was, namely an academic. From our conversation, he had appeared well-read, quoting liberally from what seemed to me like an impressive list of classic and contemporary religious works.

"No harm in it then, I don't suppose," Ian said, "and you might even get a good story out of it, who knows? Tell you what, Caroline, if you feel nervous at all, I'll come with you."

Our conversation naturally drifted away from the Professor as we tucked into my first real Hong Kong meal. My tastebuds were caressed by spicy prawn wontons, shredded chili beef, Peking duck and an avalanche of other equally delicious gourmet recipes.

The following afternoon Ian and I made our way, along with hordes of others, onto the Star Ferry and across the water to Kowloon.

At the other end we decided to split up and approach the Peninsula Hotel by separate doors in order to avoid being seen together. I entered from the near side and Ian walked around the building to enter from the far side. As soon as I walked in, I could see Professor Khan strutting up and down the lobby. There was no sign of any Chinese woman with him. I saw him stop briefly to look at his watch. I checked mine. It was exactly 3pm. Through his dark glasses he caught sight of me, waved enthusiastically and rushed over to meet me. He then whisked me back out through the same doors I had just entered where a taxi appeared to be waiting for him, engine running. I tried to slow down the pace to give Ian time to catch up but Khan was in a hurry and he managed to bundle me inside the taxi before I was fully aware of what was happening.

Now I began to panic. I instantly regretted being so impetuous. This assignment, embarked on in simple curiosity, could no longer be considered an "adventure". Unwelcome thoughts flooded my mind. The Chinese woman was probably a hoax. She probably didn't even exist. It was all just a ploy to kidnap me. The possibility of being sold into white slavery, raped, abducted or, worse still, murdered on some back street in Kowloon, now looked very real.

I tried to think clearly what I could do. As the taxi sped off I saw only two courses of action. Either I could open the door and risk my life by ejecting myself through it onto the teeming sidewalk. Or I could try to cause an accident by somehow diverting the driver's attention.

I had to think fast. *Which was it to be? Would I have the nerve to do either? Was I simply over-reacting? Or was I caught up in something beyond my control?*

My hand reached furtively for the door handle. However, even before I had time to turn it, the taxi stopped abruptly and I was unceremoniously dumped out into the street. *Was this an opportunity? Could I now make a dash for it while Khan was paying the driver?* But, the Indian had attached a vice-like hold to my wrist and I sensed the more I tried to wriggle free the stronger his grip would become. Oddly too, he made no attempt to remove his wallet, so I surmised he had either paid the taxi driver in advance or there was some secret arrangement between the two of them. This sobering thought made me more convinced than ever I was now in real danger. Khan, clutching my arm, proceeded to frog-march me down a side alleyway. I had no idea where I was. And, despite my pleas for help, the bustling hordes of Chinese going about their daily business displayed little interest in us.

At the end of the narrow alley the "Professor" propelled me roughly inside what looked like a derelict warehouse. It appeared to be entirely empty, unlit and falling apart. At the far end of the interior courtyard I could just make out a dilapidated staircase with a handrail that had been ripped away in large sections. The building must have been condemned for many years and I imagined there was little likelihood that, even if Ian sent out a search party, it would never consider looking for me in here.

My heart pounded so furiously I thought it might explode. But I was feeling so numb from fear that I knew I was incapable of putting up even a weak struggle. Breathing heavily, Khan pushed me up four crumbling flights of stairs. I was convinced now this was my last hour upon the earth unless I could somehow untangle my disordered thoughts and dream up an effective method of escape.

On the fourth floor I was pulled through a maze of small, bare rooms. I was fervently praying that, if only by the instinct of pure terror, I would be able summon up the strength to wriggle free from Khan's grasp and negotiate my way back through these gloomy, winding passages if the opportunity miraculously arose. I attempted to make some feeble excuse to leave.

"Look, Professor Khan, I didn't realize how late it was. I have an appointment at the newspaper in half an hour. I really must be getting back now. If I'm not at the office by 4.30 they'll start looking for me."

My voice trembled. I was aware how lame I sounded. And, anyway, I should have known my excuse would fall on deaf ears. The "Professor" just wasn't in the mood to listen.

"We're here!" he announced, his fist still locked tightly around my wrist.

Strangely, as is often the case in such threatening circumstances, confused and terrified as I was I now felt calm. Whatever was going to happen to me would soon be over. Everything was out of my control. It was puzzling but I found that my fate, whatever it may be, was welcome.

There was a small room in front of us. A man was sitting behind a desk reading the racing pages of a newspaper under a naked bulb swinging from the ceiling. Flies buzzed around it. I noted that beside him was a telephone so, at least, I thought, there was some form of communication with the outside world. Despite the fact that I knew I would never get the opportunity to use it, this thought provided me with the faintest glimmer of hope.

The man looked up briefly. "Good afternoon, Sir, take number 11 as usual. The lady will be with you in a minute."

From this remark it was not hard to surmise that the "Professor" was a regular visitor to this "establishment". The man behind the desk proffered a key in his hand, without looking up from the sports pages. Khan then maneuvered me roughly down a passageway lit only by another bare bulb suspended by a single wire. Cockroaches and woodlice, alerted by our approaching footsteps, scattered in all directions as we made our way down the corridor.

I noticed there were plenty of doors off each side. Some closed tight, others half open. I was able to catch a glimpse inside one or two as we passed. Each room appeared to contain a double bed, some of them already occupied by gyrating, moaning couples. It was obvious now I was in some seedy illegal brothel. Khan skillfully guided me into a room at the end of the corridor, the number 11 amateurishly marked in white paint on the door. He slumped down on the bed without a word, panting slightly from the exertion and the oppressive heat. I realized I still hadn't seen his eyes and, for some reason, this thought scared me most of all.

I perched on the rough wooden chair nearest the door, my mind calmer, trying to plan my escape. But, at the same time, I was acutely aware that any plan would probably be doomed.

"I would like to explain what's going to happen." Professor Khan abruptly broke his silence. It dawned on me this was the first time he had spoken to me since our meeting in the hotel.

"The lady will deal with me first, so you will watch. If you have any questions don't hesitate to ask. Understand?"

I nodded weakly. My mind numb. My belly tightening in panic. My heart ready to explode.

"Good. You will have to undress, of course," he continued. "Anyway you will see the procedure with me and you will do the same!"

I was too afraid to respond. I had no intention of showing him how helpless I felt. There was no doubt in my mind I had to get out of there, no matter the physical risk to myself. The question was, how? The woman would appear in the room at any minute. I could no longer delude myself that she was some amazing guru waiting to be discovered by the world. It was obvious now she was Khan's main accomplice. And, if that was the case, I knew I wouldn't stand a chance against two of them. Deep down I feared the "Professor" might become excessively violent if his sexual plans for me were thwarted.

Silently, I willed him to remove his glasses, if only for a second. How could I possibly read his thoughts without seeing the eyes behind them? As he started to undress I was momentarily confronted by two kaleidoscopic images of myself, reflections of a girl, rooted to her chair, too terrified to run.

"I have to go to the bathroom!" I gasped.

Those images of myself in his sunglasses had finally spurred me to do something. Khan waved his hand towards the adjoining toilet beyond the bed. This would have meant passing further into the room, adding unwelcome distance from my only escape route. I muttered some feeble excuse about needing privacy, bolted out of the room and back down the passageway. I knew Khan was following me. I heard his panting breath at my neck and his heavy footsteps on the uneven wooden floorboards.

"The ladies room, please!" I shouted to the man behind the desk. He pointed to a room opposite him without raising his eyes from the paper. I dashed inside and locked the door.

I made all the appropriate sounds, turning on the taps, flushing the lavatory while, at the same time, trying to compose myself sufficiently to conjure up an escape plan. But this didn't prove easy under such pressure. Panic, I discovered, has a numbing effect on the mind and, just when I needed it most, my brain obstinately refused to function coherently. All I could think of how I could I have been so stupid to admit to Khan I was alone in Hong Kong? Perhaps, that admission alone had been enough to persuade him to abduct, rape and, possibly, murder me?

There was nothing I could do. I was trapped. So, in the end, I dutifully emerged, submissively proffered my bruised wrists to the "Professor", who was casually zipping up his flies. He immediately latched his big sweaty palm onto my arm and dragged me back to Number 11, muttering all the time what I assumed must be Hindu curses under his breath.

By the time we entered the room the Chinese lady was already there. She beamed and nodded at her Indian accomplice, scrutinizing me up and down. She muttered something to him in Chinese as she locked the door behind us. I noted with relief that she had failed to remove the key. So, mercifully, there was a glimmer of hope. As long as I remained vigilant and didn't fumble with the lock, there might be a chance.

In that moment I decided I would pretend to go along with Khan's plans while, at the same time, preparing my escape. I began asking him some pertinent questions to make it look like I had a keen interest in his accomplice's work. I tried to eliminate the panic in my voice by speaking slowly and calmly. I made a point of feigning an interest in his replies. In this way the "Professor" slowly regained his confidence in me and, while answering my queries, began to remove all his clothes. He then lay on his back on the bed, stark naked, his vast dark belly protruding upwards obscuring his vision of his stirring genitals below.

The Chinese lady poured creams and oils over his legs and torso and began massaging him rigorously while reciting some soothing Chinese incantations. The "Professor's" glasses, the last vestige of his modesty, mirrored the steamy image of her plump little fingers pummeling away at his huge hairy chest and then down towards his massive thighs. And, while he was evidently enjoying the erotic stimulation from her experienced fingers, he ordered me to start getting undressed.

I had no way of knowing whether his eyes, still hidden behind the steamy glasses, were open or closed so felt I had no alternative but to obey his instructions. Very slowly I started undoing the buttons on my dress. And when I considered Khan was sufficiently overcome by the musky-smelling oils, the heat of the small room and the over-efficient pumping of the plump little fingers, I decided to make a dash for freedom.

While trying to create the illusion that I was aroused by the events taking place on the bed in front of me and anxious to do as I was told, I slowly inched my way backwards towards the door. Careful not to arouse their suspicion, with one hand I continued unbuttoning my dress while, with the other, I gently groped behind me for the key. Gradually, and without once averting my gaze from Khan, I twisted the key around desperately praying someone had bothered to grease it recently. Gently I turned the handle, felt the door silently release itself, then swung my body abruptly around and, clutching my dress around my waist, ran blindly back down the narrow corridor towards what I hoped was the main exit.

I took a few wrong turns but eventually saw the collapsing staircase in front of me. I leapt down, four or five steps at a time, praying they wouldn't give way beneath me. I didn't dare turn round, my ears constantly alert for the dreaded sound of heavy breathing and pounding footsteps in my wake. I heard a few angry shouts but was fairly confident that Khan could not be following immediately on my heels considering the state of undress I had left him in.

I tugged hard at the heavy warehouse door and finally catapulted myself out into the welcome chaos of the Kowloon alleyway outside. I remember thinking at that moment, thank God for the ten million Hong Kong Chinese. Only then did I realize that here I was, in broad daylight, in the middle of a teeming Kowloon street, with my bra exposed and my dress hanging down to my hips.

But there was no time to fix it now. I ran as fast as I could, not knowing, or even caring, where I ended up. When I felt sufficiently confident that I was out of immediate danger, I dived off the main road into a side street and through the revolving doors of a small hotel. Slipping my arms back into my dress and buttoning it up as hurriedly as I could, I fell, gratefully, into the nearest phone booth and called Ian at the newspaper.

"God, Caroline, I've been worried sick about you. Where the hell are you?" Ian sounded genuinely panicked.

"I've no idea," I sobbed into the phone. I was so relieved to hear his voice.

"I'll come and get you, just tell me where you are. Jesus, Caroline, you gave me a fright!"

"You frightened? How about me?" I sniffed. I wiped my eyes and nose on my sleeve. "God, Ian, I'm so happy to hear you."

"What happened, for God's sake? No, don't answer that. Just get me the address!" he ordered. "Now!"

I left the phone dangling off the hook and, still nervously buttoning my dress, made my way to the reception desk. The receptionist looked up at me, devoid of any expression, "Yes, can I help?"

"The name of the hotel, please, and the address. Quickly!"

The receptionist handed me a card and I returned to the phone.

"Ian?"

"I'm here, just give it to me! Quickly!"

I heard him scribbling down the details. "Now just sit tight and wait for me. Don't go anywhere, promise me!"

"I promise. Please hurry!"

Half an hour later Ian turned up. I was so relieved to see a friendly face that I broke down and wept all over again. He put his arms around me protectively.

"Don't ever do that again, Caroline, you scared the life out of me!"

Ian held on to my hand the whole way back to his flat as though he expected me to disappear again.

Like the good newspaper reporter he was, he gently probed the story out of me, every sordid detail. It was all so recent and so vivid that it made me fearful simply reliving it. I was constantly looking around me to make sure Khan wasn't somewhere nearby on the crowded ferry watching us, ready to pounce as soon as Ian's back was turned.

Back home Ian sat me down and forced a glass of brandy into my trembling hand.

"But I'm a teetotaler Ian, remember?" I protested, starting to giggle hysterically.

"Just drink it, girl! It's an order!"

I took a sip, made a face and handed it back. "No thanks. You have it, you probably need it as much as I do!"

"You bet I do!" Ian grabbed it and swallowed the contents of the glass in one gulp. "Now, Caroline, I want your permission to call my friend, Murray Todd, Superintendent of the Hong Kong Police Force. I think he should hear this story."

In fact, I needed little convincing. So Ian picked up the receiver and dialed Murray's home number. He described the events thoroughly, beginning with the Maharishi press conference and ending with his own less than heroic role in my salvation. Murray, evidently very concerned, asked if he could come around immediately to question me.

Ian looked towards me, "Are you OK to do it now?" he asked, "or would you prefer in the morning?"

I wanted to get it over with and besides, I thought, perhaps it would give the police a better chance of catching up with the bogus "Professor". And once they caught him I could finally relax and enjoy the rest of my stay in Hong Kong.

"Now's fine." I said, "Let's do it."

Chapter 18
Nothing Can Go Wrong

Less than an hour later Murray Todd arrived. He was a rather large, avuncular, red-haired Scotsman who I instinctively trusted. Falteringly I described my ordeal, yet again, omitting nothing. He listened, nodding occasionally, without comment until I had finished. While I was talking he alternately patted my knee and squeezed my hand to demonstrate his sympathy.

"Well, you've not had a very good experience on your first visit to Hong Kong then?" he joked, lamely. "I'm really sorry for you, Caroline," he said, "Dreadful ordeal! But I want to reassure you we will do all we can."

I nodded, my spirits somewhat revived.

"In fact," he went on, "we have been aware of this man, "Professor" Khan, or whatever other alias he chooses to go by, for several months now. He is a sexual pervert and has raped several women, both here and, I understand from the authorities in India, also there. So far we always get close but we never seem to catch him. But he doesn't give up easily, that's one thing about him we have managed to establish. He is very persistent and I am almost certain he will call you again. That's his pattern. Now, if he does," Murray paused, looking at me in the eye, "will you please make another appointment with him? Will you try to convince him that you didn't really want to leave him but that you had a pressing engagement, or something, and you couldn't have stayed a minute longer? Will you try to convince him you're still interested?"

The red-haired Scotsman paused to look at me intently and, grabbing my hand to emphasize his point, he continued, "We desperately need help to catch this man and this is the first time we've been in a position to do it. I'm pleading with you, Caroline, and I don't need to tell you, you'd be doing us a very great favour indeed."

I looked doubtful. How could I willingly put myself through that ordeal again? But then, on the other hand, I thought, perhaps I should agree simply for the sake of other young women who could end up as Khan's future victims.

Murray obviously read my thoughts. "I give you my word, Caroline, nothing can go wrong. A detective will be assigned to the case. He will be at your rendezvous when you meet Khan and will apprehend him on the spot. You will be risking nothing, I assure you. Naturally we would prefer to arrest him and all his accomplices at the place where they operate, but I wouldn't want to put you in any unnecessary danger." He looked towards Ian, "In fact, my friend Ian would never allow me to risk your safety. Right Ian?"

Ian nodded vigorously.

"So we shall just have to be content with arresting him in the hotel lobby or wherever else he chooses to meet you. Will you do this for us, please?" It seemed Murray Todd was almost pleading with me. "Again, I promise you Caroline, nothing can go wrong."

I looked at Ian, who smiled at me, "It'll be alright, Caroline, I promise. If you can't trust the police, who can you trust?" He winked and squeezed my hand.

So, foolishly, I agreed. Before he left Ian's apartment, Murray thanked me effusively, pumping my hand and kissing me gratefully on the cheek. He handed me his personal phone number.

"As soon as this bastard gets in touch with you and gives you a time and a place to meet, call me immediately and I shall assign our best detective to be there fifteen minutes earlier. I would also ask you to arrive there fifteen minutes ahead of time so that the detective can make a sign to you to reassure you he is around to give you protection. OK?"

"OK, I'll do it!" I answered impetuously but without a shred of enthusiasm. I felt like an unsung heroine. Here I was, I thought, offering to risk my life or, at least, my body for the glory of the Hong Kong Police Force and whether I ended up kidnapped, raped or murdered in a dingy rundown warehouse in the backstreets of Kowloon, who would ever hear about it, least of all who would care?

As Murray had so rightly calculated, Khan called me the very next morning. "What happened to you yesterday, Miss Kennedy?" he asked casually.

"I'm so sorry," I replied. Despite my fears, I was trying my best to sound contrite. "I really did have to get back to the newspaper urgently. I did warn you I might have to leave early."

Hoping he believed me, I repeated, "I really am very sorry, Professor."

For the sake of Murray Todd and any future victims of Khan, I tried to sound suitably convincing.

Khan was evidently fooled enough to ask me, "Can you make it at the same time today? The Chinese lady is very anxious to help you. She thought you appeared extremely agitated and in need of a great deal of attention."

You bet I was agitated, I thought but aloud I said, "She's probably right. I have been through a lot lately."

"How about 3pm at the Peninsula again?" he asked.

"OK, I'll be there!" I enthused as I briefly relished the spectacle of Hong Kong's serial rapist being publicly apprehended in the hotel lobby.

I telephoned Murray's private number so he could make the necessary arrangements. He called me back later that evening to brief me and to give me a physical description of Len Rogers, his "top" detective who had been assigned to the job. He told me the officer's height, his hair and eye colour and even what clothes he would be wearing so I would have no difficulty identifying him.

I felt supremely patriotic, above and beyond the call of duty, as I made my way to the Peninsula Hotel the next afternoon. I had never before been given the opportunity, in any capacity, to serve a police force and I was determined not to let Murray Todd down now by losing my nerve.

At 2.45pm, as instructed, I reached the hotel lobby. Casually I looked around me. No sign anywhere of a man matching Len Roger's description. I waited until 2.50pm and then began to experience nagging doubts. Suddenly I felt very vulnerable and very naive. *Had I got the instructions right? Had Murray really ordered Len Rogers to be on duty? Had the detective forgotten, been held up or had an accident on his way here? Had he turned up at the wrong hotel? Had I mistaken the Hilton for the Peninsula? Had he? Was he supposed to make his presence known to me first, or I to him? Would he, in fact, ever turn up at all? Or was I now on my own?*

I crossed over the lobby to the front desk, in full view of the revolving doors, grasped a phone and called Len Roger's direct line. A woman answered. That can't be right, I thought, and asked for him by name.

"I'm sorry he hasn't come in to work today. I think he may be sick."

"Are you sure? "My heart lurched.

"Can I take a message?"

"No!" I gulped.

"Can someone else help you?" the tone at the other end was monotone.

I wanted to scream at her that I was doing her police force a big favour but I didn't have time for explanations.

So I replied, "No, somebody else can't help!" All the while I was fearfully scanning the lobby in case Khan, too, had decided to arrive early.

"You could try this number," the woman offered robotically.

I was beginning to panic. I took down the other number she gave me, dialed it and, once again, asked for Detective Inspector Rogers.

"I'm sorry, Miss, we haven't seen him all day. He may be in tomorrow. Do you want to leave a message or would you like to speak to someone else?"

"No," I whispered weakly. I replaced the receiver in shock. I was now trembling uncontrollably. *"Nothing can go wrong, nothing can go wrong!"* I repeated Murray's words to myself over and over like a wish-fulfilling mantra. But, deep down, I knew that, despite his persistent reassurances, something had, indeed, gone dramatically and irrevocably wrong.

The telephone I had been using was right in the centre of the lobby and any minute now Khan would arrive and see me there. I rushed headlong into one of the darkened passages that connected to the reception area. I dived into the nearest open door, which happened to be an airline office.

"Can I use your phone?" I pleaded, visibly shaking.

"There's one in the lobby!" A girl, paying scant attention to me, gesticulated unhelpfully towards the direction from which I had just come.

I bit my lip trying, unsuccessfully, to suppress the tears that were rising beneath the surface.

"Here, use mine!" A gallant male employee, who could obviously recognize a damsel in distress, pushed a phone across his desk towards me. He pointed to a chair in front of him. "You look like you need to sit down."

I was too tense to sit so I just nodded my thanks, dialed Murray's number and asked to speak to the police chief urgently. The efficient voice on the other end asked me to hold, Superintendent Todd was on another line. It seemed hours before Murray picked up the receiver, although it was probably only a matter of seconds. I felt instantly comforted when I heard his booming, reassuring voice.

"What's the problem, Caroline?" he queried blithely, "Haven't you met our Bob yet?"

"No, he isn't here. I've been waiting for ten minutes already." I was almost screaming down the phone. Then I froze. *Bob? Who the hell was Bob? Who on earth was Murray talking about?*

"Who's Bob?" I asked, attempting to compose myself. Perhaps I was the one who was being an idiot, who had failed to understand.

"Len Rogers unfortunately couldn't make it today. He's off sick with the flu but I've sent someone else in his place. One of our best men, in fact. No need for you to worry on that score, Caroline. I'm sorry I didn't have time to warn you. Isn't he there yet? I ordered him to be there at 2.45pm prompt."

"Well, I don't know if he's there. I don't know what he looks like and I don't know what he's wearing. But no, no one's approached me yet. What do I do now?" The terror was welling up inside. My voice was beginning to sound hysterical.

Murray paused. "Well, can you go back into the lobby and wait a little longer? He will turn up, I promise you. Very reliable is Bob."

I was somewhat reassured but still apprehensive. "Don't you see, if I go back into the lobby and Bob isn't there, well, it's already 3pm. Don't you understand? Khan will be waiting for me. He'll grab me and make me leave and that'll be the end of it. I don't know if I can go through with it, Murray, honestly." My tears were about to flow again.

"Please do this for us, Caroline. I know Bob's there. He's never let me down in the past. He's probably even seen you already but hasn't introduced himself for fear of blowing his cover." He let this sink in before proceeding. "We have to catch people like Khan, Caroline, you can appreciate that. And you're in a unique position to help us. Please do this for us. Bob is there. I know he is."

My confidence had, by now, completely eroded but my sense of duty somehow prevailed. I agreed, reluctantly, to go ahead as planned. I replaced the receiver, sobbed my thanks to the somewhat startled young man in the airline office and retraced my steps into the lobby. As I approached, I took a long, deep breath to compose myself.

As I had feared, Khan was already there waiting and, as soon as he spotted me, he made his way swiftly towards me. I waited for Bob to miraculously materialize from behind a pillar, an armchair or a potted palm to apprehend him but nobody did. As far as I could see no one was paying us the least attention. Nobody, it seemed, could have cared less as I acted out my own little drama, praying that Bob would appear as if by magic and tap Khan on the shoulder.

"You're late!" Khan reproached me frowning, "Come, we'll have to leave right away!"

He seemed more edgy than the previous day sensing, perhaps, that something was wrong. He grabbed my wrist. I desperately tried to think of some aversion tactics. Risking breaking my arm, I twisted myself around and somehow managed to loosen his grasp sufficiently to allow me to collapse sideways into a deep armchair.

Jolted, he turned back in surprise, his mirrored glasses disguising his thoughts. Thoughts that I was sure were far from friendly towards me at that particular moment.

"I'm sorry, Professor," I said, "I'm feeling a little dizzy from the heat. I've been running around all day and I just realized I haven't had anything to eat or drink yet. Do you mind if I order some tea and biscuits? Really I'm dying of thirst."

And, without waiting for Khan's objections, I beckoned a hovering waiter and ordered two teas.

I desperately hoped that service at the Peninsula was as sluggish as it had been at the Hilton Coffee shop. Khan muttered something inaudible under his breath, reluctantly let go of my wrist and perched proprietorially beside me on the arm of the chair. He started drumming his knuckles impatiently on his lap, obviously frustrated by this unforeseen delay.

"You could have had some tea at the other place," he snarled.

But, thankfully, the waiter had vanished through the swing doors into the kitchen and Khan was unable to cancel the order. Still there was no sign of Bob. I had to accept it now I was entirely on my own. The tears were welling up in my eyes again so, to help compose myself, I stared down at the floor, concentrating on the pattern in the carpet. But the thoughts persisted. *Where was Bob? How could Murray let me down like this? Why hadn't Ian volunteered to come along too, just in case, as back up? Did any of them really care at all what might happen to me?*

The waiter arrived with the tea. I poured it out as slowly as I could, deliberately spilling some onto the embroidered tablecloth as a delaying tactic. I started mopping it up, playing for time, anything to give me an extra moment to prepare my next move. It was obvious I could not count on Bob any more. I would have to save myself from this situation.

As I proffered a cup of tea towards Khan I was thinking maybe I should create a scene in the lobby by shouting "Help me!" at the top of my voice and then, when I had people's attention, I could tell them that Khan was a wanted man, that he was a serial rapist and he was trying to kidnap me. Glumly, I decided, they would just think I was a nut case and apprehend me instead.

The "Professor" pushed the teacup away. "You drink yours. I don't want any," he said petulantly. Behind his glasses, he appeared to be scanning the lobby nervously. It was possible he suspected a trap. "I better call the Chinese lady to tell her we'll be late." Khan lifted himself off the arm of the chair and, without ever turning his mirrored gaze away from me, wandered slowly over to the telephone at the front desk.

There was no doubt in my mind, now was the time to run. I had worked out that Khan would have to pay for the tea and, hopefully, if he tried to avoid it, someone from the hotel would accost him on his way out. This would give me a couple of vital minutes head-start. I realized that by some miracle I had been given this one chance and it would probably be my only chance. At the same time, I was aware that both exit doors were in sight of the front desk. Khan could not help but see me leave. I looked at him and saw that, even now, his gaze had not left me for a second. Nevertheless I had no option but to run.

I jumped up and flew out of the nearest exit. I knew Khan had spotted me but there was nothing I could do. I was sobbing uncontrollably and everything around me was blurred but, for the moment at least, I was free!

I kept looking behind me. People in the street were suddenly aware of some small drama being acted out around them and briefly stopped what they were doing to stare at me. By now Khan, too, had emerged from the hotel and was giving chase, flailing his arms wildly in the air and shouting. I realized he couldn't have waited to pay the bill. If he had stopped to do so, I might have stood a chance to elude him. And now, despite his massive weight, he was gaining on me.

It was then that it suddenly hit me. I had been running away from, rather than towards, the Star Ferry. This would have been fine if I had been content to run just anywhere. But all I could think of at that moment was the safety of Ian's apartment. And now I realized that would entail doubling back past the hotel again, wasting precious minutes and, worse, risking running straight into the arms of Khan. But, being unfamiliar with the area, it was the only way I knew and, thus, I had no choice. Somehow I had retrace my steps.

I wanted to call out to everyone, anyone, to catch Khan, to impede him, that he was a criminal wanted by the police. But I had no breath and certainly no voice. All I could hear above the noise of my pounding heart and the traffic chaos of the Kowloon street was him shouting. All I could feel was the weakness in my legs and the painful throbbing in my chest. And all I could see were people staring, gaping open-mouthed as I rushed full tilt past them.

No one volunteered to help. No one came to my rescue. I doubted if anyone even cared. I cut into a side street and plunged down some steps into a crowded basement shop. I watched, cringing, as Khan's enormous legs thundered past the window. I waited a moment. *Was it safe for me to go out? Would Khan double back if he didn't see me ahead of him? Or worse still, would he suspect my hiding place and come looking for me?* He would have no difficulty trapping me inside. Perhaps he had even seen me go in and was just waiting outside the door ready to pounce on me when I emerged. Certainly, too, he would have realized that I wanted to catch the Ferry so maybe he was already making his way there.

Having established there was no telephone in the shop, I had no alternative but to leave. I glanced cautiously out of the door. Khan didn't appear to be around, or, at least, I could see no sign of him. Gingerly, I retraced my steps to the main road and then ran as fast as I could in the direction of the Star Ferry. This time I did not look back. I did not want to risk taking the wrong turn again. Nor did I want to see the heavy, sweating image of Khan bearing down on me.

As I approached the ticket office, totally out of breath, I caught a glimpse of him in the distance approaching from the opposite direction. I believed, and hoped, he hadn't spotted me yet. I joined the queue that, mercifully, was not too long, bought my ticket and passed through into the welcoming, dimly lit interior. I watched fretfully as Khan shuffled backwards and forwards in front of the entrance, apparently making up his mind whether to buy a ticket or whether to wait a little longer. He was looking at his watch. By this time there was a large crowd of passengers behind me and I tried my best to blend in with it. My distinctive clothes and my long blonde hair did nothing to help camouflage my presence.

I saw Khan eventually join the queue to buy his ticket as the line of passengers in front of me started filing through the heavy metal gates towards the dock. I followed them, praying that, by the time Khan approached the barrier, the gates would slide shut in front of him, blocking his entry. At that precise moment, he must have caught a glimpse of me and tried to roughly shove his way through the human traffic to the head of the queue. To look less conspicuous I huddled close to a group of tourists and, propelled by the crowd, we rushed past the gates and onto the waiting ferry.

To my immense relief, the large metal gates slowly started to close. I saw Khan shoving his way through the jostling mob of people, desperately trying to reach the gates before they slammed together. He waved his arms hopelessly to the attendant to keep the gates open for him but, thankfully, the attendant appeared neither to notice, nor to care. Tempting a nasty injury, Khan somehow managed to squeeze his huge bulk through the closing gates and ran full tilt towards the gangplank. But, by then, the ferry was freed of its guy ropes and had started to shunt gently out of its moorings.

To my relief I watched as Khan was left stranded at the water's edge. The engine on the old ferry spluttered laboriously. I held my breath. We were moving so slowly away from the pier, would Khan risk jumping on board? Surely he wouldn't be that desperate? If he did try it, would he make it?

Then I saw the gate attendant, fearing for his job perhaps, spring towards Khan, grab him roughly by the collar and shove him back behind the gates to wait in queue. Finally I was safe. To the surprise of my fellow passengers, I sat down on the crowded deck and shed copious tears of relief.

Within fifteen minutes I had arrived back at Ian's apartment and bolted the door firmly behind me. It remained double-locked for five days before I dared venture out into the streets of Hong Kong again. "Professor" Khan, after all, was still a free man and, as Ian pointed out, if he had my phone number, he might also know where I lived. It was possible, too, that because he had failed, he might want to exact his revenge on me. How was I to know?

Murray Todd dropped by Ian's flat later that same evening. He was extremely apologetic.

"As well he should be," Ian whispered in my ear.

It turned out that the very reliable Detective Inspector Bob had drunk one too many beers during his lunch break that day and, by the evening, Murray had fired him.

Despite Murray's very sincere regrets and offers to make amends, I swore that would be the first and last time I would ever again act as a decoy for any police force. He had seriously bungled the sting operation and put my life at risk. But I realized that I, too, had also failed. I had not successfully put an end to "Professor"

Khan's sadistic career. The evening ended with Murray giving me a bear hug and one more grovelling apology.

As he left the flat I reminded him of my father's favourite saying, "If you want a job done properly, do it yourself."

Ian squeezed my hand. In his raw Glaswegian brogue he joked, "I think it's high time you gave up being a teetotaler, Caroline. Now is the time to take a wee dram!"

Within a week, officers from both the Laotian and Vietnamese consulates had advised me that my visas would take at least one more month to process. So, all things considered, I decided it was probably now time for me to leave Hong Kong. I remembered the invitation from Betsy and Henry to attend their wedding in Manila, and that offer now seemed irresistibly attractive.

I called Betsy. "I'll be there!" I told her. I had little idea that my decision to make a side trip to the Philippines would change the course of my life forever.

Chapter 19
Art, Politics & Explosions

I arrived in Manila in late June 1968, emerging from the terminal into the glaring Philippine sunlight. Amid the confusion of hundreds of waving, shouting, whistling, jostling Filipinos who were desperately trying to attract the attention of their arriving family members, I finally caught sight of Betsy and Henry beckoning me furiously. They hustled me into their waiting car and, as we slowly made our way towards Betsy's family home in Quezon City, we chatted excitedly, eager to catch up on our news since we'd parted company in Hong Kong.

Our progress to their house was painfully slow, giving me plenty of time to take in the scene around me. From all sides, the roads were jammed with impatient, honking traffic. Dilapidated, overloaded buses belching diesel fumes, vied for space with garishly painted and ingeniously adapted World War II jeeps, known as jeepneys. A motley assortment of decrepit taxis attempted to plough their way over the potholed roads alongside ramshackle trucks, flimsy bicycle rickshaws and sleek air-conditioned limousines. Hordes of people thronged the narrow sidewalks. Nimble vendors, mostly children, zig-zagged perilously in and out of the traffic, hawking pork chicharonnes, hand towels, garlands of flowers or single cigarettes.

Amidst all this chaos, emaciated stray dogs, cats and rats scavenged for scraps of food among the numerous piles of discarded fly-infested rubbish dumped outside countless fast-food restaurants. And, circling the churches, limbless beggars and able-bodied scroungers competed with candle sellers and vendors of religious artifacts to beg a few coins from the passing shoppers-by and congregants.

In contrast, on Roxas Boulevard, stretching the full-length of Manila's eastern shoreline, Betsy pointed out her aunt Imelda's nascent building programme, or "edifice complex", as it later came to be known. The Cultural Centre, constructed two years earlier, was to be the first of many multi-million dollar buildings set on 21 hectares of reclaimed land stretching far out into Manila Bay. Only later did I learn it was built with funds brazenly extorted from charitable foundations, the Philippines treasury, the war reparations chest, wealthy businessmen and intimidated bank presidents, setting a successful fundraising precedent for all her projects that followed over the next two decades. Now, in only her third year as First Lady, Imelda was already an enthusiastic convert to the doctrine of absolutism. According to Betsy, no one was permitted to challenge the methods she used to make her mark on the city she considered was hers by Divine Right.

Like her husband, Imelda had come to believe she was answerable only to God. Yet, at this early stage, she was still naively unabashed by her own unscrupulous methods of obtaining money to finance her pet projects.

"She calls herself Robin Hood!" Betsy giggled. "That's what she said to a group of journalists recently!"

I laughed.

"She told me," Betsy continued, "that building the Cultural Center would reduce juvenile delinquency."

"How?" I asked.

"She couldn't explain!"

Within a week Betsy had made good on her earlier promise to me. She had driven me around town and introduced me to all the top editors, journalists, artists and poets in Manila. Eric Giron, the editor of the *Manila Times*, immediately offered me a weekly column in his weekend magazine. The editor of the *Manila Chronicle* wanted to publish my articles on James Michener and Brigitte Bardot.

"I'll call you Caroline London!" said the principal cartoonist of the *Manila Times*, Nonoy Marcelo. And, true to his word, within a week, there I was easily recognizable as Caroline London, in my Ozzie Clarke robes, waist-length necklaces and flowing blonde hair, incorporated into Nonoy's popular daily comic strip, "Tisoy."

"And I'll paint your portrait!" declared the prodigal painter, Frederico Aguilar Alcuaz, recently returned from several years in Germany.

"I'll take your photograph!" exclaimed top photographer, Frankie Patriarca.

"I'll put you in my next movie!" announced a local movie star, Jun Aristorenas.

"And you must be a guest on my show, *Two for the Road*, please!" insisted popular TV host, Elvira Manahan.

Added to this, as the owner of the Indios Bravos Café, the nightly hub for Manila's social and artistic elite, I soon discovered Betsy was not only at the very centre of the artistic world of Manila, but also at the very heart of the growing political movement, fired by disillusionment, resentment and dissent with the corrupt Marcos presidency. Around the main table of the Café every night, I talked art – but mainly politics, with the likes of the Philippines' high priestess of poetry, Virgie Moreno, the Philippines National Artist for Literature, Nick Joaquin, the activist poet, Pete Lacaba, US Cultural Attache Jack Crockett and visiting Guggenheim Fellowship Awardee, Jose Garcia Villa.

Under the Tiffany lamp at the Café's main table too, writers, photographers, actors, dancers, poets, journalists and artists, among them an upcoming young artist, Ben Cabrera, jostled for a seat eager to share the day's gossip and to add their voices to the growing resistance to Marcos's increasingly autocratic presidency. Joining us during these occasions was always the odd sprinkling of foreign embassy personnel hoping to be "part of the action", overseas tourists looking to experience some "local colour" and Presidential aides and politicians wanting to be considered "hip" or, more often than not, spying for the government.

"In Indios Bravos," Betsy told me my first day in town, "you will find that East truly meets West."

This was no idle boast. For, it's true to say that, on any given night, in the salon-like atmosphere Betsy had created, you could join in an animated discussion about contemporary Philippine literature, art, film, theatre and dance, listen to foreign journalists giving us the latest news from the frontlines in Vietnam or find yourself in one of the café's dimly-lit corners discussing the latest pre-historic discoveries unearthed in the Tabon Caves, off Palawan Island, with anthropologists Robert Fox and Dave Baradas.

But, mainly, during this period, the gossip inevitably turned either to Imelda Marcos's latest extravagant shopping spree or Marcos's most recent example of corruption. The air of anarchy that prevailed in the Cafe at the time of my arrival was tangible. And horror was plainly visible on the faces of the Indios Bravos crowd one night when one of the Manila Times more distinguished anti-Marcos journalists, JV Cruz, announced emphatically that the President was hatching plans to remain in power in perpetuity.

"He's worried he will lose the election next year so he's planning to rewrite the Constitution." JV told us.

According to JV, Marcos was already indulging in massive vote buying by wining and dining the Delegates to the Constitutional Convention at Malacanang Palace and handing them envelopes stuffed with cash along with promises of more to come. The other alternative Marcos was considering in order to cling to power, JV explained, was to create an atmosphere of rumour, innuendo and fear over a long period of time, by planting bombs throughout Manila and the provinces, thereby exaggerating the threat of the Communist New People's Army and, thus, gain the continued US support for his strongarm tactics.

"That way," JV continued, "the US would back Marcos for a second term, and even support him if he were to declare martial law!"

There had been whispers about the possibility of Marcos eventually declaring martial law but this was the first serious mention of it and it sent shock waves around the Café.

Soon afterward, bombs began exploding all over Manila, mainly in government buildings at night, to generate an atmosphere of fear but, at the same time, to minimize the number of casualties. The population, becoming wise to Marcos's ambitions, blamed the President and he, in turn, blamed the Communists New Peoples' Army (the NPA). Student demonstrations, until then typically a good-humoured combination of fiesta and political rally, became increasingly serious and were met with brutal resistance. I joined one peaceful protest outside the American Embassy on Roxas Boulevard against Filipino involvement in America's war in Vietnam only to be confronted with police armed with machine guns.

Despite all this, I was having the greatest time of my life as one opportunity led to another-to another–and to another. Writing jobs, TV and movie appearances, hosting my own daily TV show - the offers just kept coming in. The attention I was receiving and the excitement of the political story unfolding around me, was enough to turn any head. And it certainly turned mine.

The Philippines was certainly not Vietnam, the place I planned to be. But, at the same time, it was obvious the country was at a crossroads. I instinctively knew there was an intriguing story here for me to tell. And, with Betsy as my whistleblower into the hidden secrets of Imelda's family life, I knew I was in an unique position to tell that story. Then, of course, there was an extremely talented, handsome young artist, Ben Cabrera, who was beginning to play a very large role in my own life. And so, without the slightest remorse, my plans for Saigon were conveniently shelved and I simply stayed on in Manila with Ben and my new friends, writing my weekly column, appearing in movies and hosting my own daily TV show.

On Christmas night Betsy, Henry, Ben and I entered the Indios Bravos café after a day out on a beach in Tagatay. From outside on the pavement I could hear Christmas carols blaring out from the shop fronts all the way down Mabini Street.

"Dashing through the snow, on a one horse open sleigh…"

I stopped in my tracks. Snow? Did I hear right?

"Sleigh bells ring, are you listening?…."

Sleigh bells? No, this must be a joke, surely?

"I'm dreaming of a white Christmas…"

A white Christmas? Here in Manila where winter temperatures rarely fall lower than 18% celsius? They can't be serious! I looked at Betsy and Henry. They were chuckling at my expression.

It all seemed so utterly absurd and, yet, so typically and so endearingly, Filipino. Here I was, a visiting writer in a paradise of some 7000 islands, soaking up the warmth of my first ever sub-tropical winter, surrounded by things I could only have fantasized about from the bleak, damp interior of my London home.

Even the prostitutes, pimps and cigarette vendors hovering outside the café that night – two nights before Christmas 1968 – were wearing tinsel in their hair and sprigs of plastic holly around their necks. Inside the café a real log fire crackled and burned. And even the conversation seemed no less bizarre.

"Many Filipinos believe if we become the 51st state of America then we'll have white Christmasses," the poet Virginia Moreno said to me as I sat down beside her.

Her tiny face peered out at me through the comical oversized spectacles that had become her trademark,

My jaw dropped in undisguised disbelief.

"But, it's true!" she insisted, "Hindi ba, Nick?"

She looked to Nick Joaquin, aka Quijano de Manila, the outspoken columnist of the Philippines' Free Press, to back up her characteristically wild assertion. I was used to Virgie's outrageous remarks by then and wasn't about to be taken in yet again.

But Nick nodded in agreement.

"There's a group here, Caroline, you must understand, who really are convinced that the Philippines will become the 51st state and," he added, as he downed a seasonal glass of brandy in one swallow, "obviously, with American statehood comes snow!"

I waited for Nick to smile, to nudge me in the ribs, to kick me under the table, admit he was jesting, tell me how I gullible I was. It would not have been the first time he had made fun of me and it certainly would not be the last. But, no, this time he appeared deadly serious.

At that precise moment, General Hans Menzi strode through the door. With all this talk of a White Christmas I half expected him to be trailing an icy blizzard and a sleigh laden with Christmas gifts in his wake. This tall, shadowy figure was formerly a Swiss army officer with a dubious past, a plantation owner and publisher of the *Manila Bulletin,* before he joined Marcos to become the much-feared eyes and ears of Malacanang Palace.

Most of the regulars were in Indios Bravos on that night before Christmas, including the American cultural attaché, Jack Crockett. Jack had become such a vital part of our scene that, like me, he had been bestowed the title, "honorary Indio" by the adoring café literati.

But General Hans Menzi was never welcome. Mercifully, to date, he had been a fairly infrequent customer. His penchant for young boys had been well-recorded gossip around Manila for several years but rarely, if ever, had anyone dared broach the subject in public. To be caught voicing those rumours, whether in coffee houses or living rooms, the regulars told me, would be tantamount to treason. To even whisper them around Manila would be to risk one's life – or, at least, one's liberty.

"So keep your mouth shut!" Virgie warned me as Menzi walked towards his favourite table by the window.

But, for once, Menzi appeared to be in the Christmas spirit, almost managing to force a smile in our direction. We had suspected for some time that the only reason the General ever visited the Café was to pick up one of the many young boys who loitered around outside the door every night waiting to call a taxi for the café's customers as they left and hopefully to pick up a tip. Either that or Menzi was sent to spy on us, to report on the hippie drug scene of the Indios Bravos crowd to Imelda's "thought police". For both reasons it was always considered wiser to stay out of his way. For to annoy or displease him was to court personal disaster as many, including Betsy and Henry, would soon discover.

So, on that Christmas night, we all smiled back amiably, if somewhat reluctantly. I noticed one young photographer even politely vacated his seat so the General could sit down next to the artist Fred Aguilar Alcuaz, recently returned from several years in Germany. It was painfully apparent to those of us watching that Alcuaz had no idea who Menzi was and we didn't have a chance to warn him. After raising a convivial glass or two of his favourite drink, Menzi leaned over towards Alcuaz and asked, "Do you know where I can get any pot around here?"

The chatter in the Cafe came to an abrupt halt. Some people froze on the spot. Others stampeded towards the loos to flush their own incriminating evidence down the one working toilet. Others tumbled over each other in their haste to catapult themselves out into the street. And, yet, others, not wanting to attract attention to themselves, nonchalantly stamped out their spliffs on the floor beneath their seats. Everyone fidgeted nervously, frantically attempting to secrete their half-smoked reefers under the table, stuff their Rizlas and hash into the upturned Tiffany lampshades, or wrap them up in paper napkins and flick them into the nearest wastebin. Even the waiters turned and fled to the comparative safety of the kitchen. They didn't want to be around for any trouble.

Bing Crosby's "White Christmas" that had been playing through the speakers, had now, given way to the anti-Vietnam War carol, Simon & Garfunkel's *Silent Night*. But at that moment the needle jerked off track leaving Nixon's compelling and haunting voice-over to splutter, grind to a halt and, finally, die.

All eyes and ears swivelled towards Menzi and Alcuaz. None of us in the café could believe what we had just heard. As we all waited for Alcuaz to speak, the painter removed a pen from his top pocket and started scribbling an address onto a white paper napkin. We held our communal breath, waiting for the police to come bursting through the door to arrest the unsuspecting artist.

"There is one place," Alcuaz smiled into his disappearing whisky, "there's a shop around the corner – on del Pilar Street – they sell pots, I mean terracotta ones, but…"

He glanced down to look at his watch and we all did the same. It was almost midnight.

"Yes," Alcuaz continued, "I'm pretty sure it'll be closed now but there might be one I know in Quezon City which will be open at six o'clock tomorrow morning! Do you need the pot urgently?"

He scribbled down another address and handed it to the amazed General.

None of us knew whether to laugh or weep. Was Alcuaz just being very clever? Surely, he had been living in Frankfurt long enough now that he couldn't be that innocent? Or could he? He must have known all about hash, pot, weed, grass, ganja, call it what you will. But no. It's just possible he had no idea. I had got to know him quite well in recent weeks. I had been sitting for two portraits by him and I had come to the firm conclusion that he was just about the most socially naive person I'd ever met.

That Christmas night Menzi, in all his misleading display of camaraderie, had chosen the wrong man. And now the bogus four-star general had been embarrassed in front of all of us. We knew instinctively what this could mean. Menzi was not about to forget such an humiliating experience. For certain he would exact his revenge – in his own way and in his own time. We would pay for Alcuaz's innocence. This would mean Indios Bravos would, most likely, be raided by Imelda's Metrocom Police soon. There was little doubt in any of our minds about that. It was just a question of when.

And, yes, sure enough, a few days into the New Year, General Menzi's belated Christmas present arrived at Indios Bravos, not in the form of Santa's sleigh bearing gifts, but in the form of the Manila Metrocom, searching for drugs. Betsy was about to learn that writing unfavourably about Imelda, even at this early stage, did not go unpunished. Betsy had often said to me that if you played by her Aunt Imelda's rules she would smother you with love and largesse but, "if you crossed her or criticized her or saw her as, in any way, flawed, she would be an implacable foe."

That evening Betsy found out just what kind of a foe her aunt Imelda was prepared to be. And there was no doubting the raid's concealed Christmas message from the First Lady. Like the sleigh bells, it rang out loud and clear to all the habituees of Indios Bravos.

"Welcome to 1969. I shall be watching you!"

This was to be the first of many raids over the next few years, culminating on 14 October 1972. On that night, as Betsy later described it to me in a letter. "A raiding party of 40 Metrocom soldiers armed with M-16s burst into Indios Bravos. They ransacked the premises and hauled 19 of us aboard six trucks bound for the

Military Camp Crame. There we were stripped, interrogated and detained – some for several hours, some, like me for several days, and others for a few months."

Sadly, this last raid heralded the death knell for Indios Bravos. Its habituees were forced to meet clandestinely elsewhere. Under martial law, in an atmosphere of intimidation where a gathering of more than five people constituted a conspiracy punishable by law, where a 9pm curfew was enforced every night, where men with long hair and beards were considered the enemy and forcibly shaved on the street and where the typically-Filipino pastimes of gossip, innuendo and intrigue were rewarded with custodial sentences, the days of café society had become a thing of the past.

But, for me, offers of work were still flooding in. I was asked to appear in countless TV shows and films, alongside well-known comedians and actors such as Chiquito, Dolphy & Panchito, Leopoldo Salcedo, Jun Aristorenas, Pilar Pilapil and Elvira Manahan. I was written about in fan magazines, weekend supplements and daily newspapers. And then, to cap it all, Nick Joaquin (alias Quijano de Manila), the National Artist for Literature, decided, with my agreement, to publish a naughty "tell-all" cover story for the Valentine Day's issue of The Free Press, that was specifically designed to stir up incandescent indignation among the Filipino male population.

The article, when it appeared, was explosive, as Nick predicted it would be. And it resulted in threats of my immediate deportation, abusive language being hurled in my direction and the henchmen of a notorious murderer, local mayor, "Banjo" Laurel, turning up on my doorstep threatening my life. But it also won me a few supporters. Local newspapers fanned the flames, printing letters condemning me or praising me and, to this day, Filipino men of a certain age, remember the tempest the article caused.

Chapter 20
From Mere Mortal to Living Goddess

One cold, misty January morning, Ben and I, along with a fellow artist, Mars Galang, boarded a local Benguet bus from the Philippines' summer capital, Baguio City, bound for Kiangan in the far north of the vast Cordillera Mountain range. Ben and I had already begun travelling around the country together. So far, we had visited the Visayan Islands and Mindoro Island several times, Vigan, Batangas, Tagatay ad Pangasinjan in Northern Luzon and Zamboanga, Cagayan de Oro and Davao, in the southern island of Mindanao. Now we were both excited to be heading far further north than either of us had ventured before.

Ben knew I had travelled across Eastern Europe and Siberia, spent time in Tokyo, Hong Kong and Manila but that I had never yet had the opportunity to live among an indigenous tribe. So, for the first time for both of us, we were going to spend a week among the remote Igorot, Ifugao and Kalinga people.

I realized a week wasn't quite enough to fulfill my dream of becoming a second Margaret Mead! But it would give me an opportunity to observe and begin to learn, at first-hand, their customs and their way of life. Of course, there was no way of knowing then that I was setting out from Baguio a mere mortal but would be returning a week later as a "living goddess".

The drive from Baguio itself was a long, arduous and dusty one. There was no choice of first or second-class transport, as on buses in other areas of Luzon. All were strictly third class. There was no glass in the windows on one side of the bus and, on the other, there was nothing at all. It was completely open. This proved to be not only terrifying on these winding mountain passes but also extremely hazardous. As the ancient bus ricocheted from side to side, the passengers were catapulted from their seats to within inches of death. I found myself automatically clutching on to anything that seemed solid, human, animal or vegetable, although I realized that in the event of us tipping over the edge, this move would hardly be likely to save my life.

There were no tourists on the buses heading so far north in those days. I was told that very occasionally an American Peace Corps volunteer headed up that way to check out the area but even that was a fairly rare sight. And, as a result, I was an immediate oddity. The further north we travelled the more curious people became and the more they stared at me. The brasher ones stepped forward to touch me and then dissolved into fits of embarrassed giggles.

The seats on the bus were composed of long, hard wooden benches. Soon into the 13-hour trip, I discovered, to everyone's discomfort, that as many as twelve people could be sandwiched together side by side onto a seat that was designed for no more than six. As the bus hurtled round the hairpin bends, the conductor clambered agilely over our laps and the assorted bundles of rice, vegetables, livestock and personal effects to collect his fares. As he came to the end of a row he swung himself outside the bus, clinging precariously to its open side, defying all gravity, as it skirted the cliff face at frightening speed.

Although there were, apparently, set points along the route designated as official bus stops, the more inland we travelled, the more frequently it would come to a shuddering halt. No one along the road was denied a space if there was an inch of floor, roof or seat to be filled. Every so often people flagged down the bus, boarded it and then hopped off a mile or so further along the road. The local men, despite the cold January temperature in the cloud forest of the high Cordilleras, were clad only in their scarlet, yellow and green G-strings. They were on their way to market, many of them with their pigs and goats to sell. As if knowing their fate, the animals appeared reluctant to clamber board.

The women, bare-breasted in some cases, were wrapped in colourful skirts woven in native designs and loaded down with bulging sacks of vegetables and rice. Many of the older women displayed intricate tattoos on their arms, a sign that the male members of their family had once been proficient head-hunters. The more tattoos they displayed, the fiercer their father or grandfather had been as a head-hunter during inter-tribal conflicts. It was on this trip that I became fascinated by the variety of images used in these tattoos and, on my return to Manila, studied the subject. I ended up writing an article about them for the encyclopaedia, *Filipino Heritage,* published four years later by Paul Hamlyn.

As we proceeded on our journey the landscape changed from sloping grasslands to pine forests. The coconut plantations gave way to dense thickets of bamboo. And, dotted here and there, were native huts on stilts made from nipa palm and rattan vines and decorated with colourful window boxes and climbing bougainvillea blossoms. Splashes of gold and yellow sunflowers stood tall against the smoke grey hills and vivid green rice paddies.

All along the route, we passed stalls selling watermelons, papayas, avocados, mangos, bananas, sweet potatoes, coconuts and, even, strawberries. But, as we climbed steadily higher and closer to the interior, even these began to thin out.

We arrived finally in Bontoc, the last sizeable town before reaching the rice terraces of Banaue. Everyone was, at last, free to climb down from the bus, stretch their atrophied legs, go to the squat toilet and take a quick lunch before boarding the bus again.

As soon we stepped out of the bus into the marketplace, small children, like an army of ants, surrounded us from all sides, selling coca-cola, coconut slices, rice-cakes and local peanut brittle. Their mothers following them were selling grilled corncobs (mais) and cooked pink bananas (saba). The women, constantly complaining about their meagre earnings and their hard life, did everything they could to encourage us to buy. One woman was so determined to sell her wares that she clung to the side of the bus as we were taking our seats again. She was still hanging on when it moved off unexpectedly and she was forced to make an inelegant leap to the ground. When I turned to look out of the open window, I saw she had survived intact but her basket of pink bananas had not.

On the way to Banaue we stopped at off at the Sagada caves. These caves, the ancient burial grounds of another tribe, the Ifugao, were dank and badly preserved. Grafitti covered the walls. Names of local tribesmen coupled with those of American soldiers (from the Philippine-American war at the turn of the 20th century) were painted over the lids and sides of the primitive wooden coffins and limestone burial jars. Water dripped monotonously from the roof into a large underground lake. Stalactites clung precariously from the ceiling, threatening to fall, at any moment into the depths of the caves.

When I spoke to the local chief later he told me, "We believe that the caves were formed millions of years ago before the country emerged from the sea."

As we approached Banaue we could already see the beginnings of the fabled rice terraces. And, although I had been warned that January was not the right time of year to appreciate them fully, the visual effect was still impressive. Over the heads of the people in front of me, I called to ask the bus driver if he could stop while I took some photos. Fortunately, nobody seemed to mind. On these hazardous roads, I supposed, nobody was in a hurry.

As I stood beside the bus taking photographs, the mountains surrounding me on all sides, were disappearing and reappearing into the clouds of mist. I noticed the water in each terrace mirrored the reflection of the terraces above it and the vibrant colours – red, green, yellow and black of the native G-strings, worn by the men planting rice, formed a kaleidoscope of ever-changing patterns in the watery prisms.

The rice terraces, later named a UNESCO World Heritage Site in 1995, are known in the Philippines as the Eighth Wonder of the World. But, to the Igorote, Ifugao and Kalinga tribes who inhabit them, they are referred to as the "*Stairways of the Gods*". Reaching from valley floor to peak they exceed, in some places, 5000 feet. And, as I watched them appear and recede in the high altitude mists, it was easy to believe that they did, indeed, reach out into the firmament beyond space itself. I got back into the bus feeling a great respect for these tough, resilient people, whose daily lives were dictated by planting, harvesting and selling their rice.

Further along the route, on the way to Kiangan, the bus came to an abrupt halt. We were all instructed to disembark to help clear an overnight avalanche of rocks that was strewn over the road rendering it impassable. It was noon and, though we were high up in the mountains, the heat was surprisingly intense. The limestone dust in the air from the rock fall made it hard to breathe. I envied the local Ifugaos, who had come fully prepared and, before they even descended from the bus, had swiftly wrapped their faces and hair with wet towels. Now, too late, it dawned on me why, at our last stop, the child vendors had been encouraging us to buy towels.

It took all of us two hours to clear the mass of rocks and boulders strewn across the road. By this time Ben's black hair was almost as blonde as my own. Our clothes, too, were totally whitened by the chalk and our skin felt itchy and uncomfortable. We eagerly clambered on board again, each hoping to secure a better seat or space than our last. I was determined not to sit on the open side with the unobstructed view of the valley several thousand feet below. I managed to squeeze myself in beside a woman with two small children and a cage of complaining chickens. The driver noisily thrust the bus into gear and he drove off, skimming the precipitous slopes, twists and bends with the skill and fearlessness of an experienced lion tamer. Our friend, fellow artist Mars Galang, who had been proudly sporting a pair of brand new glossy black leather shoes, then spent most of the journey spitting on Kleenex tissues in a futile attempt to polish them back to their original shine

A few miles further on, however, we were forced to a halt by another, more recent, avalanche. This time the giant boulders blocked the road completely. It was obvious we couldn't manage alone so we waited, a little less patiently this time, for reinforcements to arrive on foot to clear the way. This, we were informed, would be a long wait. The passengers moved restlessly in their cramped seats, reluctant to give them up. Eventually, one by one, they got out to stretch their legs. The women, prepared for such an occasion, brought out picnics of fruit and rice cakes and large supplies of lethal, locally brewed rice wine. Some women squatted on the rocks and washed their hair or clothes in the crystal, icy water pools nearby. They were obviously used to these long delays and I marvelled at their patience as they began to sing, chatter or simply sit silently chewing tobacco or betel nut.

Clearing the boulders took almost what remained of that day. But, eventually, we set off again. Mars continued to polish his shoes and Ben's white hair was even whiter. Finally, by the early evening, we arrived in Lagawe, in Kalinga-Apayao territory. The road, which had twisted upwards until this point, now descended abruptly and we soon found ourselves in a rich, green valley. Trees, that had thinned out close to the summit, now profusely overhung the road and the air was refreshingly cool. There was a large avenue down the centre of town lined by lush bushes of purple and pink bougainvillea. The houses, evidently constructed originally by wealthy Spaniards, reminded me of the laconic lifestyle of the deep American South, the white wooden verandahed houses were reminiscent of my earlier visit to Savannah and Charleston.

Strangely, most of these houses in Lagawe appeared completely uninhabited. Dilapidated and overgrown with thick vegetation, their luminous porticos gleamed momentarily in the occasional light of the moon as the clouds scudded across it, adding to what was already the eerie quality of a Spanish ghost town. This atmosphere was further enhanced by the approaching dusk and, with it, the evening chorus of cicadas and the abrupt darkening of the sky as the nightly cavalcade of fruit bats flew overhead of us in search of their evening meal.

Children appeared in the road, emerging silently from behind the trees. Even they were muted as they passively watched the bus drive past. This was quite unlike the impulsive, rowdy reception and noisy greetings we had received in other villages along the route.

Two hours later we arrived, weary, dirty and aching, in Kiangan. It was already dark and much colder even than Baguio at night. We were planning to stay with Raymond and Rosario, anthropologist friends from Manila, who had rented the Mission House for their work. Our problem now was to locate the house.

"It's easy to spot," Raymond had told us before we left Baguio. "It's the only house with an electric light. On the outside, not the inside!"

We enquired at the local sari-sari (grocery) store and the owner directed the way, as best he could, with a series of gesticulations and toothless grins. The path he pointed to was made out of roughly hewn stones and, as we made our way in the complete darkness, we stumbled painfully and often.

Finally, with some relief, we spied the single electric light bulb swinging imposingly in the night breeze over the garden of the Mission House, in front of the local school. Raymond and Rosario were inside heating up some tinned food over a paraffin burner. They were already familiar visitors to this place, carrying out research on Ifugao and Kalinga-Apayao folklore for the University of the Philippines. By the light of candles, we ate our dinner huddled gratefully around the log fire, our shivering, stiff limbs wrapped in blankets, rugs and sleeping bags.

The Mission House, Rosario told us, belonged to a Belgian mission run by a nun from Brussels who had lived among these hill people for 43 years. She was solely responsible for converting most of the non-believers in this area to Catholicism.

This knowledge somewhat saddened me but had evidently gladdened the hearts of the nun's superiors back in Belgium.

That night, after we had sufficiently rested and warmed ourselves, we were fortunate enough to be asked to witness a local tribal ritual feast.

"With Catholicism many of these rituals are fast dying out," Raymond explained, "and it won't be long before there will be none left at all. So we're trying to record as many of them as we can before that day comes."

Raymond told us that the ritual we would watch that night was called the canyao, a celebration in which a carabao, pigs and chickens are slaughtered in honour of a tribal death or, as in this case, to celebrate the making of a hagabi. This wooden bench is made from one huge, hollowed out tree trunk, which is dragged down from the mountains to the village by the men. These benches are strictly for decoration and status, only the more affluent men being able to afford the labour for the length of days it takes to make one. The day it is completed and installed beneath someone's house is marked by the killing of a carabao followed by several days of feasting and rejoicing.

I waited till Raymond had finished his explanation and then took my first visit to the Mission House bathroom. It was not an experience I was keen to repeat. Although the Belgian nun apparently boasted it was "western" in concept, it differed fairly drastically in that it lacked any running water whatsoever. We had to draw water from a well outside and carry in pails, jugs, pots and, even, glasses every time we wanted to go to the lavatory or wash. This, in itself, I didn't mind. What I did find hard to cope with was that the water, being drawn straight from the nearby mountains, was icy. Exhilarating, no doubt, to some, but unbearable to others.

The following morning, with the invigorating, pine-scented air and the sudden shining dawn, we awoke at around 5.30am. After we had each experienced our local ritual in the bathroom with many pails of water, we wandered into the kitchen for breakfast. Raymond and Rosario were already at work with their tape recorder and typewriter. A local schoolteacher, acting as their interpreter, was busy translating their latest tapes. We ate quickly, anxious to follow Raymond into the village.

On our way, he pointed out the Ulag, a dormitory for young girls that were then still being used as a trial marriage house. Men were encouraged to sleep with girls to test their fertility. Some of these girls looked no more than twelve years old as they peered at us through the open windows.

"On becoming pregnant," Raymond said, "the girl is released from the Ulag to marry the man responsible for her pregnancy. This tribal custom thus prevents any infertile marriages."

A girl who sleeps with a man outside the confines of the Ulag will remain unmarried. However, inside the Ulag, a girl may sleep with as many men as she likes. A practice which, I suggested, was unlikely to receive the blessing of the Belgian nun!

We then strolled into the marketplace that was situated in a large plaza in the centre of the village. The vendors were squatting under the shade of palm and bamboo fans smoking the local tobacco. Even small children, no higher than my waist, were puffing on long thin cigarillos that were so huge they could well have served them as walking sticks. Everything there was for sale. Vegetables and fruits of all varieties, different types of rice, livestock such as pigs, goats and chickens, Ifugao and Kalinga cloths, blankets, G-strings, local carvings and assorted plastic items such as combs and beads.

It seemed the entire population of the village and surrounding areas was in the plaza selling or buying – but mostly bargaining – in shrill voices. At one moment I observed a very wrinkled, shrunken old woman on the opposite side of the marketplace. She was smiling at me, an almost seraphic, though toothless, smile and muttering loudly to herself. Hunched over and walking with great difficulty clutching a cane, she appeared to be heading straight towards me. But, as she reached me, she slowly unbent herself, threw her stick to the ground and grasped my hands in hers, pumping them excitedly. She then crossed herself and whispered something. She grinned again, turned and faltered off without her stick. Raymond's interpreter translated to me what the old woman had mumbled. "It's the Blessed Virgin, I have seen Her at last. Now I can die happy!" This was the first sign I had that I was beginning to acquire a deified status!

Following this astounding display by the old lady, who apparently was considered locally to be an oracle, there was nowhere in the marketplace I could go without attracting hordes of spectators and newly-converted religious fanatics wanting to touch my clothes, stroke my hair or clasp my hands. Even pregnant women came up to me simply to gaze. The interpreter explained that by staring at me in this fashion and making a wish these future mothers believed that the baby in their wombs would look like me!

Eventually, tiring slightly from this new-found apotheosis, we decided to head off for a walk to some less populated area. But, as we set off from the marketplace, numerous children followed me. To me, it was more reminiscent of the Pied Piper than the Virgin Mary. Small five-year-olds, barely able to walk themselves, carrying fat babies attached to their backs by yards of brightly-coloured cloth, ran, stumbled and fell in their efforts to keep up with us.

Raymond brought us to a large area of rice paddies. He prepared us to cross it because he wanted to show us a forest and a lake, some three miles beyond, which formed part of a local legend. Crossing the rice fields at the best of times would be hard. Crossing them followed by countless children weaving in and out of my path was, as I found out, impossible. It required balancing on narrow earthen walls that ran between the paddies. Failing to do this meant falling knee deep into the rich mud. A few inches to fall but a great loss of dignity, especially to someone so recently acquiring Holy status.

To avoid such personal humiliation I decided to take the cowardly option. I volunteered to return to the Mission House with Rosario to help her cook lunch. My companions, Raymond, Ben and Mars, immediately rejected this feeble excuse. They assured me that three able-bodied men would be perfectly capable of helping me across. I foolishly gave in. Raymond went first and I went fourth. It was very obvious Raymond had become something of an expert at this art for he was at least 500 yards across the field before Mars dared to put one foot on the low mud wall. It was then suggested by the amused children that we all walk crab-like with our arms outstretched for balance.

They proceeded to give us a demonstration and, giggling at our clumsy efforts, beckoned us to follow. We did so very reluctantly and very cautiously. The children dodged in and out of us obviously enjoying my agonized expressions as they playfully tried to dislodge my foothold.

By some miracle, I arrived halfway across safely but then panic set in. Should I proceed or should I return? My common sense definitely dictated retreat. But I had little public support for this idea. It was translated by all as cowardice. Some cheeky toddlers pushed me on before I was able to turn back. Too late I saw, to my horror, that some hardened earth had crumbled away just ahead of me. Panic set in.

"Jump!" I was advised.

"Sideways? I can't do it!" I said emphatically.

But then I heard my father's voice in my head, repeating his favourite mantra, "You know, Caroline, there's no such word as can't."

Momentarily resolved, I stepped gingerly on. Too gingerly, apparently, for, if I had stepped a little quicker I might have avoided my acute embarrassment. I might have managed to retrieve my footing or I might never have slipped in the first place. Or so I was informed after the event had happened.

What utter humiliation! Not so much in front of my friends but faced by scores of hysterical children, pointing their chubby fingers at this less than infallible Virgin. In their merriment they doubled up with laughter, threatening to eject their infant passengers from the snug safety of the cocoons on their backs.

I recovered my composure but defiantly refused to climb back onto the wall. Instead, with my shoes and socks still on, I waded through the squelching mud, accompanied by shrieks of delight from my small companions. After reaching the other side, with what little remaining dignity I could muster, I walked slowly and agonizingly barefoot and silent the rest of the way, keeping my eyes wide open for the occasional snake or scorpion in my path.

I regained my sense of humour somewhat when Raymond pointed out the mythical lake suddenly appearing in front of us from the centre of the surrounding forest.

"Local folklore tells us, "Raymond said, "that the female ancestor of the locals, in the form of Princess Maganda (Beautiful), rose out of this lake in a giant bamboo. Then, as the bamboo dried, it split open and the Princess stepped out. Another bamboo surfaced a few days later. This one contained a man, Malakas (Strong). This particular place appeared so enchanting to both Maganda and Malakas that they decided to stay and so became the mother and father of the Filipino people."

In the afternoon Raymond and Rosario took us to meet the Belgian missionary. She appeared very agitated, so Rosario asked her the cause of her concern.

"I worked so hard last night," she replied. "And, finally, I made my last convert. The local witch here. Lord be praised!"

Rosario explained to us later that the 'witch' in question, was well known locally for her colourful stories, her healings and her herbal medicines. She had resisted conversion these past 43 years.

"Now she will longer recount her 'heathen folk tales'," the nun continued triumphantly. "She will do and say nothing to upset the Lord. Lord be praised!"

Somehow, I found this all acutely depressing. Rosario had previously promised us a visit to this old woman but now there seemed little point in visiting her.

"And she will attend Church every Sunday from now on," the elated nun continued. "Lord be praised!"

Without conviction we congratulated the nun and left her to praise the Lord a few more times.

So, instead of visiting the old 'witch' as planned, we walked a few miles into a neighbouring barrio (village). We passed the local Fawi (Council House) where the tribal elders were sitting, discussing the problems of their villages. And, suddenly, I had this moment of elation. This is where I always wanted to be. After reading copious books in my teens about living among remote mountain tribes, here I was, actually beginning to live my dream.

Raymond pointed out the food that had been left out on the stone wall beneath a large boulder. "An offering to the spirits to keep them happy," he explained. "The boulder is sacred and where they believe the spirits live."

We arrived at the house of a rich and, previously, much-feared head-hunter and local chief.

"Sadly, this man, too, has been converted by the same nun," Rosario told us.

These recent conversions, no doubt welcomed by the Vatican, left us all feeling despondent. I fervently wished religious zealots would keep their claws off people like this and leave them with their own animistic beliefs. Beliefs that had been handed down, generation to generation, for hundreds of years.

"Surely, so much of their history and culture will be lost now?" I asked.

Rosario nodded. "That's why we came here to help preserve it," she said.

"Here, a rich man is not determined by his wealth," Raymond explained, "but by the number of goats and pigs he keeps."

"Also by how many family heirlooms he possesses," added Rosario. "Like jewellery, crocodile heads, spears, artifacts and tribal costumes."

As I glanced at the artefacts surrounding the house, it seemed, this elderly chief must be very rich indeed.

Followed by a group of men, the old man climbed down the ladder from his nipa hut, proudly carrying great baskets of his "wealth" to show us. With great care, the men helped him lay everything out on his massive hagabi bench under his house. Rare beads and stones, ancient earthenware carvings, wooden tribal sculptures and Chinese potteries, ancestral carvings and limestone jars, countless spearheads, and some faded black and white pictures of himself at his wedding, attired in a magnificent tribal dress. They stood back proudly, with folded arms, smiling broadly, as they watched us pick up each of the items and demonstrate our approval.

Through the interpreter we asked the chief if he would put on the headdress for us. It was ornately plumed and beaked to represent a magnificent giant hornbill. At first, he appeared reluctant for he was, like everyone else in these mountains, deeply superstitious. But, in the end, he needed little encouragement for also, like everyone else, he was something of an exhibitionist.

The chief and his friends were barefooted and attired only in G-strings. And, like all the mountain tribesmen I had seen, they had deformed feet. From a lifetime of gripping the bark as they shinned up the coconut palms and from clinging to the almost perpendicular slopes as they climbed the Cordillera mountainsides, the soles had spread flat and wide and the big toes turned inwards at a complete right angle.

The exterior walls of the chief's house were covered with carabao horns, spears, goatskin bags, crocodile heads and other trophies. It seemed he was very proud to show them to us and kept grinning and nodding as we admired them all.

Through the interpreter he told us, "The men here, denied their traditional head-hunting forays by law and religion, now hunt snakes and crocodiles."

And, although I had never actually seen the latter, the chief said there were, apparently, a great many of both in these highland areas of the Philippines. He showed me some crocodile heads he kept as treasures in sawali (split bamboo) containers, along with some stone and wooden figurative carvings (anitos) used for ancestral worship.

I asked the chief what happened to the snake and crocodile skins.

"Sold to agents," he answered, "who, in turn, sell them on to shops in Manila."

I had noticed a few shops in the city specializing in crocodile and snakeskin bags, luggage, belts, shoes and other items aimed at the tourist trade but had always believed they were imported from China.

Rosario was eager to record his stories. Her interpreter had been farsighted enough to bring along several crates of local beer, carried by our ever-present retinue of young children. The Chief invited us to climb the ladder into his house and beckoned us to sit down on the floor or on low wooden stools set around the log fire in the centre of the room.

Beside the fire, I noticed a cat was chained to the grate.

"To scare away the mice and rats," Rosario whispered to me.

Everything inside the one-room house was charred, grimy and blackened from years of soot. And squatting beside the cat was the chief's wife and small daughter. They smiled at us but said nothing.

It was getting dark by now and there were no candles. Only the flames from the fire lit the faces of the chief and those of his friends who had managed to squeeze their way into the cramped room. Their spirits rose at the sight of the beer. And, in no time at all, they were gulping it down. In return, the chief offered us, his own rice wine that he had brewed in huge Chinese porcelain jars that, unknown to him, could well have fetched a princely sum at any London auction house. He ladled the wine into hollowed out coconut shells and, silently, handed them around.

When the interpreter thought the men were sufficiently inebriated, she switched on the tape recorder and asked them to talk about their lives and how the Japanese occupation had affected them. They began in turn, hesitantly at first, a little bewildered by the microphone and a little shy of me. But, as the beer passed more freely from the bottles to their mouths, so their tongues got looser.

One story the Chief related to us was like a fairy tale but he obviously believed it. He said he was sleeping one evening in a tree and was awoken by a strange light. Seated on the ground surrounding the base of the tree were several duende (gnomes). They danced in a circle around him. Then, one by one, they disappeared. Again he saw the strange light but now it was further away. He followed it and it fell from the sky. At the spot where it fell, he found a Neolithic stone. He kept it ever since as an amulet against evil. The Chief then produced from his hip a small wooden canister. He opened the lid respectfully, unwrapped the small object inside revealing the precious stone.

After more stories about their lives and about the Japanese atrocities during the Occupation, the men started singing. Surprisingly to us, they were singing in Japanese. Even their own native songs, which they sang in their own dialect, were sung to Japanese tunes. And as they sang they acted out the songs in the cramped space of the smoke-filled room.

One man, a village elder, improvised a song about me. This too, although totally spontaneous, was set to a Japanese melody. Raymond taped it and, later, his interpreter translated it for me.

"I am poor and barefoot and I see you in your beautiful shoes.

I have few clothes and I see you in your beautiful robes.

I work in the fields all day and I see the corn colour of your hair.

It is alright for me to work all day knowing I shall see you on my return.

My eyes are squinting from the sun and your eyes shine brightly.

My skin burns with the heat and your skin is pure white.

My hands are calloused from my work and your hands are soft.

I work in the fields all day and I see the corn colour of your hair.

But it is alright for me to work all day knowing I shall see you on my return."

The tune was sad and lyrical. I think this was the first time anyone had made up a song about me and I was touched.

When the beer and the rice wine finally ran out, we thanked the Chief and his friends for their hospitality and left. As we made our way home across the fields, the voices of the men, still singing, echoed through the night.

The next day the old Chief came to the Mission House. The interpreter met him.

"He's offering you his collection of anitos (wooden ancestral sculptures) if you would dedicate your hair to his tribe," the interpreter told me. "He said he will keep your hair, along with his other tribal relics, as an amulet to bring the village good luck and good harvests in the future."

I wasn't quite sure how to respond.

"He asks if he can christen you the Goddess of Kiangan," the interpreter continued. All the while the Chief was shyly smiling at me and nodding.

"What should I do?" I whispered to Rosario.

"It's up to you," she replied. "It would make him very happy!"

So I agreed, although I refused to accept his precious anitos.

The Chief pumped my hand. I noticed he had tears in his eyes. And, without waiting for me to change my mind, he removed his fearsome-looking bolo (a long native, all-purpose knife) from his G-string and promptly, and somewhat painfully, gave me a "healthy" trim that would have sent the high-class hairdressers of Mayfair reeling in dismay.

And so, perhaps, to this day, some golden tresses, wrapped carefully in crumbling palm leaves and tied with rattan vines, lie in a small wooden ceremonial box buried deep in the rice terraces in a small Kiangan barrio, along with a fading photograph of me with the Chief. Maybe one day an anthropologist will discover the box and wonder about its contents. Perhaps too, the image of me as Goddess or Virgin, (even though my 'heavenly' feet slipped into the muddy rice paddies), has been written into the local folklore of that remote village along with the mysterious Princess Maganda who rose up out of the forest lake in a giant bamboo.

Chapter 21
Tired Of Waiting

"I'm tired of waiting. I want them to end it for me. I don't care what they do to me. I just want it finished."

The voice, coming from the young man in the corner of the cell, lacked all emotion. I watched as his fingers groped for a brown plastic comb in his jeans pocket and, with defiant strokes, he attempted to sleek back the obstinate lock of brylcreemed hair dangling over his eyes. In the gloomy, fetid corner of this tiny room, a welcome stream of sunlight from the high window filtered over one side of his face illuminating his sallow complexion.

I was visiting Death Row at the New Bilibid State Prison in Muntilupa, Alabang at the invitation of the Governor, Alejo Santos. I had met Santos, a tall, elegant man with graying hair and freshly manicured nails at a dinner party some weeks before. He told me he followed my column avidly in the *Saturday Mirror* magazine and asked if I would consider writing something about "his prison."

"Despite all this," he explained, swiveling his eyes around the opulent interior of our hosts' North Forbes Park home, "no one seems to care about my prison. They don't mind spending millions of dollars on private residences, public buildings, corporate offices and high-profile projects but nowhere is there money to be found for Bilibid."

Bilibid was built in 1944, in the then verdant suburbs south of Manila. It was considered inhospitable territory, overgrown, swampy and mosquito-infested, suitable only to house the archipelago's most dangerous criminals. It was a forlorn place where hopes of escape were the futile dreams of desperate men. But, by 1968, Manila's tentacles were fast spreading out into its rural surroundings. Alabang, about 20 miles to the south, was no exception.

Under Marcos's presidency the rapidly growing middle classes had fuelled an unprecedented building boom. Their greed for large plots of land on which to build their, often sumptuous, family compounds, demanded more and more space. And Muntinlupa, bordering the notorious Bilibid Prison, was choice land – easy to build on and within commuting distance of the city. Within five years it was unrecognizable, transformed into some of Greater Manila's most sought-after real estate, complete with facilities the upper middle classes had come to expect - swimming pools, tennis courts and manicured golf courses. The sound of builders at work behind the high electric fences of Alabang's nouveau-riche mansions, could clearly be heard from inside the walls of Bilibid on the day of my visit.

Back in the cell, Santos introduced me to the nervous young man in the corner. Eyes downcast, shifting uncomfortably from one foot to the other, he replaced his comb and proffered his hand. He told me his name was Apolonio Adriano, he was twenty-five years old and he was one of 12 residents currently confined to Death Row. In a voice hardly above a whisper he told me the reason for his incarceration. His crime, by any standards, was horrific and unforgivable. He and three of his friends had hacked to death five security guards of the Rice and Corn Administration when they had tried to prevent the four men robbing its treasury.

"We have all been on Death Row now for…" His eyes lifted towards the Director for an answer.

"Almost ten years, *hindi ba*?" Santos finished the sentence for him.

"Yes, sir, ten years." Mariano Domingo, one of Adriano's co-conspirators, stepped forward, his slippers shuffling almost soundlessly across the cement floor.

He spoke very little but his expression, a permanent scowl, expressed the depth of his anger. But whereas Mariano was, according to Santos, still praying for an unlikely last-minute reprieve, Apolonio had almost certainly given up all hope. So far, every time the dreaded moment had arrived where they would come face to face with the electric chair, there had always been an eleventh-hour stay of execution and the interminable waiting had begun all over again. This cruel game of suspense by the authorities, Apolonio said, had literally driven several of Death Row's inmates insane.

The Row, itself, was hushed unlike the other wings of the prison where raised voices, even laughter and singing, could be heard. Although Death Row prisoners were not kept in solitary confinement, the inmates were under the constant scrutiny of heavily-armed wardens. They were permitted to walk around inside and chat quietly to each other but they were not allowed to leave the main cell without permission. Any infringement and they would immediately be locked up inside the nearby solitary block and their few privileges removed.

"But there's nothing to talk about." Mariano's frown eased for a moment. "What can we say to one another with a death sentence hanging over our heads? What can we say to each other when our families have forgotten us – when they don't visit us anymore?"

The only thing these men had in common, it seemed, was their ultimate fate – the electric chair, or "death seat", as they referred to it. It had been transported from the Old Bilibid Prison in Sampaloc, downtown Manila, where death by electric chair was first introduced by the United States in 1888. It was now situated at some distance from the present cellblocks, in a stark concrete chamber, on the other side of the prison. Most of the inmates had never even seen it. But, despite many descriptions from those few who had, Apolonio said he still couldn't or, perhaps, didn't want to visualize what it looked like. The only certainty was its permanent, ominous presence and that one day soon each of the twelve men would have their chance to see it for the very first and, probably, the very last time. This is the only thing they shared – this was the recurring nightmare of Death Row.

I asked Apolonio and Mariano about their crime, about how many times they had asked themselves since, "Why did we do it?" "How did it happen?" or "Where would we be now if?"

Apolonio's reply was curt and unexpected. "No. Never. I had my reasons then. They haven't changed."

Apolonio introduced me to one of Death Row's most recent occupants, Jaime Jose, a slender, shy boy and, despite his twenty-two years, displaying no hint of a beard. Jaime, along with three of his friends, had been convicted of abducting and gang-raping a young actress, Maggie de la Riva. Abduction and rape were two of the twenty-four offences currently punishable by death under the Marcos regime and so the Court, ignoring the defendants' plea for leniency, had shown them little mercy. On 6th February 1971, a little more than a year after my visit, it would hand down its verdict – death by electric chair with no right of appeal.

Although it was obvious from the way the others treated him, Jaime was the star personality on Death Row, he appeared lonely, introverted and subdued. There was no doubt he had brooded long and hard over his actions that night of heavy drinking four years earlier and regretted it.

"I'm not an animal," he murmured to me, almost as an aside, "I just don't remember what happened."

I asked him if he'd ever thought of writing to the victim to apologize.

He nodded. "Many times but the others – they said, no, don't do it, it'll prove you're guilty. I just wish I hadn't listened to them."

I told him there was still time but he shook his head. "No, it's too late now." He turned and wandered off, a forlorn figure receding into the darkness of his cell.

Within a year of the verdict being announced, amid a carnival atmosphere and in the full glare of TV cameras allowed into the death chamber to film an execution for the very first time, Jaime Jose and two of his co-defendants were electrocuted. Although I refused to watch the "festivities" on television that day, I shed a tear for the shy, slender boy I had met on Death Row.

It saddened me that the authorities had chosen to ignore the fact that Jaime had shown genuine remorse and, thus, was very unlikely to re-offend. They also refused to take into account that he was only a boy when the crime was committed and under the influence of bad company and alcohol. I felt that, if only given the opportunity and with his new found "celebrity" status, he could have forged a successful career in any area he cared to choose. In the end, due to the huge amount of publicity surrounding the case, his victim's career took off and Maggie de la Riva became one Manila's hottest actresses.

Another inmate joined Alejo Santos and me as we made our way around the cells. Alejo introduced him as the former action movie star, Pancho Pelagio. Pancho was a large man, with broad shoulders, an expanding belly and a contagious laugh. He wasted no time in telling me he had murdered someone in a fit of anger. That, he said, was why he was here on Death Row. He seemed almost proud of the fact. I gulped. I wasn't quite sure what to think. And then, just as swiftly, he patted me on the back, guffawed and said, "I'm joking, of course!"

Smiling at my obvious discomfort Pancho slid his arm up my back and around my shoulder. I automatically stiffened. We walked out into the prison grounds. I was glad for a bit of sunlight and fresh air.

"Did you believe me then?" Pancho asked, his eyes twinkling at his practical joke.

I felt off-balance. "I've no idea what to believe," I replied. And I didn't.

"He's an actor, remember, Caroline," Santos interrupted. "Maybe he even acted in court. Who knows?" He winked at Pancho who clutched his ill-fitting trousers and erupted into one of his belly laughs.

"No, the truth is, Caroline," Pancho said, "I planned a robbery. I was the look-out. I waited at the gate."

"That's your story, Pancho," Another young man had joined our group and butted in. He held his hand out to me, "Excuse me, m'am, my name is Dominador. Dominador Aguilar. Don't listen to Pancho."

"But it's true." Pancho scowled at the interloper. "The judge believed me. My friends went inside the house – and my other friend went to hail a taxi down the road so we could make a quick getaway. I stayed at the gate, watching out."

"And? What happened?" I relaxed briefly. I was curious now.

"Pancho saw someone coming out of the house. Not one of his friends. So he ran." Dominador's voice was brimming with sarcasm. He was obviously enjoying himself.

"Yes, I admit. I was afraid." Pancho retorted, "I thought this guy would call the police. So I left."

"Not very brave, huh?" Dominador joked. "Big Pancho, brave Pancho, ran away! Just like he did in the movies!"

"And did he?" I asked.

"Did he what?" Pancho was stalling, deliberately keeping me in suspense.

"Call for the police, of course?"

"He did. The others were just making their getaway in the taxi and suddenly the road was blocked by a jeepney coming from the opposite direction. A man got out and walked towards their taxi. One of my friends recognized him as a police officer. They shot him. Pumped him with bullets. He was killed."

"So you had nothing to do with the murder?" I asked.

"Nothing whatsoever – honest." Pancho began stroking my shoulder a little too intimately to be reassuring. I wanted to believe him because I was not quite sure how I would respond if I knew a cold-blooded killer had his hand so close to my neck. A little further, I imagined, and his fingers could be caressing my throat.

I turned to Santos for protection. But he had stopped briefly to speak with a guard who was hovering over a group of prisoners at the edge of the path. Dominador, too, had lingered behind to mingle with the group. I could see now why Pancho had taken this opportunity to be a little too familiar with me. I moved slightly away from him.

Pancho followed close behind. "You know, Caroline," he whispered into my ear, "I have your picture on the wall of my cell. The one with you and Jun Aristorenas – from your film, *El Tigre*. I'm not the only one. Other guys in here have your photos too."

I tried to compose myself. "Really? I'm flattered."

The truth was I felt more awkward than flattered. I wasn't sure if the sexual vibes I thought I was sensing from Pancho were real or imagined. Were they the understandable act of a predatory male removed from the company of women for the past twelve years or the slightly masochistic fantasy of a young girl in an all-male environment? I decided it was in my mind. Pancho was probably just trying to be hospitable. He had obviously been given orders by Santos to look after me and he was simply carrying out his task. Nothing sinister intended.

I changed the subject. "So what was your sentence?"

"I've spent twelve years on Death Row just waiting for my execution."

Thankfully Santos caught up with us at that point. "Pancho's appeal will come up very soon and we're hoping the Supreme Court will modify his conviction from robbery with homicide to simple robbery. Isn't that right, Pancho?"

"Yes, Sir," the actor grinned. "And Mr. Santos says once the Supreme Court reaches that decision I will be released immediately because of my good behaviour all these years. I'm a trustee, you see."

He turned to face the Director. "So, not long to go now, Sir, and I'll be leaving you!"

He laughed, removing his arm from my shoulder to once again grab hold of the trousers that had been threatening to fall down around his ankles. He shrugged his shoulders at me and winked. "No belts, pins or ropes allowed in here! Not even for a trustee! And look I've lost weight too!" He breathed in deeply, sucking in his large stomach and tugged at the over-generous waistband. It was true the trousers appeared to be several sizes too big.

"Mind you behave yourself in the meantime, Pancho." Santos warned, "Don't go ruining everything. Think of your family."

Family? I guess I hadn't thought of any of these men as having families. I dwelled for a moment on the notion of Pancho being a patriarchal figure. For some reason, despite the fact he had participated in a chilling, premeditated crime, I could somehow imagine him being a dependable father, perhaps even a caring one. I wondered if his crime had been a one-off, a momentary act of recklessness by a man desperately needing to provide for his children.

I turned my thoughts to the others I had met that day. *How many of them, too, had come from a normal family life? Did Apolonio and Mariano have devoted wives, girlfriends or daughters waiting for them outside Bilibid? Did Jaime have an adoring mother praying every day for his release?* It was strange that when I now thought about them this way, as family men, I could no longer think of them as the ruthless, cold-blooded burglars, rapists or slayers I had read about in the newspapers. To see them and to talk to them was to be convinced they were incapable of harming anyone. *But then, maybe. they were considered so dangerous they were kept sedated inside these walls?. Or, perhaps, after all these years on Death Row, their spirits had been broken? Perhaps they were vastly different now from the men they had once been?* I wondered aloud to Santos if I was just being naïve, seduced by their charm, their smiles, their sensitivity or their quiet demeanour, much as their many victims must have been.

Santos chuckled. "I'm taken in by them every day, Caroline. Killers can be very manipulative, very persuasive, very charming, you know." Somewhat indulgently he added, "But I must agree with you – I wouldn't want to believe they would do it again if they went free."

"But, Sir," Pancho interrupted, "why do people in favour of capital punishment always argue, if people kill once they'll do it again – and again? How do they know?"

"You know all these men well enough by now, Pancho, do you think that's true?" I asked him.

"Not true." Pancho replied without hesitation. "The ones who are dangerous are those, still outside, in society, the ones who haven't yet committed a murder. Isn't that right, Sir?"

Santos smiled, "If you say so, Pancho."

In one respect, Death Row appeared pleasant. At least it was clean and each man was allowed his own bedding. In contrast to the place we were now entering – the admittance hall. The quarters housing the new remand prisoners where each man was forced to sleep, side by side, on the concrete floor of a metal cage waiting to be assigned their respective cells. In the last four weeks, Santos explained, the prison had received a further 1200 new prisoners and there was little he could do to alleviate their distressful living conditions.

"It's madness," Pancho sighed, "There's just no place to put them all."

I watched the new prisoners for a few moments, huddled together, unclassified, undignified and anonymous. Here they were expected to languish in herds until their papers had been processed and there was bed space available.

What the prison had always suffered from, Santos continued, was a severe lack of funds. Not only money was in short supply but food, clothing, kitchenware, bedding, medical and sanitary supplies too were all desperately needed. To save on the food budget the inmates were encouraged to grow their own vegetables. He led me towards the gardens.

I was surprised. Without exception, they appeared neat and well-tended. And the atmosphere, for the most part, was not as intimidating as I would have imagined. The prisoners were polite, mostly soft-spoken and respectful to their Director. As the three of us walked past them they immediately stood up to greet us. Being a figure of authority they may not have loved Santos but it appeared they certainly respected him.

Across from the vegetable gardens, in the center of the main block, Pancho pointed out the distorted, huddled silhouettes of men clinging to the iron bars of their windows.

"That's the psychiatric ward," he explained, "some of them used to be on Death Row."

I remembered what Apolonio had told me. It was sad to imagine that some of these pathetic figures were possibly former cellmates of his driven made by the endless waiting. Their eyes stared vacantly out at us across the garden, probably unaware of their surroundings.

Next door to the psychiatric ward, Pancho led me to the TB and leprosy wing. Santos confessed he would prefer me not to enter either. Later Pancho whispered to me, "It's bedlam in those places! It would scare you. It's not a pretty sight!"

I didn't admit it then but I was quite grateful both wings were deemed off-limits.

I simply peeked around the door of the psychiatric ward. Other than a few patients aimlessly milling about there was little to show that it was, in fact, a mental facility. The building was dilapidated, squalid and uninviting. From what little I could see there were no medical supplies in evidence, little equipment, very few drugs and sadly inadequate living space.

"As the Director probably told you, there are currently 9000 inmates in Bilibid," Pancho told me. "Our cramped conditions means we have a vital need of medicines and medical support. We live in such close proximity with each other germs and diseases spread swiftly and furiously." Patting his stomach he continued, "We've all been ill here. Many times."

I could imagine what he was referring to. And from a cursory inspection, the sanitary facilities looked less than hygienic.

"Without hospital equipment and drugs," Santos shrugged, "there is little our doctors can do to prevent it, I'm afraid."

According to Pancho, not all the current inmates at Bilibid were guilty of committing a crime. A great many of them, he informed me, were fall guys, paid or hired by more affluent and powerful individuals to admit to a crime they did not commit. Others were imprisoned solely because they possessed neither the money nor the contacts to get decent legal representation. And still others were framed. Some of these men were condemned to spend most of their lives or, in many cases, ending their lives, inside a metal cage knowing that the men they were protecting, the men who actually committed "their" particular crime were living normal, possibly very privileged, lives outside.

"Can you begin to imagine how that must feel, Caroline?" Pancho asked.

It was a painful thought but it was easy for me to see that in the kind of society they were living in – a society of drastic contrasts between the haves and the have-nots – there was almost nothing people like Pancho could do to put an end to such injustices. Money, contacts and a good lawyer were all necessary requirements for avoiding prison sentences. I realized, sadly, that if all of the inmates I had met that day had any one of those luxuries at their disposal there was no doubt they would never be inside Bilibid Prison. And I knew from talking to them at length that every man, in his own way, had learned to accept this fact, no matter how unpalatable.

But the reality was that 9000 men were incarcerated there, some guilty but very many innocent, who all deserved, at least, the right of a clean mat to sleep on and a bar of soap to wash himself. For every man who escaped the death sentence, there would always be another, more unfortunate, individual who would be executed in the "death seat". It made me both sad and angry to think what if these men were, as Pancho was insinuating, entirely innocent?

"Please try to help me and my friends. You know we're tired of waiting." Pancho whispered as he kissed me goodbye. Santos had already said his goodbyes and had returned to his office for more pressing administrative duties.

Engulfed by Pancho's huge bear hug I was powerless to prevent his fingers from straying down to the very base of my spine. When he eventually released me he laughed his big, generous laugh. "Send me your photo, Caroline, please. A personal one, with a personal message. And wait for me. I'll be out soon. OK?

"Sure," I said. "And thanks for taking me round, Pancho. Good luck!" As I left, I turned my head. He was standing there watching me leave, his fingers gripping the waistband of his baggy trousers, his large head thrown back and a big grin on his face.

Chapter 22
A Date with the Pope

The second time I visited Bilibid Prison was under very different circumstances. In fact the day following my second visit one of the Manila papers referred to it under a typical tabloid headline: *"Balloons and Bibingka for Benjamin's Birthday."*

My friendship with the Bolivian surrealist artist, Benjamin Mendoza, began in late 1969. At the age of 25, I considered myself an old Manila hand, and was regarded by many locals as an "honorary Filipina" and by the Indios Bravos crowd a resident fixture of the Cafe.

Benjamin Mendoza was the new guy in town. As with most newcomers, particularly artists, it did not take long for him to gravitate towards the artistic crowd in Indios Bravos. I met him on his first visit to the coffee shop. He was sitting alone and I instantly recognized him as South American. He had the dark, elongated face, the fine aquiline nose and the thin lips, all familiar facial characteristics of the Quechua peoples of the Andes. I introduced myself and joined him at his table.

I was curious to find out why he had come to Manila, what had brought him there?

"The art!" he told me, "I read books and magazines. I read about the vibrant art scene in Manila. I wanted to see it for myself. After all, Latin America and the Philippines have a common background – Spanish conquistadores and Roman Catholic priests. I wanted to see if our art was similar too."

He pulled out some small paintings from his battered briefcase and passed them across the table to me. They were miniature oil paintings, mainly of animals and religious subjects, in dark, brooding tones, the only light emanating from them were painted shards of broken glass around the edges.

"What do they say to you?" he asked as I tried to look like I was studying them seriously.

I was tempted to say I had no idea but I was certain a psychiatrist would have found them challenging. But not wanting to appear impolite, I smiled.

"They're good. I like them." And then I turned the question back to him. "What did you want me to see in them?"

"Vignettes of life. Hope, despair. Good, bad. Love, hate. Anger, serenity. Life is made up of contrasts. You can't have one without the other."

He looked at me sideways as he stabbed a toothpick into the fried spring roll on his plate.

"Haven't you ever ended up hating someone you really loved? Had moments of immense happiness that resulted in tears? Had instances of unparalleled pleasure that turned into pain? That's what I'm trying to say in my paintings."

His voice was hushed, barely audible. Not because of the background music, "Hey Jude", by the Beatles, playing loudly from the café's sound system. But simply because that was the way he spoke. Benjamin was gentle, thoughtful, if slightly morose.

Over the following months, we forged a friendship of sorts. But whereas Benjamin was a solitary person, I was the opposite. He joined the Manila artists' group, participating in their weekly gatherings while, at the same time, remaining very much on the periphery. Belonging but apart. Many found him aloof, slightly weird but harmless. Betsy and I enjoyed his company and he soon became yet another regular in the cast of characters unique to the Indios Bravos Cafe.

One evening Benjamin and I were sitting at his table discussing religion, one of his favourite topics.

"You're so lucky, Caroline," he mused, "you weren't brought up in fear. You weren't forced to accept something you didn't believe in. You weren't punished for rejecting God. You weren't threatened for questioning the Church's motives. You didn't feel you were sinning when you took precautions….birth control, I mean."

"I'd hate to imagine where I'd be without the Pill!" I joked, "It would have cramped my style considerably. I'd probably have given birth to a complete basketball team by now!"

I was trying to make light of the discussion because I noticed the rising intensity in his voice.

"Exactly. But in my country and in all poor Catholic countries women die – here too, probably – because they are expected to go on and on having children. Just to keep the Church happy."

I felt his anger. I reached across the table to touch his hand, attempting to mollify him.

"I'd be angry too, you know," I said.

I was grateful at that moment that the only Catholics in my family, my mother and my sister, had never tried to convert me.

Benjamin stared into his glass without saying a word. I could sense he was fighting back the overwhelming urge to share his anger but, being naturally reserved, he was not the kind of person who would ever consider upsetting the mood of the evening.

But on the morning of the 27 November 1970 that impression of him was about to change dramatically or, at least, called into question. I was back in London watching the world news on television.

Curiously enough there were several firsts that day. In London the first Gay Rights demonstration, a candlelight vigil against police harassment, was taking place in Highbury Fields.

"A milestone in gay history," said Peter Tatchell, one of the 150 participants. "Today instead of fear we feel pride and defiance!"

In Plesetsk, Siberia the communications satellite Molniya 8 was launched successfully into orbit. This was followed by the news of a plane crash in Anchorage, Alaska. A Capitol Airways DC 8, flight number 472, crashed on take-off, killing 48 and injuring 226.

And in Manila 180 Bishops had convened for the first ever Pan-Aseatic Bishops' Conference. They were shown at the Manila International Airport waiting for the arrival of Giovanni Battista Montini, Pope Paul VI. Curiously, despite the Philippines 400 years of Spanish Catholic colonization, Montini was the first Pontiff ever to set foot on Philippine soil.

Leading up to the Pope's visit there had been much speculation in the local and international Press as to whose guest the Holy Father would be – the Catholic Church or Ferdinand and Imelda Marcos. For the only predominantly Catholic country in Asia, this visit was considered to be a momentous occasion and the kudos to be gained, both politically and commercially, from having the Pope stay with the Marcoses in Malacanang Palace was immeasurable. By hosting the Pope, Marcos hoped it would be viewed among the population as an endorsement of his increasingly dictatorial rule.

In the months leading up to the Papal visit, the value of the peso had plunged, food was in short supply and jobs were scarce. Civil disorder, student demonstrations and organized rallies had become commonplace. These confrontations had been met by violent, sometimes bloody, resistance by Marcos, his constabulary and his armed forces. Marcos was more unpopular now than he had ever been and he blamed many in the priesthood for fomenting political unrest among the students.

Here was an opportunity to demonstrate to his predominantly Catholic nation and to the world that he had the full approval and support of the Vatican. Both Ferdinand and Imelda were determined to exploit the event to the full. But neither had counted on the formidable personality of Cardinal Santos, whose increasingly vocal opposition to the Marcos regime now turned into open warfare. His stand against the Marcoses on this point was very public, vociferous and humiliating. He stuck his ground, declaring this was purely a pastoral visit by His Holiness to address his flock and to attend the Bishops' Conference. He went further, insisting the Holy Father would not be staying at the Palace nor would he be driven from the airport into the city in the Presidential limousine. Fuming, the First Lady, too, refused to give way, claiming it was she who had extended a personal invitation to the Pope during her visit to the Vatican the previous year.

The heated battle of the two adversaries was still deadlocked on the day of the Pope's arrival. Whether His Holiness knew of it or not, separate itineraries had been prepared for him by both his Cardinal and the First Lady. But it was all deference, bell-pealing, flag waving and smiles as the frail seventy-year old Pontiff stepped off his Alitalia plane at Manila International Airport.

Waving to the crowd, the Pope stooped for a moment to accept a bouquet of white flowers from Irene, the Marcos's youngest daughter. He shook hands with the President and First Lady and began to cross the red carpet towards the dais. The crowds roared their welcome and pitched forward upsetting the barriers, hoping to get closer to their Pontiff. Under strict instructions from Cardinal Santos, the Catholic hierarchy moved in immediately to flank and protect the diminutive figure of Paul VI.

One by one the Cardinal and Bishops bowed down to kiss the Pope's ring. The Marcoses, who planned to demonstrate their closeness to His Holiness in front the world's TV cameras and the masses of Filipinos who had assembled at the airport to witness this historic occasion, had to be content to walk behind the Pope. I watched the news report live as Paul VI slowly made his way along the red carpet towards the dais, stopping to shake hands with all the dignitaries lining his route.

Among the many faces I recognized, the politicians, the journalists and the clergy, there was one face that made me sit up and take notice. *No,* I thought, *it can't be, I must be mistaken.* I peered closer hoping for a better look. And there he was. With his hand outstretched towards the approaching Pontiff and dressed in a long, black priestly sutane, the person I saw was my erstwhile friend, the Bolivian artist, Benjamin Mendoza. *But, surely, it couldn't be? Why on earth would he be there? How did he get past security? Was I just imagining things? Or was it one of his surrealist jokes?*

I tried to convince myself that Mendoza must have been on my mind because I had just received a postcard from him a few days earlier saying he was planning to return to Bolivia. So, perhaps, this man, whoever he was, was simply an Andean priest, part of the Vatican's entourage. I continued to scan the screen but the image I was searching for was obscured.

Suddenly there was pandemonium, a glint of steel, screams, shouts, gasps and lunging, writhing bodies scrambling to the ground. I had no idea at that moment what had happened. An hysterical voice on the news report informed us an attempt had been made on the Pontiff's life by an unknown assailant armed with a knife. Silence. Then we were told that, mercifully, the Pope was safe. The assailant had been overcome by Papal security guards. This last piece of information was vital considering the story put out less than twenty-four hours later by President Marcos.

Several times that day I watched for further news to learn the identity of the assassin. Finally I was both rewarded and shocked to learn that the would-be killer was none other than a Bolivian painter by the name of Benjamin Mendoza y Amor. I was stunned. Even more extraordinary was Imelda's revelation that she had witnessed her husband saving the Pope's life by delivering a karate chop and a flying kick to the would-be assassin, knocking the 10-inch knife right out of his hand at the crucial moment.

There must be some mistake, I thought. I knew Benjamin disapproved of the Catholic Church but he would never have gone this far, I could have sworn it. It must have been a practical joke gone very wrong or, more likely, a scenario dreamed up by the Marcoses to upstage the Cardinal.

The next day film footage was released showing Benjamin Mendoza attending a very obviously pre-rehearsed press conference at the Philippine Constabulary Headquarters at Camp Crame. He was being grilled by members of NBI, the Philippine's National Bureau of Investigation and the Philippine Armed Forces.

In an uncharacteristically animated voice Benjamin said, "I feel disappointed for failing to kill the Pope and would do it again if given another chance."

The NBI Director leaned towards the artist and asked, "And who saved the Pope's life?"

"I had thought it was President Marcos," Benjamin dutifully replied, intently looking at his interrogator and sounding well-coached, "but I wasn't too sure. But then when I saw the pictures you showed me, I am convinced it really was the President who prevented me killing the Pope."

In fact the photos that were published showed the President far too distant from both the Pope and the artist to have either saved the one or delivered a crippling karate chop to the other.

Members of the Catholic Church who had surrounded the Pontiff at the time all agreed with the Bishop of Sarawak who, on his return to Indonesia some days later, stated categorically,

"I was very close to His Holiness at that moment and I do not remember seeing President Marcos give the Bolivian painter a karate chop and a kick."

He went on to say, "It was one of the two papal security guards who played the vital role of saving the Pope for it was he who stuck out his hand to parry the attacker's lunge and pushed His Holiness away – right into my arms. I held him tight, pulling him away until the security men grabbed the assailant and dragged him away."

Despite this credible rebuttal, the filmed interview with Benjamin Mendoza at Camp Crame was replayed on a loop all week on every channel of Philippine television. For the time being, it seemed, in the eyes of the majority of Filipinos, President Marcos was presenting himself as the hero of the hour. Since Benjamin Mendoza had played right into the President's hands, he was treated leniently. He was sentenced to four years in Bilibid Prison with deportation upon his release.

When I returned to Manila in early 1972, I got in touch with Benjamin. Because of my previous visit to Bilibid, and my friendship with Governor Santos, I was allowed to speak directly to him without going through the military authorities. Benjamin sounded content. He told me he was well looked after but that he was looking forward to returning to his family in Bolivia.

"It was a surrealist gesture, Caroline," he told me, answering my unspoken question. "I had no intention of killing him."

"And Marcos," I asked, "where did he come into it?"

"Now that's a question you know I can't answer," Benjamin chuckled. "You'll get yourself into trouble if you ask me such things and I'll get into trouble if I tell you." Abruptly he changed the subject. "When will I see you? Will you visit me?"

"Of course," I answered, "when?"

"Well, next Sunday's my birthday. I'm thirty-seven. Why not come then?"

"It's a date," I said, "and I'll get the Indios Bravos group to come along too."

I replaced the receiver and immediately started planning. Betsy and Henry jumped at the opportunity. Ben and a few of the other artists, writers, dancers and poets were ready to join in the fun. Together we assembled gifts galore, hampers full of picnic food and a birthday cake with thirty-seven candles. In the early afternoon we started out from Indios Bravos towards Bilibid in a convoy of jeepneys festooned with coloured balloons and streamers announcing "Happy Birthday Benjamin". People in the street watched in amazement as we passed by, our horns blaring and the tape decks blasting out loud music.

My feelings were mixed when I approached the gates. There would be many new faces but few of the old familiar ones. It was only three years later but Pancho had been released early and Jaime, Dominador, Adriano and Mariano had all been executed.

Security at the prison that day was lax. Everyone, officers, prisoners and guards, were all determined to have a good time. It was odd seeing Benjamin in his ill-fitting orange prison overalls. It was strange to see him squatting on the ground outside his cell and not sitting at his habitual table at Indios Bravos.

We spread the picnic around him and called all the guards and prisoners within hearing distance to join us. We lit the candles and methodically Benjamin blew them out, screwing up his eyes and making a wish as he did so. Everyone immediately burst into song. I found it ironic that here they all were singing Happy Birthday to possibly the most hated man in the Philippines and the wider Catholic world, the man who, in their eyes, had almost succeeded in assassinating their beloved Pope.

Benjamin must have noticed my astonished look. He leaned over and whispered in my ear,

"Yes, and there are a lot of born-again Christians in here too. Funny, isn't it?"

I laughed. "Do they give you a hard time?" I asked, concerned that religious fanatics might single him out for harsh treatment.

"No. They love me," he smiled, "I'm a celebrity, remember. And more than God they love celebrities in the Philippines, you know that, Caroline!"

It was true, of course. I should have known. Imelda had known it too from the beginning of the Marcos presidency. Consequently, she had exploited the cult of celebrity to the hilt.

"Escapism for the masses" she called it. "It gives them something to brighten up their dreary little lives!" She also discovered it was a useful tool to smokescreen a multitude of sins carried out by the Marcoses, their government, their relatives and their cronies.

It was a memorable day but it was tinged with sadness as I realized it would probably be the last time I would see Benjamin Mendoza. Soon after our visit his sentence was suspended and he was driven straight to the airport to board a plane back to Bolivia. I received one more postcard from him and then silence. I never knew how he was received back home, as celebrity, as prodigal son or as religious enemy.

I often wondered about it. And as to my unspoken questions, *did Ferdie or Imelda organize the whole episode to win the hearts and minds of the Filipino people in her war with Cardinal Santos?* Possibly. *And if so, why would Benjamin have agreed to it? Money?* I didn't think so. *Notoriety?* I doubted it. *Or simply, as he said himself, "as a surrealist gesture against the Church's policy in impoverished countries such as Bolivia and the Philippines?"*

In my opinion, that was far more likely. But whatever the reasons only Benjamin Mendoza knew them and he was keeping them to himself.

Chapter 23
The Boy Wonder of Tarlac

Very soon after my arrival in the Philippines I had become aware of a brash, young politician, Benigno "Ninoy" Aquino, the only Liberal Party Senator who had survived Marcos's landslide victory in 1965. Every day, it seemed, Ninoy spoke out loudly against Marcos's increasing stranglehold on the country's political, judicial and commercial institutions. He was an unashamed loudmouth, uncompromising in his speeches and fearless in his personal attacks. He knew how to use the media and he used it effectively. And, as a hopeful future President, he used the floor of the Senate and travelled all over the country to wage his personal war against Marcos, despite the increasing risks to himself.

Not a day passed without some news coverage of Ninoy's latest tirade against corruption, crony capitalism, the development of a police state or tax evasion. As a former reporter and foreign correspondent for the *Manila Times*, the young Senator had many friends within the media who were equally worried about Marcos's expanding powers and who were more than willing to devote many column inches to Ninoy's accusations. Like many others I, too, was fascinated by anyone who was brave, or foolhardy, enough to stand up and oppose Marcos and I relished the opportunity to meet him.

So, when a journalist friend, Sylvia Mayuga, called me up with an invitation to join her and a group of reporters to stay overnight at Ninoy's home in Tarlac I grabbed it.

"What's your interest in him?" I inquired.

Sylvia was, undoubtedly, one of the most astute young journalists in Manila and I was eager to hear her opinion on the "Boy Wonder of Tarlac", as the newspapers had dubbed him.

On the other end of the phone Sylvia laughed. "You know, Caroline, he is going to be our next President. That's my interest in him!"

The emphasis on the "is" intrigued me. It was evident by the sarcastic tone of her voice Sylvia was not a Ninoy fan. Although I also knew from our nightly political discussions in Indios Bravos that she was also vehemently anti-Marcos.

"I've been reading some of Ninoy's speeches," I said. "He's got a big mouth, that's for sure. How long can he continue getting away with the things he says?" I asked her.

"Good question. But your guess is as good as mine," Sylvia replied. "He truly believes he's the saviour of the Philippines so I imagine he'll carry on his crusade until he's either President or dead! Most people believe he'll be President."

It was amazing to me that so many people assumed the next election, due later that year, was a foregone conclusion. Other than Ninoy, there simply was no one else to challenge Marcos. If I believed what I read in the papers it would be a one-man race. Members of the opposition parties, having been trounced so soundly in 1965, were simply not prepared, it seemed, to raise their necks above the political parapet.

Sylvia told me we were to leave from the domestic airport on the dot of four o'clock on Sunday afternoon. She stressed that Ninoy had made it clear that anyone not present at the appointed time would be left behind.

"The Senator," she chuckled, "considers tardiness one of the seven deadly sins."

Naturally, not wishing to miss the opportunity to meet this larger-than-life personality that the press described in such glowing and reverential terms, I was inside the airport terminal with time to spare.

But four o'clock was approaching and there was no sign of the Senator.

"He's flying in from a meeting in Batangas!" whispered one fawning aide in my ear as though that explained everything.

One minute to four – still no sign. It couldn't be, surely, I thought, that the conscientious Senator who could not abide tardiness in others was actually going to keep us waiting? No, surely not.

Just then an agitated courtier rushed in from outside.

"The Senator's arriving now!" he announced breathlessly.

That was obviously the cue for us to form a welcoming committee on the tarmac to greet the Boy Wonder of Tarlac. Dutifully, we filed outside. Sure enough, amid a whirlwind of dust and grit kicked up by the rotor blades, there was the Senator's helicopter alighting right in front of us. I looked at my watch – on the dot of four. I had to admit it. I was impressed.

My first glimpse of the Senator was of him descending from the helicopter. I watched as he rushed, head bowed, towards the plane that was waiting, engines revving, alongside the terminal building. There was no time for introductions. The Senator was in a hurry. And his aides hustled us across the tarmac.

I looked at him. At 36, Ninoy could easily pass for his late twenties. He was chubby, no doubt, with a fleshy, boyish face framed by his trademark black-rimmed glasses and topped by a full head of dark hair with no tinge of gray. He wore a barong-tagalog, clean, well-pressed and probably new. And in his plump fingers he clutched a shiny new walkie-talkie.

"Come in Charlie! Come in Charlie!"

The machine gurgled and spat back at him.

"Yes, Sir, Senator, Sir. Can I help you, Sir?" a deferential voice at the other end crackled.

"Charlie, where is my car right now? Will it be at Luisita Airport in time to pick us up?"

The machine spluttered and hissed again.

"Yes, Sir, Senator, Sir. Just a minute, Sir. Someone in the office spoke to the driver five minutes back, Senator, Sir. I'll check to see what the message is, Sir!"

There were some more spluttering in the background and then, "Hello, Sir! Jaime just spoke to your chauffeur, Sir. Apparently he is traveling on the main highway at 80 kilometres an hour, just before the turn-off. He will be there precisely at 4.27 to collect you! Anything else, Sir?"

"No thank you, Charlie. Over and out!"

Fifteen minutes later we were there. And still not a word from the Senator to his traveling companions. As we disembarked from the plane someone tried to strike up a conversation of sorts.

"Uh, Senator, Sir, I wonder if uh,.."

But the Senator wasn't listening. He was striding down the steps playing with his walkie-talkie, informing the staff at home we had arrived and totally oblivious of any commitment he might have to his guests.

The minute we landed in Tarlac the weekend started to unfold like I imagined a weekend at the Kennedy's Hyannis Port compound would be. The accent was focused on ego, wealth and sport. No sooner had we been shown our rooms than we were whisked off to be given the grand tour of the vast estate of Hacienda Luisita. The Senator had changed from his formal barong-tagalog into an impeccably tailored riding habit courtesy, I was informed, of a renowned men's outfitters in Savile Row. Despite his bulk the Senator certainly looked elegant! And I thought what a perfectly fitting outfit for presenting us his string of polo ponies each one, he told us with pride, flown over from Ireland.

Ninoy pointed in the direction of a lush meadow where a magnificent looking steed was munching grass and whisking away the myriad flies with its tail.

"That's my Arab stallion," he boasted, "It cost me $160,000. He's the best stud in the Philippines. For his stud service alone I earn an annual income of around $26,000." He beamed. And then added. "I charge $2000 a time!"

He moved on and, like faithful hounds, we followed. In an adjacent field Ninoy pointed out a one-month old foal.

"I've already been offered $30,000 for that one on the day it was dropped. But I'm thinking why should I accept $30,000 for it when I can easily enter it in the sweepstakes and walk away with $120, 000?"

Why indeed, Senator? I thought. I was getting confused with all this talk of money. Maths had never been my strong subject.

"Anyone for a ride? Sylvia? And how about you, Caroline?" For the first time, the Senator actually noticed us.

Abruptly Ninoy jolted me back to the present. I could see he was itching to show off his prowess in the saddle.

But nobody wanted to ride, least of all me. I had no intention of making a fool of myself. The others felt the same. The Senator looked disappointed. So, instead he bundled us all into two brand new Super de Luxe Land Rovers to complete the tour of his vast property. He failed to say the land was actually part of a 5,000-acre estate belonging to his wife's family, the Cojuancos. (A few years later, the Cojuanco estate would be confiscated by Marcos under his Presidential Decree Number 27 on Land Reform.)

With a sweeping gesture Ninoy informed us, "I employ eleven thousand workers here. And I provide for each one of them." Actually, he was exaggerating. I had done my homework. He and his wife actually employed 6,500 workers.

Just then the Senator jammed on the brakes to point out a few historic landmarks of Hacienda Luisita.

"There's the church I built for my employees. There's the community centre where they dance, sing, play the piano and play billiards, whatever it is they do. And, over there, that's the school. By the way, each child receives free education up until high school. That's their bank. And that building there, that's their movie house. And over there, that's their town hall where they can hold political meetings. There's the surgery and the hospital. They have free medical and dental treatment and.."

The Senator was on a roll. There was no stopping him!

I was almost beginning to wish I lived in this utopian heaven where everything was provided for free. But I was more anxious to interrupt this self-congratulatory monologue so I asked, "How about birth control, Senator?"

I'll Be There

My question failed to faze him. As the consummate politician Ninoy had a ready answer.

"Well, each woman is provided with a free loop."

Of course, I should have known. But I was in a combative mood. I wasn't going to allow him to get away with it that easily.

"You mean to say, Senator, that you actually give 5000 women no other choice than to use an IUD when they know their church's feelings towards birth control? Do some of them hesitate or is your word more final than the Pope's?"

"Around here it is!" Ninoy beamed back at me triumphantly.

"And what do you ask in return from your employees?" I persisted, unwilling to be beaten in this altercation.

"Very little. That they work on the sugar plantation, which I shall show you in a minute. And that they vote for me, naturally!"

Well, from that I deduced, without much difficulty, Tarlac could not hope to have any political future other than Senator Aquino for many years to come. After all, at 22 he had already been elected the youngest Mayor of the local town. At 28 he had been appointed the youngest provincial vice-governor and, at 30, he had won the gubernatorial election by the highest majority ever. At 32, ever in a hurry to fulfil his destiny, Ninoy became the youngest Senator. So, much like his nemesis Marcos, Ninoy's rise to power had been mercurial.

After he had called ahead on his faithful walkie-talkie to the refinery to warn them of our impending arrival, Ninoy proceeded to inform us about the many different strains of sugar grown at Hacienda Luisita. *At least I was being educated,* I thought. It had certainly never dawned on me before that sugar came in anything more than just the three varieties, refined white, golden demerara and dark molasses.

"At the time I took it over it was a sinking ship. But I never gave up hope and I managed, single-handedly, to bring it back into full production." He paused waiting for this message to sink in. "It's now thriving and making money, thanks to me! And we produce around 10% of the country's sugar."

His lack of modesty was almost beguiling. I was shocked to find that, despite my natural inclination to dislike him, I found I was now in danger of being captivated by his famous charm. *Perhaps it's true,* I thought, *what they say about money and power being a potent aphrodisiac.* I was in danger of proving it so.

The two Super de Luxe Land Rovers braked outside the bright yellow refinery, yellow being the colour of the Senator's Liberal Party. Proudly, Ninoy led us all inside where there were mountains of brown sugar rising to the ceiling like massive sand dunes. Ninoy asked one of the workers to pass around plastic spoons so we could taste the various specimens. It was quite an experience to plunge our spoons into one sugar-mountain after another, risking a possible landslide.

Ninoy was beaming. He was obviously in his element. He climbed the stairs to his office and beckoned us to follow. There, with the help of close-circuit TV monitors, he showed us how he was able to view what was going on over the entire plantation. He demonstrated the intricate new alarm system he had installed recently. He wasn't taking any chances, he said. His crop had already been sabotaged and his refinery vandalized.

"Manpowered security just doesn't work," he explained. "I've had to lay off quite a few workers now with this new system in place but it's going to be worth it. There's only one other machine like it in the country. Not even Marcos has one!" He chuckled. "It cost me thousands of dollars, I can tell you, but it's also going to save me thousands of dollars!"

After we had been given the full Boy Wonder treatment, been inculcated by a dizzying array of facts and figures about the sugar business and been fed hundreds of his personal success stories, we felt in need of some refreshment. Ninoy packed us back into the two Land Rovers and we sped up the road towards the main house.

No sooner had he pulled to a stop outside the front door than the Senator looked around at us, "Anyone for a swim?" he asked.

The motion was discussed, swayed and carried. Everyone, excluding Sylvia and me, doffed their swimsuits and assembled at poolside. Naturally, the ever-energetic Senator was the first to take the plunge. I noticed that he was still clutching his now, water-resistant, walkie-talkie. Surprisingly, it never left his ample grip all weekend. He would use it now and again whenever he thought we were gazing at him attentively. As a matter of fact, to do the Senator justice, I believe everybody was spellbound, except me and, perhaps, Sylvia. If he had hoped to win Sylvia over to his camp this weekend, so far, he had failed. There had been a fleeting moment when I was almost ready to succumb to his evident charms but that moment had long passed.

The Senator was now setting the pace. He swam two lengths of the pool. Everyone swam two lengths of the pool. He clambered out of the pool so everyone clambered out of the pool. He changed for dinner so everyone changed for dinner. He came downstairs and his guests followed him. He had a drink so everyone picked up a glass.

His wife, Cory, appeared briefly in the living room before we filed into dinner. As we sipped the last of our drinks she shook our hands and smiled graciously at us and then, just as abruptly, disappeared.

"Where's she gone? Isn't she going to have dinner with us?" I whispered to Sylvia.

"Oh, that's normal here, in most Spanish mestiza households," Sylvia replied. "When they have guests the wife will spend her time in the kitchen just to make sure everything's OK. She'll supervise the food, make sure it's served properly, that kind of thing."

Over soup, entrée and dessert Ninoy gave us a glimpse of his more heroic past. From the beginning to the end of the meal he didn't stop talking. The reporters were silent as they lapped up his every word.

"When I was seventeen I was a national hero!" he proceeded. "I was the youngest newspaper reporter in Korea. None of the other Philippine journalists wanted to go to war because they had wives and families. So I volunteered. The *Manila Times*, agreed to send me and so I left the next day before the editor had a chance to change his mind!"

I contemplated Ninoy as the youngest war correspondent and then, for some reason, my thoughts turned to Marcos who had always claimed to be the youngest war hero. Again, in my mind, the similarities were striking. Although, to give Ninoy credit in this case, despite his exaggerations there were elements of truth in this particular story while every claim that Marcos made about his heroic past were later proved to be entirely bogus. Marcos, too, was very much aware of their similarities which is why he feared Aquino as a political opponent. He also knew that many in the US government favoured Ninoy over himself. And Aquino had never been shy to boast about his friends in the CIA.

I looked at the Boy Wonder of Tarlac. He was still talking, still basking in the admiration of this handpicked group of journalists.

"Once there I became the darling of the generals. I was in on every important meeting, informed about every campaign strategy. I knew every proposed plan. All the top people confided in me. I was the baby of the press corps and they indulged me."

He paused for audience reaction. I tried to assume an awestruck gaze such as I saw on the faces of my other dining companions. However I was unable to sustain it for long. The cynic in me refused to go away.

The Senator continued. "When I returned home after the war I was a national hero, really."

Just in case we didn't understand the true meaning of being a national hero, Ninoy gave us his personal definition.

"I was so famous I was asked to escort Miss Philippines here, there and everywhere. Can you imagine that, at the age of seventeen?"

Now I understood perfectly what it was to be a national hero. You got to escort Miss Philippines to all the discos.

"And numerous men threatened me for driving their girlfriends to a dance." Ninoy continued, "One man even came into the office with a gun once and actually fired it at me!"

I'll bet he did, I thought. *T'was a pity he wasn't a better shot.*

"But, despite that, I continued escorting Miss Philippines every year." Ninoy's hands fidgeted with his walkie-talkie. "Even Imelda, as a matter of fact, when she was Miss Manila. But then I said to myself, why should I settle for a Miss Manila when I could have a Miss Philippines?"

Why indeed, Senator? I turned around and saw everybody, except Sylvia, nodding in awed approval. Perhaps they were simply enjoying the unlikely thought of Imelda being spurned in favour of a prettier girl with a more international title.

Basking in the silent adulation Ninoy continued to flaunt us with his heroic exploits, naming all his newspaper chums who supported him. I realized then why the Senator never received bad press. Most of the columnists were his buddies from way back when he was a true Filipino "hero". I was shocked that supposedly sane, intelligent men could be deceived by what appeared to be so monstrous an ego.

Finally, clutching his walkie-talkie, the Senator rose from the table. Pushing back their chairs everyone else rose too.

"I'm afraid to disappoint you," he explained, "but I have to be in bed by 9.30pm because I'm in the office by 7.30am every morning."

Don't be afraid, Senator, I thought. *You're not disappointing me.*

Aloud I said, "Excuse me, Senator, before you go!"

"Yes?"

"I just wondered if I might thank your wife for the dinner, if it's OK?"

Ninoy paused in the doorway. He looked surprised at this request.

"Well, I suppose, yes. You'll find her in the kitchen. It's down the hall there!" He waved a pudgy finger in the direction of the long passageway leading off the dining room.

"Thanks, Senator. Good night!"

With Sylvia at my heels, I proceeded down the corridor towards the kitchen. As we arrived Cory was busy helping to clear away the dinner plates.

"Sorry to disturb you," I said, unsure whether I was doing the right thing, "Sylvia and I just wanted to say thank you for the delicious meal."

Cory smiled. "I'm glad you enjoyed it. Perhaps you're not used to Filipino food yet?"

"I love it," I assured her. "We're off to bed now. I hope we'll see you in the morning to say goodbye?"

"Perhaps," Cory replied. "I hope you're both comfortable in your rooms. Sleep well. If there's anything you need, let me know."

Sylvia and I withdrew from the kitchen with the distinct feeling we had disturbed Cory in her own personal domain.

"Don't worry about it, Caroline. We'll probably never see her again!" Sylvia said.

As far as political prophecies go Sylvia couldn't have been more wrong. We certainly didn't see Cory the next morning. She was, according to Ninoy, busy in the kitchen preparing the cooked breakfast for us all. But as Sylvia and I stood beside her in the kitchen the night before there was no way either of us could have predicted that, less than twenty years later, it would be Cory, the shy, retiring housewife from Tarlac and not her husband who would be sitting in Malacanang Palace as President of the Philippines.

As we headed back to Manila the journalists began talking among themselves about the strange weekend. The one thing they did seem to agree on was the brilliance of our host, Ninoy Aquino. Despite his egotism, his infatuation with himself and his glaring need for adulation they had all ultimately fallen victim to his charms.

I couldn't wait to write the story up. And my editor, Eric Giron, couldn't wait to print it.

"Let's do it!" he announced beaming at me from across his desk. "It'll be the first time anyone has dared write anything derogatory about Ninoy Aquino! Let's see what the reaction is!" He clapped his hands as though he could already visualize the result.

The article turned out to be a devastating piece provoking endless debate in the press and over dinners in restaurants and private houses throughout the city and possibly beyond. For the first time in his political career Ninoy fell totally silent. For a full six weeks he kept his mouth shut except to consult with his advisers and to call up Eric to complain bitterly about the injustice.

"Ninoy is flabbergasted, Caroline," Eric laughed, enjoying being at the centre of the unfolding melodrama and not untouched by the sudden leap in the popularity of his magazine. "He told me you were an uninvited house guest and how dare you accept his hospitality and then write all those atrocious things about him! I won't even tell you the words he used about me for printing them!"

"What did you reply?" I asked.

"I just listened. He was ranting on about wanting to get his own back, write his own version of the weekend. But apparently his friends advised him against it. He said he would have started it this way," Eric paused, "and these are his words:

I just met a hippie. I thought hippies were people who were large in the hips. But this one is bigger in the head!" Eric laughed again. "So what do you make of that, Caroline?"

"Hardly the stuff great politicians are made of!" I sneered.

"Well, I think you should come down to the office and read all the letters we've received. You'll be surprised how many of them support you. Listen, this will make you feel good."

I heard Eric rustling through some papers. "Here, this one…It says, 'writer Caroline Kennedy seems to be a brilliant British hippy sort of Mary McCarthy, or even latter-day Evelyn Waugh. She sees through the falsity of many of our values with piercing wit, discernment and, in her writing, has so little ego that she takes as many cracks at her own hippy self as she does at our Establishment.'"

"Now that one I like!" I giggled. "You better frame it for me!"

Six weeks later the furore had still not died down. Eventually Ninoy's brother, Butz, called me up to extend an olive branch.

"Can we meet?" he asked, "I'll take you out for a meal. We do need to talk!"

I agreed. My friend, the notoriously fiery political commentator Roger "Bomba" Arienda, accompanied me to offer his support should I need it.

Over lunch Butz told us, "Ninoy's crushed, Caroline. He doesn't know what to do. He wanted to rebut your article but we advised him against it in case it made him look like a sore loser."

Butz lowered his eyes. I almost felt sorry for him. He seemed uncomfortable in his role as mediator. "Why I'm here, what I've been asked to do, Caroline, is," Butz paused for a minute reluctant to relay the message he'd come to deliver. "Could you possibly write another one? I mean, a more favourable one?"

I couldn't believe what I was hearing.

"But it was all true!" I protested. "Ninoy knows that. Why would I want to change it? Trouble is your brother is a show-off. He can't help it. He asked for it, really he did." I looked at Roger. Now was the time I needed his support.

Roger nodded. "It's true. Caroline doesn't tell lies!"

"I know. I know," Butz replied, "but it's hurt him badly. Couldn't you just…?"

"No, I'm sorry!" I was emphatic. I had sympathy for Butz but none for the Ninoy. Roger, a firm believer in free speech, squeezed my hand under the table.

A few days passed and I received a message from Malacanang Palace requesting permission to reprint the article in the run-up to the upcoming presidential election. Again I refused. There was no way I would allow the Marcoses to use it as propaganda material. I had never intended it for that purpose and I could not agree to it. In the end, as it turned out, any propaganda against Marcos's diehard opponent proved entirely unnecessary.

Six months before the election Marcos had a far bigger propaganda card up his sleeve. In July 1969, on a whistle-stop world tour, the recently elected U.S. President, Richard Nixon, stopped off in Manila and pledged his personal support of Marcos. And, lest that should not be enough to clinch the election, Marcos stole millions from the Central Bank in order to pay bribes all over the country in exchange for votes while, at the same time, barring his official opponent, Sergio Osmena, Jr. access to his own funds. He also took control of all the election stations up and down the country. And in the week prior to the elections the President declared an extended national holiday and closed down the newspapers and television stations.

Now, for the second time in his political career, Ninoy fell silent. Without his media friends to devote television coverage, air waves and column inches to him there was no way his voice could be heard. There was no way he could successfully challenge the incumbent President. And there was no way he could prevent Marcos from becoming the first President in Philippine history to win a second term.

This first conscious step by Marcos to remove all democratic institutions heralded the downfall of Ninoy Aquino. On the 21st September 1972 Marcos declared Proclamation 1081 instituting martial law throughout the Philippines. During the previous night many of Marcos's political opponents including Ninoy Aquino, religious leaders, journalists, politicians, businessmen and academics were rounded up and put in prison.

In the lonely confinement of his cell Ninoy, accused of murder, rape, illegal possession of firearms and subversion, wrote feverishly in his diary. Occasionally, he managed to smuggle out his writings. In them he spoke of his religious conversion.

"It was as if I heard a voice saying, 'Why do you cry? I have given you honour and glory which have been denied to millions of your countrymen. I made you the youngest war correspondent, presidential assistant, mayor, vice-governor, governor and Senator and I recall you never thanked me for all these gifts. Now that I visit you in your slight desolation, you cry and whimper like a spoiled brat!' With this realization I went down on my knees and begged His forgiveness. In the loneliness of my solitary confinement, in the depths of my solitude and desolation I found my inner peace. He stood me face to face with myself then helped me discover Him."

To me, reading his words, it sounded so staged. But, then, I knew it was quite common for incarcerated people to experience a religious conversion. *Could Ninoy have truly "found God", or was it simply Ninoy politicking again?* If he had hoped the US would back him, he would be disappointed. After, a demand by President Jimmy Carter, for the restoration of democracy in the Philippines, the US President gave his tacit support to Marcos. And Vice President, Walter Mondale, on a visit to the Philippines, met up with Opposition leaders but decided not to speak to Aquino. This was seen as a win for Marcos and an humiliation for the Boy Wonder.

During his solitary confinement Ninoy had lost a great deal of weight and had been experiencing severe chest pains. The tests revealed he required immediate surgery. This, Marcos thought, was the opportunity to rid himself of his most hated opponent for good. The President offered him safe passage to the United States hoping Ninoy would never be well enough to return to the Philippines and run for political office again.

But the politician in Ninoy hadn't completely disappeared. He still believed he had a political destiny to fulfill in his country. Now it was just a matter of biding his time. After the successful heart operation Aquino took up a fellowship at Harvard for the next three years. And, by the summer of 1983, Ninoy received word that Marcos was severely ill, perhaps dying, from lupus erythematosus, a disease of the immune system that had already seriously damaged his kidneys.

Although Marcos had taken great pains to hide the facts about his ill-health, Ninoy's informer, the nephrologist Dr. Mike Baccay, told him that Marcos had undergone an unsuccessful kidney transplant at the National Kidney Center and was not expected to survive. For his indiscretion Dr. Baccay was later abducted, tortured and executed in a ritualistic-style killing.

Ninoy was now, more than ever, determined to return to his country. He was now even more convinced that this was "his" time. It was obvious to me that, despite his religious conversion, he had lost neither his ambition nor his sense of destiny.

Thus, on 21st August 1983 Ninoy boarded China Airlines flight 811 bound for Manila. As the pilot prepared for landing, the former Senator donned a bullet-proof vest.

"If they hit me in the head, I'm a gonner!" Ninoy joked to the accompanying journalists and film crew.

Along with thousands of Filipinos around the world, I was watching TV when the plane touched down. I watched as armed officers of the Philippine Armed Forces walked up to escort Ninoy into the terminal. And I watched as he emerged from the plane and slowly started to descend the steps. Seemingly, from out of nowhere, there was a momentary hail of bullets. One of those bullets entered Ninoy's skull behind his left ear. In front of the world's TV cameras, he slumped forward. And then, within seconds, the body of Marcos's nemesis, the Boy Wonder of Tarlac, along with the hopes and dreams of many of his fellow Filipinos, lay lifeless on the tarmac below.

And, yes, despite the fact I knew in my heart that Ninoy was just another ambitious politician, I cried that day. This was not the way it should have ended. And I thought that, perhaps, following his life-threatening surgery and his religious conversion, Ninoy really had become a better man. And, when I next met up with his wife, Cory, I apologized for my article years back and congratulated her on becoming the first female President of the Philippines and for redrafting the Filipino Constitution to remove the dictatorial structure created by her predecessor, Ferdinand Marcos. I told her I was grateful she had restored democracy. And I hoped it would survive

Author James Michener & wife, Mari Yoriko Sabisawa

Author John Steinbeck

My friend Christina Paolozzi

My godmother, Olga Horstig with Brigitte Bardot

My friends, John Wells (bottom Left) with John Bird and Barry Humphries (far right)

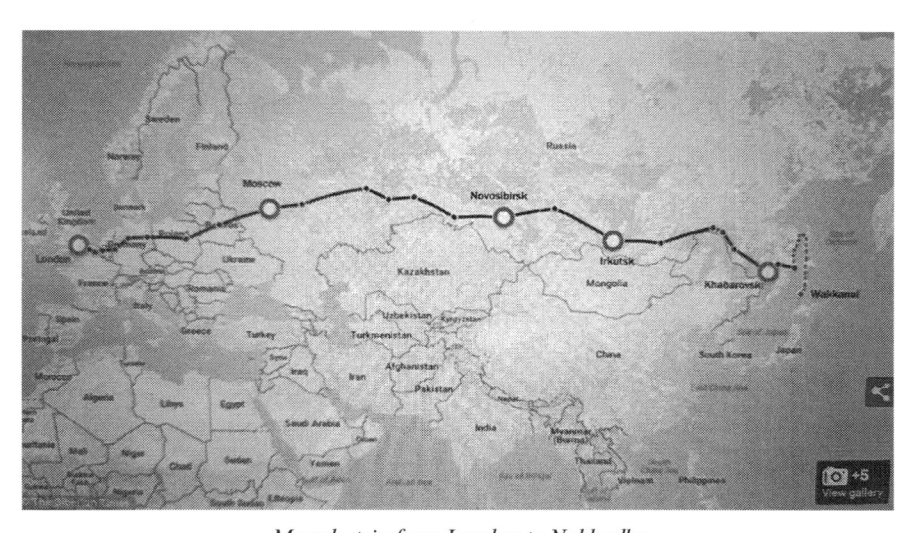

My solo trip from London to Nakhodka

Actor Masumi Okada.

My friend Betsy Romualdez Francia

Caroline Kennedy

Photographer Daido Moriyama

Press Clipping from International Herald Tribune

Press Clipping in Hong Kong

A Kalinga family in the Mountain Province

Ifugao man in the Mountain Province

Open-sided bus in Mountain Province

Me, Robin Aristorenas & Leopoldo Salcedo in El Tigre.

Jaime Jose is executed at Muntinlupa Prison.

Caroline Kennedy

Benjamin Mendoza and me at Muntinlupa Prison

Cory & Ninoy Aquino

Attracting crowds in Kathmandu

Elisar and me

Caroline Kennedy

Rita Gam visiting London

Christina Paolozzi by Richard Avedon

I'll Be There

Me by Richard Avedon

Chapter 24
Two Arrivals

In the summer of 1969, Ben and I bade our friends in Manila a temporary goodbye and left to follow the "hippie trail" through Thailand, India and Nepal, en route for Paris, where Ben would be representing the Philippines in the Paris Biennale, the international exhibition of paintings held, every two years, in a different country.

Following our shared passion, Ben and I eagerly scoured the antique shops in Delhi and Kathmandu for early carvings, bronze sculptures and thanka paintings. And, in the thrift shops of Rome, Madrid and Milan we searched for early maps and prints. So, by the time we reached Paris, our antique collection had increased dramatically, necessitating the purchase of a few extra suitcases, but our funds had virtually dried up. We ended up in a cheap hotel on Rue Dauphine, too small and seedy even to deserve a mention in our guide book but stumbled upon on our stroll around Saint-Germain-des-Pres. For a double bed we paid the equivalent of $2 a night, with a cold shower costing us an extra 25 cents. And that didn't guarantee a "private" shower, as I found out on one occasion, to my acute embarrassment.

Now, on his first ever trip abroad, I was curious to see Ben's reaction when he was able to view world famous paintings that, until then, he had only ever seen reproduced in art books. We spent hours in the galleries of the Louvre, the Musee d'Orsay and the Petit Palais, lingering in front of works such as the Mona Lisa, Van Gogh's Self Portrait and Ingres' The Death of Leonardo da Vinci. Now, instead of simply appreciating a coloured illustration on a page, he was able to marvel at textures, brush strokes, mediums, perspectives, depths and sizes. And, when his brain was over-stimulated by the sheer number and variety of fine art on display, we strolled along the banks of the Seine or explored the back streets of the Left Bank.

Once the Paris Biennale was over, at the end of September, Ben and I finally headed for London. My family were all anxious to meet my Filipino artist fiance. After spending money for my "coming out season" in London to "meet the right type of man", my mother was extremely curious to know why I had travelled halfway around the world to find a husband. And my father, in his very British way, was equally keen to get to know Ben. So, within a week of our arrival, he invited us to lunch at the Savoy Hotel.

When the day came, Ben, slightly intimidated at the prospect of not only meeting my father but meeting him in such a fashionable venue, was justifiably nervous. And it certainly didn't help when we arrived at the door of the dining room, and with my father already visible seated at a table near the far window, Ben was denied entrance for not wearing a tie. He was, in fact, wearing a very elegant "barong Tagalog" which, in the Philippines, is traditional menswear for a smart occasion. But, despite explaining this, the Maitre d' refused to budge and Ben, at the age of 27, was forced to wear a tie for the first time in his life.

I had warned Ben in advance that the first question my father would ask him would be, "Well, young man, can you mend a fuse?"

This is what he had asked all my boyfriends over the years and it had become a standard joke between us.

And, sure enough, he did put that question to Ben. But, saving Ben the embarrassment of answering in the negative, I was the one who replied. "It's OK, Dad, I can mend a fuse. You taught me how to do it!"

At least, that broke the ice and we all laughed. And, despite Ben feeling like a fish out of water, by the end of lunch he had earned my Dad's wholehearted approval.

My mother's concern evaporated as soon as she laid eyes on Ben. One thing about Mummy was that she could never resist beautiful people! So when she met the handsome artist from the Philippines, she welcomed him with open arms and whispered in my ear, "You'll have beautiful babies!"

I knew she had been secretly wishing to have - what she referred to as "Eurasian" grandchildren.

"Eurasians are the most beautiful people in the world," she had often told me.

So, needless to say, she was happy at the thought of our impending union. And, being a good Catholic convert, was prodding me to start producing her some "beautiful" grandchildren for her as soon as possible.

The wedding itself, on November 3rd, 1969, was a small family affair at Chelsea Registry Office on the King's Rd, just five minutes away from my flat on Draycott Place. My mother hosted the reception at her Eaton Square duplex. However, she had forgotten to order a wedding cake. So my sister, Tessa, who was heavily pregnant with her fourth child, rushed out to buy one. She came back with a birthday cake as that was all that was available at the local bakery.

Over the next few months, I introduced Ben to my many friends. Through my old friend, Linda Lloyd-Jones, he was offered an exhibition at the Institute of Contemporary Art (ICA) on the Mall. Through another friend, Glenda Jackson, he was given the first exhibition at her brand new gallery in Greenwich. Princess Elizabeth of Jugoslavia, gave him a one-man show at her private home on the King's Road. And, through my friends, Teal and Karen Traina, he was given another private exhibition at their home in New York. So, within a year, Ben could really boast he was an "international" artist, as he was already being referred to by his adoring media in Manila.

After two early miscarriages, I finally gave birth to our first child, Elisar, on May 16, 1971. Like every first time mother, I was thrilled, proud and deliriously happy. Even though I was never one for setting down roots anywhere, children had always been on my agenda. I assumed I could travel just as easily with babies in tow as without them.

Our friend, Jaime Zobel, the Philippines Ambassador to London and his wife, Bea, came to the Avenue Clinic in Hampstead to visit me.

"Isn't it the most wonderful feeling, holding your first baby in your arms?" Bea asked.

I had to agree with her. It was a very special feeling.

"Somehow," she continued, "it didn't quite feel the same with my seventh baby!"

Within his first weeks of life, Elisar, strapped to my back or carried by Ben in a Moses basket, became a regular at evening gallery openings, early morning antique markets and weekly auctions. During the week, Ben and I had a stall in the Chelsea Antiques Market and, every Saturday, a stall on Portobello Road, selling Indian, Nepalese and Tibetan antiques. We were fortunate that Elisar was so placid and so adaptable. He never made a fuss, never complained that voices were too loud, that places were too crowded or that nights were too late. He simply smiled or slept through it all. And, before he was three months old, we took him to my mother's new house in Mallorca for a summer holiday.

Soon after we returned to London, my old friend from New York, Rita Gam, unexpectedly entered my life again. It was past 10pm, I had just put Elisar to sleep and had fallen into bed exhausted. The phone rang. I instantly recognized Rita's voice.

"Caroline, darling, I'm in London. I know you're newly-married and you have a baby, but I was hoping to stay with you for about two weeks. I've got some business in London, some interviews with television companies and I need a place to stay. I won't get in your way, I promise. You can just give me the keys and I'll let myself in and out of the house and you won't even know I'm there. These interviews are really important. I have some ideas the TV companies are interested in. Would it be OK? Actually, I'm in a taxi, from Heathrow, and I'm on my way to your house right now."

I guess there was no way I could say no. I thought of Joe. Yes, that's Rita being Rita, alright.

An hour later the doorbell rang. Huddled in the porch out of the rain, there was Rita shivering on my doorstep.

"I don't have any money to pay the taxi. Do you have 40 pounds?" she purred.

My husband, Ben, shook his head. I ran back upstairs to look in my purse. Elisar started crying, having been startled at the sound of the doorbell. Thankfully I had enough money and rushed back downstairs.

"Could you?" said Rita to Ben, indicating she wanted him to step out into the rain in his pyjamas, pay the taxi driver who was impatiently stamping on the accelerator and bring her three matching pieces of elegant Luis Vuitton luggage inside.

"You're a darling," she said, as Ben struggled up the stairs carrying the three suitcases. "By the way, we haven't met before. I'm Rita!"

I showed Rita our spare room, overlooking the garden.

"Can we talk?" she asked. "We've got a lot to catch up on."

I shook my head. "I'm exhausted, Rita. You unpack and settle in and we can talk tomorrow morning."

She hugged me. "Good night! Sleep well!"

I closed the door, went to pacify Elisar, gently rocking him back to sleep. Then I went into my bedroom, closed the door and passed out. An hour later, there was a knock on our door.

"Caroline?" Rita whispered aloud. "Caroline, are you awake? I really need to talk to you. Can you come into my room for a moment?" Worried that she was going to wake Elisar again, I reluctantly obliged.

I crept out of bed and went into her room and sat on a chair by the window, rubbing my eyes, waiting for her to apologize for disturbing my much needed sleep.

But then I realized this was Rita and it probably didn't even occur to her that she had done anything wrong.

As I sat there in silence, she started to undress. Despite our long friendship this made me feel uncomfortable so I looked away.

When she was down to her bra and panties she said, "Look at me, Caroline! Tell me truthfully, how is my figure? Am I fat?"

"Rita, you've never been fat. You never will be fat!" I replied, without turning my head.

"But, tell me, do I look old? Does my skin look old?"

"Rita, you always look wonderful!" I desperately wanted this conversation to be over so I could go back to bed.

"But you haven't looked properly!" she persisted. "Look at me!"

She stood in front of the long mirror and examined herself.

"You see, here!!" She pinched the skin on her upper arm. "This is sagging, isn't it? Tell me the truth!"

"Rita, you look fabulous. Besides, 43 is a great age for a woman. I hope I look as good as you when I'm 43!"

"Oh, you're just saying that to be kind!" she said. "I probably need some surgery!"

"At your age? Don't be ridiculous, Rita. Honestly, you look beautiful!"

And I wasn't flattering her. I didn't have to. She did look beautiful.

Rita sat down on the bed and pulled a pair of fluffy pink slippers out of her suitcase. She held them up, looked at them intently and then burst into floods of tears.

"My mother made these for me!" she sobbed. "And I'm so horrible to my mother! I'm so ashamed!"

I got up from the chair and sat beside her on the bed, placing my arm around her shoulders.

"Your mum loves you," I said.

"I know," she sniffed. "That's the problem. I'm so mean to her and she still loves me. And she made me these for my last birthday. And I don't think I ever said thank you to her. Does that make me a bad person?"

What could I say? "I'm sure she understands," I said, trying to console her. "She knows you're a busy person. Mothers understand these things. You can always call her from here."

That was a mistake! The next day Rita took me at my word, picked up the phone and called her mother in the US. The call lasted over an hour and the phone bill soared with every minute. I kicked myself for being so naïve!

Although Rita had reassured me that she wouldn't be a burden on me and my little family, I instinctively knew she wouldn't be an easy guest. So I started conjuring up ways to share the load by introducing her to new friends.

I knew my neighbour downstairs, Lou Secchi, was an avid movie buff, particularly of movies from the 50s. And his wife, Judith Bruce, happened to be an actress. Perfect, I thought, I'll introduce her to Lou and Judith.

As I suspected he would be, Lou was absolutely thrilled when I mentioned who my houseguest was.

"Rita Gam?" he exclaimed. "I'm a huge fan! Oh, my God! You must introduce us. We'll take her out to dinner! What kind of food does she like?"

"She doesn't eat!" I replied. "She's always on a diet! But I must warn you, she does steal from other people's plates!"

So Lou and Judith took us all out to dinner at Keats in Hampstead. Lou was laying on the charm with Rita and they hit it off immediately. Over drinks they chatted excitedly and I realized Lou had either done his homework extremely diligently or, as he divulged to her, he really had seen every film she was in. He was able to cite every single movie, TV drama and play, even remembering her first Broadway role opposite Marlon Brando in *A Flag is Born*. Rita, of course, was thrilled and flattered.

By the time we came to order our food, Lou and Rita were firm friends.

"What would you like?" Lou asked her, handing her a menu. "Order anything you want!"

Rita hardly glanced at the menu.

"I'm not hungry," she said. "I don't think I'll eat. But don't let that stop any of you! I don't mind sitting here and watching you all eat. Honestly, I'm used to it!"

I kicked Judith under the table. "You see," I mouthed. "What did I tell you?"

As we ate our food, Rita looked on, watching us down every mouthful. All of a sudden she picked up a fork and plunged it into my salmon, extracting a large piece of flesh.

"You don't mind do you, darling? It looks so good," she said as she swallowed it whole.

She then did the same to a piece of juicy steak on Ben's plate.

"That looks good too!" she said, spearing the steak with her fork.

She then turned to Lou who had selected a garlic prawn dish.

"Oh, prawns, my favourite!" Rita exclaimed, "My absolute favourite!"

She plunged her fork into one of Lou's king prawns and transferred it from his plate into her mouth.

"Oh, now that is delicious!" she exclaimed, with her mouth full and raised her fork to plunge into another one.

"You don't mind, do you, Lou? I find I am quite hungry after all!"

Lou smiled indulgently.

"No, no, it's OK, take it. I don't mind, honestly. But why don't you let me order the same king prawn dish for you?"

"Oh no, I couldn't possibly!" she replied, "I don't have the appetite for a whole dish!"

Meanwhile she continued to spear Lou's prawns until there was only one left.

"Finish it!" Lou said, his exasperation showing, "I'm not hungry either!"

"Are you sure?" she asked, "I don't really need it. I'm just being greedy. But they're so good!"

So Rita hastily finished off Lou's king prawns before he could change his mind.

The odd thing was that following our dinner at Keats Lou never asked after Rita again. A friendship was forged and broken over a plate of garlic king prawns.

But that was Rita to a T. That was the effect she had on people. Over the years I had become very fond of her. But she could be exasperating. She could be self-centred. She could be thoughtless. She could be absolutely unaware of other people's feelings. But she was always kind. She was always caring. And she did want to help others. It was just that, more often than not, she didn't know how.

She had been a pampered starlet for as long as she could remember. She had married two wealthy men and been protected, cosseted and spoilt rotten by both of them. Now, in her 40s, she was learning how to cope on her own, how to make decisions without consulting a movie agent, a producer or a husband.

She told Joe once, during one of her midnight calls, "I don't know how to pay the household insurance. How do I do it?"

It turned out the household insurance wasn't the only thing Rita didn't know how to do. Cooking, cleaning and paying bills were all skills she was ignorant of and only just, very reluctantly, beginning to acquire.

"How did you reserve your plane ticket here," I asked her one morning over breakfast.

"I called up Tom's secretary and asked her to book it," Rita confessed. "I guess I shouldn't have done that, should I? I should really try to show him I'm independent."

"Easier said than done," I said, trying to reassure her.

"Next time I'll do it myself." She sipped her tea and looked at me. "Or perhaps you could help me. Show me how to do it?"

"It's not that hard, Rita," I replied. "All you need is a travel agent. That's probably what Tom's secretary uses anyway. Get a travel agent and he, or she, will do everything for you. You just tell them what day you want to travel, what day you want to return and that's it!"

"As easy as that? Really?" She took another sip of tea, wiped her bright red lips on the napkin and got up from the table.

"I need to get going," she said. "I have an appointment at the BBC in an hour. Can I order a taxi?"

"I wouldn't do that," I replied. "It's expensive. You can take the tube into Central London just as easily. I'll explain how you get there. It's really simple."

"How do I buy a ticket?' she asked. "Can you call and get me one in advance?"

I laughed. Rita was the second American who had asked me the same question.

"You don't book the tube ticket in advance," I explained. "You buy it at the station."

"You'll show me, won't you?" she asked anxiously.

I nodded my head. "Of course! I'll walk down to the station with you."

A week later, with a promise of a speedy return, Rita was gone. Our small family unit could finally settle down again to some kind of normalcy.

But we were never really settled. In less than a year, much to my family's disappointment, the three of us headed back to the Philippines for Ben's much-heralded "*Larawan*" exhibition to be held at the Luz Gallery.

Chapter 25
The Offending Emeralds

On 23rd September 1972. Marcos finally declared Martial Law. In the build up to that day, street crime was rampant, an air of anarchy prevailed and the economy, once the pride of Asia, was in tatters. The standard of living, once envied by other south-east Asian nations, was now comparable to some of the most impoverished countries in the world. By stealing from the Philippines Treasury, Marcos and his cronies had deliberately crashed the economy. TV stations and newspapers were shut down. Political enemies were rounded up and imprisoned. And, his most vocal critics were either intimidated into silence or were seduced with promises of jobs or riches.

Our friend, journalist JV Cruz, one of Marcos's loudest dissenters, was offered the Ambassadorship to London. The Café regulars were both surprised and disappointed how quickly JV accepted this offer.

Another newspaper friend and regular in Indios Bravos, Francisco "Kit" Tatad, who, in his columns, had daily denigrated Marcos, was offered the post of Minister of Information.

Kit arrived at the Cafe one night and asked me, "Should I take it?"

The mere fact he was asking that question, shocked me and the rest of the assembled crowd.

"Absolutely not!" I replied

And, yet, within a week or two, Kit became the Minister of Information in the new martial law government, with his office inside Malacanang Palace. He came to the Cafe a few times after that, pretending that he had not changed, that he was still the same old Kit he had always been. But there was nothing we could say to him. We could not trust him. To us he would always remain a traitor.

JV and Kit were just two of the many journalists who switched allegiances. To say that we were disillusioned is an understatement. *From then on*, I thought, *could we trust anyone?* Spies were many and the price of opposing Marcos was high. Detainment in military camp, disappearance, torture and death were now all very real possibilities.

Since there were no more independent newspapers, most of them having been taken over by Marcos, there were few offers of writing jobs for me. But I was commissioned to write several articles for the encyclopedia on the Philippines, entitled, *Filipino Heritage* on subjects such as "*Early European Travellers in the Philippines*", "*Tattoo Art of the Mountain Province*" and "*The Manila Galleon Trade*". And I still did get the odd invitation to appear on TV, mainly on Elvira Manahan's program, *Two for the Road*. Elvira was a friend of Imelda and, thus, was allowed to continue hosting her nightly TV show as long as she stayed clear of politics.

One night Elvira made the huge mistake of inviting me on with Imee Marcos, the Marcos's eldest daughter. Imee arrived at Channel 3 studio that night with an arm encrusted in vast uncut emeralds. It seemed an extraordinary coincidence because there was a story doing the rounds in Manila at the time that several Andean miners had lost their lives excavating the world's largest flawless emeralds intended for the First Lady of the Philippines, Imelda Romualdez Marcos.

I couldn't take my eyes off the huge green rocks encircling Imee's wrist. And, being in a playful mood, I just couldn't resist the temptation to remark on them.

"Those are the most magnificent emeralds I've ever seen, Imee," I said. "Did you ever find out exactly how many men died digging them out of the Colombian mountains?"

Flustered Imee hurriedly tried to obscure the offending jewels by covering them with her other arm.

I could see she was uncomfortable but I had started, so I persisted. "I heard your mother has yet to pay the bill, is that right?"

Elvira, who was one of Imelda's coterie of "blue ladies", pulled one of her characteristic Phyllis-Diller-type expressions and let out a nervous giggle. I waited for an answer but Imee looked straight through me. For once the bright, intelligent First Daughter, who was being groomed to succeed her father, didn't have a ready answer.

Elvira coughed and tried to change the subject. But I knew my friends would expect me to pursue the subject until I got an answer. And youthful arrogance got the better of me. Besides, I was enjoying myself.

"How much do you think they're worth – $50 million, $100 million? What would you say, Imee?"

Composing herself, Elvira reprimanded me: "Now, Caroline, that's an unfair question. Imee wouldn't have any idea. They were gifts from her mother."

While I was wondering how Elvira knew that for a fact, she turned to Imee. "Now tell me about your life, Imee, are you planning to continue at Princeton in the Fall?"

I was tempted to say, *"If the Philippines can afford the bill!"* It was well known that funds to educate the Marcos children were extracted not from Marcos's modest presidential salary of $6500 per annum but from the Philippines treasury. Like everything else in his life, Marcos automatically expected his political dynasty to be paid for by the people.

I was also tempted to ask Imee about the rhinestone-encrusted jeans she had been reported wearing during a recent summer barbeque in Long Island. Except that, another guest reliably informed me, they weren't actually rhinestones at all but real diamonds. Sadly, at this point, my instinct for self-preservation got the better of me. I had almost been deported once, Betsy, Henry and many of my friends had been jailed and now I had the safety of my own family to consider. So I let it go and we twittered on about innocuous subjects that required little soul-searching, little animosity and zero confrontation.

From that moment on, I suspected, Imee had become my avowed enemy. And that, I was very much aware, could be dangerous because she was her Daddy's favourite. I was to meet her again in a different country, under very different circumstances. And, for her, it would be pay-back time.

On 8th November 1973, I gave birth to our daughter, Mayumi, at the Makati Medical Center. She was delivered, head first, by Elvira Manahan's obstetrician husband, Constantino Manahan. In those days of martial law, every week had its designated name. And Mayumi was born in *National Volleyball Consciousness Week*. I was actually quite relieved she hadn't been born a week earlier, in *National Rat-Catchers Week*. Whether these epithets meant anything or not, I couldn't say. Or whether it was simply a martial law folly, designed to amuse the masses and detract attention from the dire things that were happening in the country, I simply had no idea. And there was never any explanation.

Mummy, Billy and my sister, Marina, came over for the birth . As I knew she would be, my mother was thrilled that I had produced her first Eurasian granddaughter.

"She's going to be an absolute beauty!" she declared emphatically, without the slightest hint of doubt.

Mayumi was precocious from the start. By the age of three months she had pulled herself up the side of her cot and fallen out. A month later she was standing up, holding on to the furniture. And, by six months she was walking holding my hand.

Fortunately, Ben's *"Larawan"* exhibition had been a huge sell-out success that year, despite the extreme austerity conditions that were pervasive in the Philippines at the time. But, after a great deal of soul-searching, we finally decided we had no wish to bring up our two children under martial law. So, once again, we said our temporary farewells to our friends and headed home to London.

I'll Be There

But, after two years of domestic bliss, I began to get itchy feet again. Ben and I had taken occasional brief trips to New York, Dubrovnik and Mallorca but I was eager to travel somewhere new, somewhere I had never been before. Soon after Ben and I had married, my brother, Alexander, married a Colombian beauty, Doris Garcia, and this presented the perfect opportunity for the four of us to visit South America. Leaving Elisar and Mayumi behind with Daddy and Daphie was a wrench. It was our first separation. But I had no doubt my little ones would have the best time with their grandparents at Lowsley House.

So, with Doris as our guide, we set out for Bogota, San Augustin, Cartagena and then on to Peru to see Macchu Pichu, Puno, Arequipe and the floating villages on Lake Titicaca. In 1975, Macchu Pichu was fairly inaccessible. There was only one lodge to stay in, whereas today there are numerous hotels to choose from in the vicinity. So we were fortunate to have Macchu Pichu all to ourselves at dawn as we trekked up the Inca trails to the summit. The memory of the spectacular sunrise from the top of the mountain with a 360% view, has remained with me all these years.

South America at that time was gaining an international reputation for drug smuggling. And, as a consequence, customs officers in almost every airport around the world, detained people returning from there. Ben and I proved no exception. We were taken aside by officers at Heathrow looking for cocaine. We were both questioned, strip-searched and held for over two hours. My hair was pulled to make sure I wasn't hiding drugs under a wig. My bag was searched, letters read, lipsticks and make-up ruined. And then, the most humiliating experience of all - the cavity search. Ben weathered his interrogation stoically. But I, of course, was totally indignant. Instead of remaining silent and submissive, I continually protested. Why were we chosen? What made us look more suspicious than our fellow passengers? What rights did they have to simply haul us off? I tried to explain to them, they had selected the wrong victim. I was a teetotaller, I was a non-smoker and I didn't do drugs. How could they be so wrong? But, of course, they didn't have to explain themselves. They had every right, so they said. There would be no apology for any indignities suffered. There was no one I could complain to. And I simply had to "grin and bear it."

Meanwhile, Daddy, Daphie, Elisar and Mayumi, who had come to meet us were totally ignorant of what was happening behind the scenes. And, since we were considered suspects, we were not allowed to convey a message to them outside the Customs Hall. Eventually, we were allowed to leave, brutalized, dishevelled but intact. From that moment on, I have always been very wary of but very deferential to Customs officers.

The mid 70s was a time of mass departures from the Philippines. Due to martial law, many young people, high school graduates, trainee nurses and domestic workers, all wanted to leave the country for a better life elsewhere. In England this mass migration coincided with British workers refusing to do what became known as "dirty jobs". Jobs such as janitors, hospital auxiliaries, public toilet attendants, all necessary jobs but with very low salaries. Since English people refused to take them, the migrant Filipinos were happy to step in.

Sadly, at the same time, there were many unscrupulous middle men, such as recruiting agents, travel agents and dubious lawyers, all willing to cash in on the sheer number of Filipinos escaping their country for a better life abroad. These middle men filled in job applications, passport applications and visa applications, many of them falsely, and pocketed the money.

Consequently, many of the Filipinos arriving in the UK found they were in the country illegally. The British government responded by starting a programme of deporting them back to the Philippines. That was when Ben and I stepped in. Together, we published a monthly newspaper, *Balita*, for the Filipino diaspora in the UK, not only covering all their social activities but also offering those threatened with deportation all the resources they would require to stave off their departures.

I wrote most of the articles. Ben took most of the photographs and did the layouts. Some Filipino friends wrote guest articles or sent in photos of birthday parties, weddings and christenings. And then, at the end of each month, I would drive around town, delivering the newspaper to newsagents and supermarkets where there were large Filipino communities.

In February 1977, our youngest, Jasmine, was born. My waters broke at home, just after I'd dropped Elisar off to school in the morning. I called an ambulance and, with Mayumi in tow, was carted off in the middle of rush hour, to University College Hospital. By the time I reached there, I had almost given birth. No time for painkillers or an epidural. Within an hour I had my new baby in my arms. For some reason, Ben and I actually had no name chosen for her. We hadn't been able to decide on one we both liked. So, when my sister, Marina, and my neighbour, Judith, both brought jasmine plants to my hospital room, we agreed that would be the perfect name for her.

Chapter 26
An Edifice Complex

In June 1979, I took Elisar, aged 8 and Mayumi, aged 6, to a matinee performance of *The King and I* at the London Palladium, starring Yul Brynner. Afterwards we went backstage and, somewhat timidly, I knocked on the door of Yul's dressing-room. After all this time I wasn't even sure he'd recognize me.

"Remember me?" I asked as he opened the door slightly and peered out.

"My God, Caroline Kennedy!" he beamed. "Of course, I remember you!" He tossed some make-up tissues towards a bin beside the dressing table. "With our wonderful Christina in New York. How long ago was that? Have you seen her recently? How is she?"

"Oh, she's fine" I replied. "I heard from her very recently, in fact. She's well. She's as she always is. She's Christina, isn't she? Still raising eyebrows and still creating wonderful mayhem wherever she goes."

"I can't believe it. It's so good to see you again, come in, come in!" He stepped back and gestured for us to take a seat among the mountain of clothes that were hastily being removed by his dresser. I ushered my children through the door.

"By the way Yul, these are my children, Elisar and Mayumi!" I announced proudly. He bent down and cuddled each one in turn. They eyed his bald head and exaggerated stage make-up suspiciously.

"So," Yul announced, "you've done the same as I have. Well done, Caroline!"

"What? What have I done?" I asked puzzled.

"Got yourself two of those," he replied.

"My children, you mean?"

"Yes. I adopted two Vietnamese children too, didn't you know?"

I did know but my maternal pride bristled to think he hadn't even recognized them as my own.

"They're not adopted, Yul!" I retorted. "Nor are they Vietnamese. They're all mine. And their father is Filipino!"

For a moment Yul appeared dumbstruck. Then his face broke into a huge grin.

"Well, good for you anyway. They're just beautiful - both of them."

We had well and truly broken the ice after so many years. It was good to see him again. I told him how I had enjoyed his film *Westworld* where he had played a robot cowboy. It was a brilliant portrayal and had rightly won him many accolades in 1973. He gave the children an impromptu demonstration strutting robotically up and down the dressing room, stopping abruptly to aim a pretend gun at his image in the mirror. His performance looked all the more absurd since he was still dressed in his *King & I* costume. The children giggled. He had won them over. We reverted to discussing Christina for whom, it was obvious, he still held enormous affection.

I reminded him of the second outrage Christina had performed on stuffy New Yorkers - posing nude for the fashion photographer, Richard Avedon, in Vogue magazine. For this deliberate offence to respectability Avedon catapulted to fame but Christina was immediately struck off Earl Blackwell's Celebrity Register, the bible that every society-conscious New Yorker desperately wanted to be included in.

"Christina couldn't have cared less." Yul laughed loudly. "She said to me, "Me respectable? You know me better than anyone, Yul, I wasn't born to be respectable, was I?"

I am sure I left Yul that night reminiscing on his old flame. To all of us Christina was beautiful, capricious and affectionate. Her passion for life, her compulsive flirtations and her need to test traditional boundaries were judged by most New Yorkers as distinct character flaws but to us, her friends and admirers, they were considered all part of her undeniable individuality and charm. I truly missed her spontaneity. I missed New York.

Ben was also missing the Philippines. And his family were anxious to meet the children. So, in late 1980, we made plans to return to Manila for an extended holiday. We agreed to rent a beautiful period bungalow in Bayside Village owned by our ballerina friend, Alice Reyes. Situated right on Roxas Boulevard, we were able to walk along the ocean promenade every day or buy fish from the local fishermen when they arrived at dawn with their nightly catch.

It didn't take us long to adapt to Manila life again. We were both sucked in immediately. Ben, with offers of another major exhibition at the Luz Gallery, and me with various writing and TV work.

From Bayview Village, too, it was a short walk to the area around the Cultural Center where Imelda Marcos was now rushing to build her International Film Center for the opening of her Film Festival. To prevent boredom at home she had begun to aggressively pursue what became known as her "edifice complex".

Perhaps, like the Pharaohs, she intended to leave the world monuments to remember her by. She built the Cultural Centre in 90 days as a venue for the Miss Universe contest, then came the International Convention Centre to give a forum for overseas investors and businessmen, a Folk Arts Centre, ready in time to accommodate the Ali-Frazier *"Thrilla in Manila"* world heavyweight fight, a fortress like Metropolitan Museum to house her personal collection of paintings, a University of Life, a Heart Centre for Asia, a Lung Centre, fourteen luxury hotels and the Coconut Palace to accommodate her jet-setting guests and to permanently display – although not to the public – her priceless collection of jewels and icons.

But the building that topped them all was the Parthenon-like structure dominating the center of Manila Bay and housing her Film Centre, built for her International Film Festival, conceived by her to rival Cannes.

I watched mesmerized as this mammoth building was constructed by literally thousands of underpaid workers struggling day and night to make sure it was completed on time.

A week or two before the grand opening a catastrophe happened. A huge section of the native bamboo scaffolding collapsed resulting in 169 workers plummeting headlong into the quick-drying cement. And as their fellow workers scrambled desperately to free the victims, the order came from Imelda that there was no time to dig them out, work must continue otherwise the opening deadline would have to be postponed and her foreign guests would be "disappointed".

Offending legs and arms that were not completely buried by the cement were, allegedly, ordered to be chopped off and destroyed while the widows and families started assembling at the scene for an impromptu candlelight vigil which was to last for months.

All the foreign guests invited to the Opening Night had been assigned local "guides". I was allotted the Israeli actor Topol, fresh from his success in *Fiddler on the Roof*. Dutifully, I escorted him to various sights around Manila. But then, when the evening of the opening arrived, I was curiously excluded from the event.

"It was a bit strange," Topol told me afterward. "I was sitting there alone and there was an empty seat beside me which was probably meant for you."

Instead, Ben and I watched the opening on television. It was a surreal event. Cocteau himself could not have dreamt up a more grotesque one. Despite violent police attempts to remove the grieving families, the vigil outside defiantly continued. As men and women were forcibly removed, more arrived to take their place, a never-ending stream of wailing mourners.

Meanwhile I watched as minor celebrities from the United States and ex-royalty from Europe began arriving at the Center in their stretch limos, ignorant of the disaster and unaware of the grim reception committee that awaited them.

Despite last-minute threats and financial inducements by Imelda to the hostile workers to finish the building on time, the roof was incomplete on the opening night. And, despite the fact that the rainy season was long over, that particular night, of course, it chose to rain. Journalists huddled to keep dry outside as guests were ushered inside. Some seats that were exposed to the open roof were already soaked, but there was nothing Imelda could do. That night there was no let up. It seemed to us watching from the comfort of our homes that heaven was resolved to mourn its dead.

Imelda was, as usual, the last to arrive. On stage a chorus of hastily assembled patients from her Heart Centre began to sing as she entered the hall and swept down the aisle. They sang The Hallelujah Chorus from Handel's Messiah, "And he shall reign for ever and ever!" Except they replaced the word "he" with the word "she".

At the end of their song, to the disbelief of the audience, each one stepped off the stage, bared their chests and walked among the front rows of the stalls displaying vivid purple scars from recent heart operations. Shocked gasps were followed by an embarrassed silence. People didn't know which way to look. The emcee on stage proudly announced that these people had all received their operations at the new Imelda Romualdez Marcos Heart Centre.

At this point, of course, the audience was expected to burst into rapturous applause. But, by this time, the wailing from the mourners outside echoed eerily through the hall as rumours of the disaster began to spread. The bizarre ceremony on stage made the audience uneasy and most gave hasty excuses and left.

"This is the first and last time I will visit Manila," Topol joked to me afterward. "Once is definitely enough!"

Later in the year, Tony Bennett gave his first concert in the Philippines at the Cultural Center. Again, I was designated to act as one of his guides for the duration of his visit to the country. This time I was allowed to attend the performance. And, as a thank you for showing him around, Tony invited me onstage to sing *"I Left My Heart in San Francisco"* with him. At least now I can say I have something in common with Amy Winehouse, Billy Joel and Lady Gaga!

The following week, on a nostalgic visit back to the Indios Bravos Café, I found out it had been bought by a former Peace Corps volunteer and renamed The Hobbit House. It was staffed exclusively by dwarfs. Jim, the new owner, thought that being served by little people who had to mount ladders to wait on tables or climb on chairs to ring up bills on the cash register would be such a novelty that it would attract tourists in great numbers. To me it was a sick joke.

A visiting German documentary crew asked if they could film me in my old familiar garden, the courtyard behind Indios Bravos, where the "hobbits" now had their living quarters. In miniature squatters' huts, made from corrugated board and cardboard boxes the employees of the reinvented Indios Bravos Café lived, played and made love.

I spoke to some of them about the good old days, the days before the current curfew when friends had walked through the courtyard to climb the fire escape to my room for all night gossip sessions. I told them about the days when we were still allowed to sit around the centre table smoking pot until all hours discussing sex, politics and religion without being robbed of our rights, our freedoms and, in some cases, our lives. I told them about the days before the imposition of martial law.

It was about this time, too, that a friend of mine, Jun Gonzalez, an art restorer, told me he had just been invited to Malacanang Palace by Imelda to see a 12 X 12 foot painting by Holbein and would I like accompany him. I was curious. I had seen a wall-to-wall painting that had been started by Holbein and completed by his student, Rowland Lockey, in a stately home, Nostell Priory in Yorkshire, owned by an old friend Roland St. Oswald. It was a portrait of Sir Thomas Moore and his family. Roland was the direct descendant of Thomas Moore's daughter, Margaret.

"How on earth could Imelda have bought a Holbein?" I was incredulous. "Surely, the whole world would know when a Holbein had been purchased on the international art market? Where did it come from? Who sold it to her - or has she been duped - yet again?"

That was not all she owned, Jun told me. In her collection I would see Canalettos, Chagalls, El Grecos, Rubens, Rembrandts and Titians, to name just a few. When I returned to London later in the year, I called up the art critic, Brian Sewell, and told him, "Have I got a scoop for you!"

Brian listened as I described to him what I had seen with Jun. I had since found out that many of those paintings had been acquired for Imelda by an Italian friend of Princess Margaret, Mario D'Urso. I suggested Brian do a little more research because I knew, for a fact, than many of the paintings in her collection were fakes. It could be a big, big story.

Unfortunately, by then, Brian Sewell, had spent a couple of summers in the Philippines and had become firm friends with many of Imelda's "blue ladies". He was wined and dined there and was even planning to buy a property. His response to my "scoop" was derision. He told me, "It sounds like you have a chip on your shoulder about Mrs. Marcos."

"Not exactly," I replied, "It just irks me when she spends the Treasury's money, money that is supposed to be for the Filipino people, on paintings that aren't even authentic."

Sewell thanked me for my call and ended the conversation.

I would like to have seen the expression on his face in April 1986 when, on the front page of the *New York Times*, was a full page shocking revelation on *"Imelda's Collection of Fake Paintings"*.

Chapter 27
Payback Time

Within a month, I received a phone call from our former journalist friend, JV Cruz, the Philippines Ambassador. He informed me that Imee Marcos was coming through London with her husband, Tommy Manotoc.

"They're on a round the world tour," JV explained. "And they're here in London for a week. I have strict instructions from the President to look after them every day. And Imelda said I must not let them out of my sight."

I smiled at the thought of the once fierce critic of the Marcoses now becoming the Marcos family babysitter.

"Poor you!" I joked.

"I've arranged a week of parties, sightseeing and dinners for them but I am busy on Thursday evening. I just can't take care of them then. Could you and Ben take them off my hands just for that night, please?" JV was pleading now.

I told him I would think about it and let him know. Personally, after our last meeting on TV, I had absolutely no wish to entertain Imee. But rather than refusing outright, I replied I would ask Ben how he felt about it. Although Ben proved fairly easy to convince when I discussed it with him later, I was still extremely reluctant.

"Come on, Caroline," Ben coaxed me, "it won't be that bad."

So, very reluctantly I agreed. My brother-in-law, the film producer Elliott Kastner, had a new musical, *Marilyn*, about the life of Marilyn Monroe running at the Adelphi Theatre on the Strand so I reckoned I could invite Imee and Tommy to that. By going to the theatre I imagined, we could keep the conversation to a minimum thus avoiding dredging over old animosities. I called Elliott, explained the situation and he reserved some complimentary tickets at the box office for us. He suggested I call the manager of the theatre to warn him that I would be bringing the daughter of Ferdinand and Imelda Marcos.

The manager was extremely courteous and offered to make all the necessary security arrangements, take us into the private VIP bar during the interval and arrange for us to meet the actors backstage at the end of the show. I knew two of the main actors, Stephanie Lawrence, playing Marilyn and my former neighbour, Judith Bruce, playing Marilyn's mother, so I called them to say we would be dropping in after the performance. Everything was in place.

"Sorted", I thought.

I was almost looking forward to the evening. But how wrong I was. I should have known that nothing involving any member of the Marcos family is ever that simple.

I spoke to Imee the day before the event. I gave her the name and address of the Adelphi Theatre and told her exactly what time we should meet there. And, in order to avoid misunderstandings I asked her to write it all down.

"Everything's clear," she told me.

"And please make sure you're there ten minutes before curtain's up!" I said as politely as I could. And then, more pointedly, "Theatre always starts on time in England."

"Sure, no problem!" she replied and put the phone down.

At the allotted time, Ben, the theatre manager and I were waiting patiently in the lobby. Five, ten, fifteen minutes, half an hour passed and still no sign of Imee. Yet again, just as it always did in Manila, the theatre curtain was forced to wait for a member of the Marcos family.

As the audience inside began to hiss and boo, the red-faced manager could wait no longer. He gave the nod for the show to begin. My heart sank. I visualized Ben and me waiting in the lobby all night. I was indignant. This was discourteous not only to the management but also to the actors and the audience.

Finally, after what seemed like an eternity, seven stretch black limousines swept into view, coming to a screeching halt outside the theatre. Doors flung wide open and uniformed men, carrying machine guns, spilled out onto the pavement. I watched in horror as some of the armed minders rushed inside and others surrounded the perimeter, effecting a cordon sanitaire both inside and outside the theatre. And, then, once they decided the venue was safe, they snapped their fingers, whispered into their walkie-talkies and nodded the go-ahead for Imee and Tommy to emerge.

By this time people in the street had stopped dead in their tracks. They stared incredulously, probably wondering who on earth deserved such a massive security operation. I, too, couldn't believe my eyes. This was like finding myself in a cheap gangster movie. I couldn't help thinking that nobody in London would even recognize Imee Marcos, let alone care who she was or what happened to her. Nobody in London was ever likely to threaten her physical harm or kidnap her. Well, nobody that is, except, of course, her own parents who had already proved they were more than capable since they had managed to "kidnap" the hapless husband, Tommy Manotoc, following their daughter's hasty marriage to him. And all for the simple reason that Imelda didn't approve of him.

When the scared young man was finally "released" after a month in his secret mountain cave and when his supposed captors, the NPA Communist guerrillas, had been suitably "punished", Tommy emerged into daylight for the benefit of the television cameras looking healthier and more robust than he did before he "disappeared".

But nobody was about to drag Imee off the streets of London and hold her against her will. Nobody was about to make an attempt on her life. Nobody was going to hold her hostage. This was exhibitionism at its most vulgar. This was simply a very successful attempt at drawing attention to herself. And, whether it was her own idea of making a dramatic entrance or "Daddy's" orders for protecting his anointed heir, I never did find out.

By now the manager was at his wits' end. Armed guards were illegal in London and with them posted inside and outside the theatre so flagrantly he felt he was bound to get into serious trouble with the law.

"Can't you ask her to get rid of them?" he whispered to me, as Imee swept into the lobby.

"I doubt it," I replied, "the Marcoses are a law unto themselves. Nobody tells them what to do! That's tantamount to suicide where they come from!"

I greeted the newlyweds and introduced them to the manager. There were no apologies but then I didn't expect any.

There was more hissing and booing from the audience as we entered the auditorium in the middle of Scene 2 and blindly groped our way in the dark towards our seats in the front stalls. I cringed as people, making space for us to pass, were forced to stand up, dropping their bags, coats and boxes of chocolates, their seats swinging shut with loud thuds.

Feeling no guilt at all, Imee then whispered to me: "What's going on? What's the story so far?"

Trying to keep my voice as low as possible I whispered back. I could feel the glares in my direction as I explained the plot. I desperately wanted to leave, preferably in the dark, so no one could see me and point the finger.

In the interval, as promised, the manager led us around to the private bar. He offered us drinks and then left. I started to make small talk. Where had they visited, who had they met on their travels, that sort of thing.

I finally plucked up the courage to ask Imee the question that had really been on my lips. "Didn't you feel bad leaving your baby behind?"

"Oh, yes, I miss him terribly," Imee replied.

"Surely you could have brought him with you, I mean with a yaya (nanny) so you could still have gone out and enjoyed yourselves?"

"Yes, but Daddy wanted me to leave him. He thought it would be safer."

"But," I persisted, "I heard you were breastfeeding. Did you have to stop, just like that?"

I was really dying to know the answer to this. But, before Imee had a chance to reply, the composer Tim Rice and the actress Elaine Paige turned round to talk to us. More introductions and more pleasantries and then the bell rang and it was time to return to our seats.

When the play was over, I escorted Imee and Tommy backstage. Imee was at her sparkling best. She talked, she laughed and, like her mother, she turned on the charm. But, if I or the actors were hoping for an apology for her late arrival, we were destined to be disappointed.

Judith Bruce turned to me and whispered, "Well, Caroline, I've known you a long, long time but you always manage to surprise me with the people you know! Who on earth will you show up with next?"

Graciously, like a well-rehearsed politician, Imee made her excuses to leave. Ben and I walked her back to the lobby where the theatre manager was waiting for us. As soon as they spotted Imee the bodyguards sprang into action, raised their guns, swivelled their eyes to scan the lobby and the street outside and fell into step behind her. She shook hands with the manager, thanked him for his arrangements and made her way through the glass doors out onto the Strand.

The seven cars were waiting, engines revving. As she stepped into one of them, the minders piled themselves into the others and, with horns blaring and screeching tyres, they were off down the street. Ben and I stood, beleaguered, on the pavement. There had been no goodbyes for us, no thanks for arranging the evening and, despite the seven stretch limos, no offer of a lift home.

Later that same summer I found myself sitting on a sofa next to Imee's younger sister, Irene. She and her new husband, Greg Araneta, were visiting London on their honeymoon. I now had a perfect opportunity to ask Irene why Imee had left her baby, Ferdinand, at home.

"Daddy thought it was safer for him to stay in Manila," Irene replied.

"But I think I heard her saying she was still breastfeeding?" I said.

"Yes, she was." Irene sounded bored.

But I was intrigued. "How on earth did she continue to do that when she was travelling around Europe?"

Irene glanced at me as though I was stupid. "Simple, Caroline!" she laughed. "She just expressed her milk every day and then Daddy sent a Philippine Airlines plane to wherever she was and it would bring the milk back!"

Irene shrugged her shoulders as if to say – isn't that what every mother does when she's away from her newborn baby for several weeks?

Now I understood why all my friends had been complaining during that time that their Philippine Airlines flights to and from Europe had either been delayed or cancelled. The solution was obvious. The presidential dairy run was abducting the planes and flying Imee's precious breast milk back to Manila. This is when it really dawned on me that the Marcoses lived on a totally different planet to the rest of us.

Chapter 28
A Floundering Marriage

With three children, it was now imperative for us to have a regular income. Ben's income was intermittent and only helped support us when he had an exhibition. Also, our marriage was beginning to crumble, mainly due to his many affairs and the undeniable fact that he really missed living in the Philippines. He had loved being exposed to the museums, galleries and art shows that Europe had to offer. He loved wandering around the antique markets and attending auctions. He loved seeing all the arthouse movies, the type of movies that never got screened in Manila. But, underneath, he was desperately homesick. There was a burgeoning art scene happening in Manila and he, understandably, wanted to be a central part of it. And the longer he stayed in London, the more his own art became influenced by Filipino subjects. He wanted to return to his country for good.

The problem was I still wasn't prepared to live in a country under martial law where many of our friends had been imprisoned or "disappeared". Nor did I want our children to grow up as spoiled brats, like so many of our friends' children in Manila. And, unlike Ben, I did not want to live in a place where owning a firearm was necessary as a way to protect one's home and family. This was not how I wanted to live. And it became a constant source of contention between us.

The cracks in our marriage were becoming more obvious, not only to us as a family, but also to our friends. A fissure that no amount of glue or band-aids could conceal. And, when Ben returned to the Philippines for an exhibition in 1983 and stayed for over a year, that heralded the end. My mother had learned to tolerate long separations from my stepfather, Billy, and felt I should be able to do the same. But I was not so accepting as her. Unlike her, I was not brought up in a world where a husband's needs took precedence over a wife's needs. As a Catholic convert, she tried her hardest to dissuade me from leaving Ben.

"He's the father of your children," she told me. "You made your bed, you must lie in it."

And I thought to myself, well, that's rich, coming from you who left my father when you fell in love with Billy. But, at the same time, I knew what a sacrifice she had made to do that. So I remained silent.

"He's a good father," she persisted, still trying to convince me.

I couldn't argue with that. Ben had been a good father. And I knew he loved his children. But I always felt his art and his legacy came first. And although, as an artist, I understood how important that was, it was not how I expected it to be. To me, no matter what, our children should always come first.

Finally, in the summer of 1984, at the age of 40, just before Ben returned home from Manila, I started a brief holiday affair with a neighbour in Mallorca. When Ben arrived back I spoke to him about it. I thought, wrongly, that having had so many affairs himself he would be understanding. But, instead of discussing it rationally and finding a solution, he erupted. And I thought if there was this kind of anger within him, then there was little left worth salvaging in our marriage. He wasn't the only one to blame. I realized I had been so independent all my life, that I was probably not the easiest person to be married to. So Ben headed back to Manila again and I filed for divorce. In early 1986, I was granted a decree nisi at the Royal Courts of Justice in Fleet Street, on the grounds of an irretrievable breakdown.

And now I began my life as a single mother of three. The big question was, how would I earn money to support them? After a series of rejection letters, I was finally hired as a freelance researcher for the new TV station, Channel 4. My first assignment was looking into the medical applications of meditation. The programme was entitled *Leave Your Baggage at the Door*.

For the show I first interviewed a young Australian veterinarian, Ian Gawler, who had been dying from a very aggressive bone cancer. His oncologist advised him to meditate up to five hours a day. With the encouragement of his wife and young daughter, he followed this strict regime. And, miraculously, his cancer did disappear.

I interviewed a fifty-five year old woman who had developed an extreme case of agoraphobia in her early 30s and had never set foot outside her home since. When no medical or psychiatric treatments worked, she was advised by her local parish priest to try meditating for at least 2 hours a day. By the time, I interviewed her, she said she was almost ready to take her husband's hand, walk out of her front door and drive to the supermarket for the first time in more than twenty years.

I also spoke to a well-respected psychiatrist, Professor Ainslie Meares, who had shocked his peers by claiming a blend of hypnotism, mental homeostasis and meditation could cure most cancers. He advocated using an intense regime of all three alongside traditional treatments to get the most successful results. For this, he had been vilified by the medical establishment. But, the majority of his patients, had proved him right.

Now, with some knowledge on the subject, I was hired to research a documentary about the Cancer Care Centre in Bristol, whose healing regime for their advanced cancer patients included diet, meditation and lifestyle changes. All this got me thinking back to my days in Hong Kong. I reckoned Professor Nadir Khan, or whoever he actually was, would have been proud of me! By the end of my research, I probably knew a lot more about meditation than he did. I wonder what happened to him.

The British film company, Zenith, offered me a research job for a filmscript based on the Profumo affair which would be written by the successful comedy writing team of Laurence Marks and Maurice Gran. I never suspected it at the time, but this job would, once again, have long-term consequences on my life.

Chapter 29
It's Rita Again!

That same year, I received a phone call from Rita Gam in New York to say she would be coming to London as part of her worldwide campaign to encourage the Pope, John Paul II, to canonize her friend, Princess Grace of Monaco, who had died in 1982. Rita, at her most persuasive, was trying to convince me to join her efforts.

"You and your family knew Grace very well," Rita said, "you should really be part of this."

"I just don't have time, Rita," I said, "I'm a single mother of three and I've got a research job, remember?"

This was not my only reason. I hated to tell her that her plan was almost destined to fail. She refused to be discouraged, however. She asked if I knew any newspaper people in London who might help her publicize her campaign. I suggested my old friend from my Hong Kong days, Ian Black, who was now back in London working for the Daily Express. She thanked me profusely and said she would call him.

A few weeks later, Rita with three pieces of Luis Vuitton luggage in tow, arrived on my doorstep again. Wearing a hat and dress that perfectly matched the colour of the pink blossoms on the cherry tree in our driveway, she told me she had set up a meeting with Ian who, she gushed, appeared very interested to publicize her project.

The following morning Rita appeared at the breakfast table at 7am in full make-up, even though her appointment with Ian was not until 2pm. At that moment I was busy feeding Elisar, Mayumi and Jasmine, getting them ready for school and preparing their packed lunches. But, Rita being Rita, was oblivious to anyone else's time constraints.

She sat herself down, cleared the space in front of her and placed three hats on my French farmhouse table.

"Which one shall I wear?" she asked, making sure she got my attention by speaking uncharacteristically loudly. "The blue, the black or the red?"

"I don't know," I replied, hardly able to look up from smearing peanut butter on the slices of bread in front of me.

"But, look!" she said. "You know Ian, which one would he like best?"

"I haven't seen Ian in years," I said, which was true. "So I have no idea what his taste in millinery is. Choose the one you feel most comfortable in."

"But he will have a photographer there," she insisted, "so I need to look my best."

"Can we discuss this later, Rita?" I pleaded. "I have to finish these lunch boxes and get the kids to school in less than 10 minutes. And then I'm off to work!"

"I only need you to say which hat you like," she replied. "The blue with the veil, the black with the wide brim or the red pillbox?"

Without even looking up I said, "The red. It goes with your colouring."

Rita swooped up the hats, came over and hugged me.

"Thank you, you're a real friend."

In her long silk nightie she sashayed towards the door and then, as they do in so many movies, she stopped dramatically, looked back and said, "I am so excited to meet Ian. Do you think he'll like me?"

"I'm sure he will," I said. "What is there not to like?"

Well, I only found out later that day that when Rita had asked, "Will Ian like me?" what she actually meant was would he find her sexually attractive. I had absolutely no idea at the time that an English boyfriend was exactly what she was looking for.

Rita returned from the appointment excited and happy. The interview and photoshoot had gone so well that Ian had invited her out to dinner that night.

"I'm so grateful to you for introducing me to him," she gushed. "I think he's the one!"

"He's the one what?" I asked innocently.

"I really like him," she said. "And I think he really likes me!"

I didn't want to hurt her feelings and suggest Ian might just want to sleep with her, especially if she was throwing herself at him.

"I've got to change for dinner. What shall I wear?" She took my hand and dragged me upstairs to her room to choose something suitable.

"You know him," she said. "What do you think I should wear?"

She wanted me to go through her whole wardrobe but, with three young children waiting for their supper, I didn't have the time. I picked out a pale green chiffon dress and matching shoes.

"Green's his favourite colour," I lied, because I had no idea what Ian's favourite colour was. "Wear this one!"

An hour later she emerged from her room and found us downstairs in the kitchen eating supper.

She did a twirl and we all oohed and aahed.

"You look gorgeous, Rita!" I said. And I meant it. She did look gorgeous.

She gave me a hug. She was as excited as a teenager on a first date.

"If I don't come back tonight, you'll understand, won't you?" she asked.

"Of course," I said. "Have a great night!"

"I think this could be the start of something big," she said. "You know, I've always wanted to live in England!"

"Listen, I love you, Rita, but don't you think you're jumping the gun just a little bit?" I asked. "You've only just met him."

"But I have this strong feeling," she replied. "I just know he'll want me to come and live with him!"

That's when I began to feel really sorry for Rita. I think she honestly believed - no, she was such an innocent on so many levels, that I know she honestly believed she and Ian were going to set up house together and live happily ever after. As she closed the front door behind her, I wondered if Ian was aware of that.

Well, she didn't come back that night. Or the next night.

And when she did come back she was flushed and smiling. The date had obviously gone extremely well.

"I'm in love," she announced. "Totally in love!"

"That's wonderful, Rita. I'm so happy for you." And I was. But I also knew Ian, so I was skeptical.

The children were still at school and, since I didn't have any pressing research work scheduled, she sat me down to fill me in on the intimate details of her prolonged date.

"Have you spoken to him?" she asked. "What has he told you about me?"

"I haven't talked to him," I said.

"Oh, but you must. I want to know what he says about me. I think he really loves me!"

"Are you going to move in with him then?" I asked.

"I'm sure I will!" she said, "I told him I just need to return to New York first to sort out the apartment and to get all my things. You'll have to introduce me to people in London, of course. Do you know any actors? I need to look for stage or movie work here."

"I could probably introduce you to Glenda Jackson," I said, "Although she's giving up acting now and getting into politics so I'm not sure she'd be that helpful."

"But you work for a film company, Zenith, don't you? How about someone there?"

"I don't think I can do that, Rita. Besides, they make very English films. But I do have a couple of friends who have a rehearsal space and are putting on fringe productions, you may want to meet them."

"Please, please introduce me!" she said. "When can I meet them? Do they have a production on now?"

"I'll call them," I said. "I'm sure they'd love to meet you."

And so I introduced Rita to Charles and Christina. And it just so happened that they were in the planning stages of a production of *Macbeth* that was scheduled to be performed at the Tower Theatre in north London.

"Oh, Charles, I'd love to be in it," Rita gushed, "I'll be spending a lot of time in London from now on."

In fact the affair with Ian lasted less than a month. Rita cried real tears. And I was genuinely sorry for her. It was obvious to me then that she had really been smitten and had high hopes for a lasting relationship. But I had known Ian for many years and knew he was a loner by nature. And there was no way he would allow anyone, let alone a fading, though still beautiful, Hollywood movie actress, to share his life.

So then Rita turned her sights on Charles which was slightly awkward as she appeared to be blind to the fact that Charles was in a very happy marriage with Christina.

It was made all the more awkward by the fact that Charles and Christina had planned to cast themselves as the main characters but Rita automatically assumed that, by seniority and celebrity alone, she would automatically get the role of Lady Macbeth.

"Imagine," she said to me over dinner that night, "many more people would come to see the play with my name attached. I still have a following, you know!"

"I know that Rita," I said, "but this is Charles' and Christina's production. They are putting up their own money. So I think they are entitled to cast themselves."

"You will try to speak with Charles, won't you?" she asked. "If you talk to him maybe he'll listen."

"I'll sound him out but I can't really do much to persuade him."

So Rita's plans to find an English husband, move to London and resurrect her stage career were abandoned along with her campaign to elevate her best friend, Grace Kelly, to sainthood.

We kept in touch, of course. And I applauded her a few years later when her book, *Actress to Actress* was published. And then, towards the end of her life, I celebrated with her when she managed to get a major TV documentary series off the ground. Rita, I felt, had finally come of age.

Chapter 30
A Number One Best Seller

It didn't take long for Zenith to realize their film about the Profumo Scandal was never going to make it to the screen. Initially, I was upset, thinking that not only would all my hard work be going to waste, but I had also been looking forward to becoming a valuable part of the production team. Added to that, it meant I now had to look for another job.

In retrospect, of course, it was a blessing. Even while I was involved in the research, I had harboured genuine doubts about whether Lawrence Marks & Maurice Gran would do the story justice. My main reason being that, although I recognized them both as excellent writers, I was also aware they intended to turn it into an anti-Establishment farce, whereas I viewed it very much as a tragedy. But also, knowing how a screenplay completely condenses a story, I was convinced, too, most of the research I had taken such pains to uncover would have simply ended up discarded or ignored.

The real story of the "Profumo Scandal" had hit the national and international headlines in the early 1960s. It contained all the right ingredients for the thirsty tabloid papers – sex, politics, espionage, revenge and abandonment. The Minister for War, John Profumo, had been sleeping with a beautiful show girl, Christine Keeler, who had also been sharing her bed with a Russian Intelligence officer, Yevgeny Ivanov, assigned to the Russian Embassy in London.

At the centre of this trio was a social butterfly, the osteopath, Stephen Ward. Ward was a man who befriended people from all walks of life, the down and outs and the rich and famous, many of the latter also being his patients. Ward claimed to have been recruited by MI5 and, through his friendship with Ivanov, had been asked by them to act as a go-between between the Russians and the British government. This was at the height of the Cold War, during the Cuban Missile Crisis, and things started to go disastrously wrong. John Profumo lied to Parliament about his affair and was forced to resign. The government was about to fall. And the Prime Minister, Harold Macmillan, needed someone to blame.

So, for the first time ever, the government, the police, the Security Services and the Establishment decided on one victim, Stephen Ward. They denied he ever worked for MI5. They claimed he was a fantasist and they arrested him for living off immoral earnings. On the day of his sentencing, after his friends from all walks of life had abandoned or disowned him, Ward had committed suicide.

That was the story as it was written in 1963. Twenty-five years later, when I conducted my research, I found many of Ward's former friends, both rich and poor, from Peers to prostitutes, whose lips had been sealed until then, who decided to speak out. The story I began to glean differed dramatically from the contemporaneous one. Politicians, members of the Metropolitan police team, Ward's defense counsel, the MI5 officer who recruited Ward, friends of Ward's from his early years and up until his death, spoke to me openly, happy to finally have the chance to assuage their guilt for having deserted him at the time.

From his good friend, Pelham Pound, who I visited in his house in Lincolnshire, I was given reel to reel tapes with Ward speaking from jail about his life, the betrayal by his friends and his terrible predicament. Ward stated that if he was found not guilty on the current charges, the police were holding over other, more serious charges. Ward instinctively knew he would end up in jail for a long, long time. And, for a free spirit such as him, this thought was intolerable.

"I've kept these tapes for the past 25 years," Pound told me, "in the vague hope that someone like you, one day, would try to find out the truth."

Instinctively, I knew I had a gripping story to tell. But then the question was, who could tell it? There was only one person who stood out to me at the time – David Yallop, a former investigative journalist and the author of several best-selling non-fiction books, such as *To Encourage the Others*, *The Day the Laughter Stopped* and *Beyond Reasonable Doubt*.

I didn't know David personally. But I was determined to meet him. So I called his publisher to find out the name of his literary agent. I was given the name and address of Jenne Casseroto. I then called Jenne asking her if David would possibly consider reading all the notes and transcripts of my interviews and listening to the Ward tapes.

"This is a story that must be told," I said. "And I really would love David to write it."

Intrigued, Jenne must have passed on the message immediately. Because, within a day, I received a phone call from David asking me to visit him and bring all my research materials with me.

I remember David's first words, as he and his wife Anna, greeted me that night at the door of their home in Wood Green.

"If the material is half as good as you say it is, this story will be dynamite!"

We then all sat on the floor. I spread all the pages of handwritten and typed notes around us, handed him a tape recorder with the Ward tapes and he switched it on. I could see from their expressions that both David and Anna were absolutely shaken to the core, as I had been, by hearing Ward's distinctive voice for the very first time.

"Listen," David said, "I would love to write it. But I am already behind on my book, *In God's Name* which I was supposed to deliver last month. But your Ward story must be told. And you must write it!"

I had published lots of articles over the previous two decades and, although I had received a contract from Heinemann's to write a book about my earlier travels, I had never actually written that or any other book. I simply didn't have the confidence to do this one justice. And I told him so.

"I don't feel up to it! It really needs a professional like you," I said.

"Nonsense!" David retaliated. "You can do it. I will be there to help you!"

We continued going through the documents and tapes of other interviews. And, by the end of a very long evening, David announced, "Tomorrow, I am going to take you to my publisher Tom Maschler, of Jonathan Cape, and you can show him exactly what you've shown me tonight. He will absolutely love it, I promise you!"

Amazingly, David kept his word. The very next day David and I were sitting in Tom Maschler's office and showing him all my material. And, as David had rightly predicted, Tom immediately fell for it.

"I love it!" he declared. "I want to publish it. I will publish it!"

"And Caroline will write it," David beamed at me. "Won't you?"

I was nervous as hell. Tom's reputation as a maverick and a visionary in publishing was already legendary. I had no pedigree as a writer. And Tom knew it. He looked at me from across his desk.

"You can write it if you want," he said gently, "and I will publish it. It will sell maybe around 4000, 5000 copies. But, if you really want a blockbuster bestseller, and I know that is what it can be, then I suggest we find someone else to write it. Someone with a name and reputation. And it won't be David because he has to finish his current book."

"I agree," I said. "And I don't mind even if I am not credited at all. I just want someone to do Stephen Ward justice. I want his story to be told."

"Good." Tom pounded his desk in excitement. "We have a deal. I'll get on to it straightaway and get back to you as soon as I can."

And Tom was as good as his word. He selected the very well-respected Sunday Times investigative journalist and author of several best-selling books, Phillip

Knightley. Within a week Phillip and I were both sitting in Tom's office being introduced.

I insisted on handing over all the material to Phillip. But, being a gentleman, he said, "You are going to write this with me, Caroline. There is no way I am taking this entirely off your hands. You write very well and there is no reason you shouldn't write some of the chapters."

Tom gave his consent to this arrangement.

So, for the next few months, Phillip and I were in daily contact. I took him to interview some of the people I had already talked to so they could confirm their stories to him. And, since he was an expert in politics and the Intelligence world, he offered to write the more serious chapters of the book, leaving the more frivolous ones about Ward's personal and social life to me.

Once it was completed and we had submitted it to Tom, I took myself off on a gentle trip up the Nile, in preparation for the coming publicity assault and the many TV and radio interviews that, Tom warned me, would follow the book's publication.

Once word got out that this story was about to be published and that Phillip and I were ready to point fingers at those who had behaved maliciously at the time, we started getting threats from various people who wanted to place an injunction on the book. But they were up against Tom Maschler, who was known in the publishing world as, not only as a maverick but also as a crusader and a fighter. And he fought on our behalf and won.

Around this time, too, I sensed my phone was being tapped. Two of the good friends I had made during my research were "Lucky" Gordon, a former black lover of Christine Keeler, and Frank Critchlow, a well-known black activist and the owner of the famous Mangrove Café in Notting Hill where Stephen Ward had often visited with Christine. A couple of times when I spoke to them over the phone, we heard ominous clicks on the line.

"Did you hear that?" I asked Lucky, when he called one day to invite me and my children to dinner at Island Records, in Notting Hill, where he was currently working as a chef.

Lucky laughed. "I sure did! It's familiar. It happened before, during that time, you know. They always kept tabs on me!"

Frank said the same. "They always like to know who I'm talking to. But maybe this time they want to know who you're talking to!"

The book was published in May 1987 and serialized in the Sunday Times, over the following four weeks. And, within a week of publication, it became the number one best-seller.

I remember the thrill of sitting on a bus and seeing a couple of people near me avidly reading the Sunday Times serialization. I remember sitting in my car on my way to picking up Mayumi from one of her modelling assignments and, when stopping at a traffic light, seeing the driver in the car next to me, reading my book while he waited for the light to change. And I remember walking into the bookstores of Harrods, Selfridges and Hatchards and finding our book displayed there in the centre of each store on the top of their pyramid of best-selling books.

And, since, Phillip had a day job as a Sunday Times investigative journalist, he left it to me to do most of the numerous radio and TV interviews to publicize our findings that, far from being the bad guy, Ward was, in fact, a victim of extreme malice by the Macmillan government, the Metropolitan Police and the Security Services. I was interviewed by Jeremy Paxman on Newsnight, by Ann Diamond on GMTV and by Kirsty Walk on BBC Breakfast Time, among many others.

I was invited by Cunard Lines to give two lectures on board the QE2 on a transatlantic crossing from Southampton to New York. One, of course, was about the Profumo Scandal and the framing of Stephen Ward. And the other was on my other favourite topic, the Marcoses and the Missing Filipino Millions. Both lectures were fully attended and ended up with standing room only. Even the Filipino crew members took time off to listen to the lecture on the Marcoses and I got a standing ovation each time. On the main deck, later, I signed copies of the book and sold them all.

One elderly lady came up to me, saying, "My family and I are great fans of your family."

Before I had a chance to correct her, knowing she had mistaken me for the daughter of John F Kennedy, who was also called Caroline, she continued, "My husband and I had been saving up for this cruise for years. He died a few weeks back. I wasn't going to come on this trip without him but my children insisted I should go. I am so happy now that I did because I have met you. Please can I have a photograph with you?"

She seemed close to tears. And I was about to tell her I wasn't JFK's daughter. But my friend, who was travelling with me who also happened to be a psychotherapist, whispered, "Don't disappoint her. You will ruin her cruise. Just go along with it."

Unfortunately, I allowed myself to be persuaded and kept up the charade. I signed the book for her, had a photograph taken with her and wished her happiness. I just hated to think once she returned home, had her photos developed and proudly displayed them to her children, they would tell her, "But that's not the real Caroline Kennedy!" I felt like a complete jerk.

From the moment the book was published, it became the "definitive" authority on the subject of what had become known as "the Profumo Scandal", the story that just refused to die. The book was quoted again and again over the next 25 years, in newspapers, books, TV programmes and even in Parliament.

And, in 2013, it became the basis for a musical by Andrew Lloyd-Weber, entitled *Stephen Ward*. Lloyd-Weber told me he had been so affected after reading our book that he couldn't let go of the subject. He even spearheaded a campaign with the respected human rights barrister, Geoffrey Robinson QC, to obtain a posthumous pardon for Stephen Ward. Robinson's 195 page brief, liberally quoted from our book to prove their case. Sadly, the Ministry of Justice in David Cameron's Conservative government refused, yet again, to allow the Cabinet Papers surrounding the Profumo Scandal to be unsealed, thus making it impossible for the pardon case to move forward.

In September 2021, Tom Mangold, who had been a young reporter on the Daily Express covering the Ward trial in 1963, presented a BBC Panorama Special to accompany a dramatized film about the perjury trial of Christine Keeler.

Tom interviewed me about the very crucial secret meeting, my research had uncovered, between Macmillan's Home Secretary, Henry Brooke, the head of the Metropolitan Police Force, Sir Joseph Simpson and the Director of MI5, Sir Roger Hollis, where they had all decided to publicly deny that Stephen Ward had ever been recruited by the Security Services and that the police would do their utmost to find some charge against him in order to silence him. This was the crux of our story, the very heart of the malevolent plot to go out and "get Ward", by whatever means possible. This meeting, which we revealed for the very first time in our book, had sealed Ward's fate.

Chapter 31
The War in Dubrovnik

Now, thanks to the publication of the book, I had a little income of my own. Until then, because I was receiving no alimony or child support from Ben, my mother had generously been helping me and the children financially, even paying for their private school fees.

At age 18, Elisar had just taken his "A" levels, was about to leave St. Paul's and was planning his future as a film director. Mayumi and Jasmine were both still at boarding school in Wiltshire. In the holidays Mayumi was pursuing her modelling career with Models One. The three of them had been very patient and understanding while I was driving around the country and, even, travelling abroad, researching the book so I decided it was time to indulge them a bit.

My stepfather, Billy, had died a few months before the book came out. Although I was obviously very saddened at his passing, I thought it was probably a blessing since I was very much aware the book would have acutely embarrassed him by accusing his friends and colleagues in Macmillan's government of wrongdoing and, by their misdeeds, had driven Stephen Ward to suicide. Two of Billy's best friends had been Harold Macmillan's son, Maurice, and his son-in-law, Julian Amery which, I realized, would have put Billy in a very awkward situation.

In his Will, Billy left me a bit of money that was enough to take Elisar, Mayumi and Jasmine on safari in Kenya. And, since he had been such a wanderer all his life, I thought it was the perfect way to remember him. A year or so later, I took them to India and Nepal. I was happy to finally have the chance to expand their horizons and show them places I had already visited but which now gave me the opportunity to see them again through their young eyes.

In 1991, I began researching a screenplay with my friend, Ulla, about a young man, named Varian Fry, who was sent to France during World War 11, by the American Friends of German Freedom, to rescue writers, artists, sculptors, philosophers and musicians from the Vichy French. Fry was given a list of 200 names and he ended up rescuing over 2000 people, walking them across the Pyrenees, to freedom and, from there, into the United States.

Ulla and I travelled to France to see the escape route for ourselves and to interview any of those participants who were still alive who had helped Fry in his clandestine work. We bought the rights to Fry's story from his widow who, two years later, invited us to the opening to the Holocaust Museum in Washington DC because it had a room dedicated to the incredible work Fry had done.

Some of the more well-known people Fry had saved were Alma Mahler, Franz Werfel, Hannah Arendt, Marc Chagall, Heinrich Mann, Andre Breton, Wanda Landowska, Jacques Lipchitz, Claude Levi-Strauss, Andre Masson, Max Ernst and Marcel Duchamp. He also saved Nobel Prize-Winning chemists, mathematicians and scientists. We entitled our screenplay, *Are There Cows in America?* as that was the first thing that Chagall asked when Fry advised him that it was too dangerous for him to stay in France and that he must leave immediately for the United States.

Later that year, on October 23rd 1991, I watched the television news report a fierce attack on the town of Dubrovnik on the Dalmatian Coast. Dubrovnik was a town I knew quite well. My mother was from there and I had visited the beautiful 16th century walled city several times. The Bosnian War had started in April but it was only now when I realized Dubrovnik could be totally destroyed, that I really became aware of how serious this conflict was about to become.

At first the camera showed a distant view of the this beautiful, medieval city, clouds of dust and smoke rising above its terracotta rooftops, towers and turrets. Then I watched as the camera zoomed in on a nearby street of half-ruined houses and of soldiers carefully picking their way through the debris.

If it had been some unfamiliar city, it would have been unlikely to set my pulse racing. But this shook me to my core. And, when the camera closed in on a little house with two smoldering black windows I felt as though I had been punched in the stomach. I recognized the house next door to it. I had been to that house just a few summers before. This day was a particularly fine day and the burned shell of this ruined house stood outlined against a deep blue autumn sky. It was not just anyone's house that lay there in smoldering ruins. It was the next door neighbor of someone I knew. That moment was like an epiphany to me. It sent a rush of cold blood through my veins. It touched a raw nerve and made me think I must do something to help the victims of this particular conflict. I must somehow get involved.

A little further on, in front of the house, the television camera panned in on a child's swing, its empty seat banging monotonously against the tree to which it was attached. I felt panic rising up in my throat. My imagination ran wild. Instantly, I could visualize a child, only a short time ago, sitting there, laughing, looking up at the sky, legs dangling. And I could imagine the mother, a baby in her arms, perhaps, at the door of her house watching, smiling. And, as she turned her head away the bomb had dropped, her child had screamed, and then there was a terrible silence. She and the baby had died where they stood. No time to hug her child. No time to call her husband's name. No time for goodbyes. I tried to delete the image from my mind. I felt sick.

On that same day in North London, a former Canadian fashion model, Gill Silvester, was also watching the news report. And, in the leafy south London suburb of Esher, a former emergency nurse, Shirley Ludlow was glued to her television set too.

We didn't know each other then. But we discovered later that we all had personal memories of holidays in Dubrovnik and agreed that the news reports about the attack on the city had shocked us into action. We were appalled that not only had war come to our doorstep in Europe but it had come to a place we all knew and loved. And the three of us, at the same time, in different parts of London, had decided we had to do something about it, become involved, help in whatever way we could.

Gill immediately set up a small charity, Brit-Aid, to bring supplies down to Jugoslavia. Shirley and I, independently, looked for convoys we could join to provide medical, sanitary and food supplies to the hospitals, refugee camps and orphanages.

At the same time, in Peacehaven, on the south coast of Britain, a former charity shop worker, Mick Roberts, was thinking he could put his three vans to good use by filling them with necessary supplies and driving them down to Croatia. He just had to find some drivers.

On LBC Radio that same night, an emergency call went out for drivers for a convoy leaving in a week's time. I decided I would phone the number the next morning. Shirley had heard the same emergency call and phoned straightaway. She got a place on the convoy. I did not. Not to be deterred, I scoured newspapers for information about other convoys and read about an organization named Crisis Support, run by a former ambulance driver and charity worker, Mick Roberts from Peacehaven, that was looking for drivers. Not wanting to miss out this time, I hurried down to the south coast to meet up with Mick.

Looking back, I realize I was probably a bit too eager, too fearful of missing out on this opportunity. So, from the outset, I failed to notice the warning signals. On the surface, Mick appeared to be an unassuming man, in his fifties, with dyed black hair, bushy black eyebrows, and a quick smile. He talked a lot about his previous seventeen years of charity work and, instead of asking him for references, I took him at his word. It never occurred to me that someone who had been involved in charity work for so long would be in it for entirely the wrong reasons. Naively, I believed that, like me, he genuinely wanted to help people.

So, although never having driven a truck before, I agreed to be one of Mick's drivers. And we made plans to leave in early December. That gave me time to collect clothes, shoes, non-perishable food, sanitary supplies, toys and medicines. An American friend, Virginia Schultz, offered to accompany me as my co-driver. A week before we were due to leave, one of Mick's young associates, Andy, drove up to London to collect everything Virginia and I had assembled. We boxed and labelled all the items and loaded them onto Andy's truck.

Then, at dawn on December 12th, Virginia and I drove down to Peacehaven. Mick and Andy were already busy sorting out all the boxes and packing them into the three vans. Finally, all was ready and we set off on our first convoy.

My mother's younger half-brother, Marco, who was working as an interpreter for the UN in Rijeka, had put together a list for us of hospitals, orphanages, rehabilitation centres and refugee camps that needed help. The number one camp on the list was Culineca, an unauthorized camp on the outskirts of Zagreb, the capital of Croatia. There were, apparently, approximately 6500 people living there with no clean water, no electricity, no cooking facilities, no sanitation and no medical support. And, although a small improvised clinic had been set up by the time we arrived, there appeared to be no one in charge. According to our interpreter, typhoid, hepatitis, head lice, scurvy, respiratory and intestinal ailments were rampant, not to mention untreated cancers, kidney diseases, heart conditions and diabetes.

It was chaotic. As soon as our trucks came to a stop, we were surrounded by people desperate for help. It was very much a case of each one for himself, with the stronger ones pushing their way to the front. With the help of an interpreter, we asked the refugees to form a line. Again, the weaker ones were pushed to the back by the able-bodied ones. I was determined, though, that those unable to come to the front, did not miss out on the boxes of food, clothing and sanitary supplies. So while Mick and Andy, handed out boxes at the front of the line, Virginia and I drove our van to the rear and started handing our supplies to the weaker ones.

Standing alone, I saw a young Muslim girl who appeared to be in shock. I asked our interpreter to approach her and ask her name.

"She says her name is Merima," the interpreter told me. "And she is all alone."

Slowly, the interpreter managed to coax Merima into telling us her story. The young girl was suspicious and hesitant at first. But, once she started, the full story emerged.

"I was naughty that day", she began, dabbing her eyes with her sleeve, "I was wrong and now I shall never be able to tell my mother I'm sorry. I came home from school so late. I stayed behind to play with my friends. I arrived home about dinner time. It was winter. It was dark. I couldn't see anything. I couldn't see my house. I didn't know what to do. But then someone grabbed me, told me to run with them.

Told me there were trucks leaving, that we had to get on them. There was no time to look for my family They told me the mosque had received a direct hit. The mosque was right next to my house. They had seen my father come out of the house. They had seen him fall. And that was it."

A couple of months prior to this, Merima said, her two older brothers and her father had been rounded up and taken to Tronopolje, one of the worst of the Serb concentration camps where her mother heard they had been subjected to the most brutal torture. Nothing more had been heard from her brothers. But her father, who had been suffering serious health issues on top of his torture, had been released by his Serb captors in a rare display of compassion.

"We were very happy to see him alive," Merima continued. "But then, a week later the bomb dropped."

That had been 18 months ago and, since then, Merima had been transferred from one refugee camp to another, finally ending up at Culineca.

"I don't know anything about my parents," she said. "Maybe they are alive. Maybe dead. Maybe in another camp. Maybe with relatives in Slovenia. I don't know." Merima was sobbing loudly now.

I wanted to hug her. But I felt she still regarded me with suspicion. Her story had touched me deeply. I was determined to find out where her parents were. Since Marco, was working with the UN, I thought there was a possibility he could trace them for me. I also knew I could make contact with Muslim refugee organizations in the UK and other parts of Europe who might have some news of them. I managed to persuade Merima to lend me the only mementos of her family she possessed - some small faded photographs she kept in her purse. I told her it was a long shot but I was committed to giving it a try.

The following day, I visited some of the main aid agencies in Croatia. I gave them her parents' names, told them Merima's story and showed them her photographs. One by one, they all shook their heads.

On my return home I was given the name of a contact working for Islamic Relief Worldwide, an organization based in Birmingham that, I was told, had been arranging mercy flights for severely injured Bosnian Muslims to receive medical treatment in the U.K. This was even more of a long shot. But God or Allah must have been on my side that day. Someone there recognized the family name. They were fairly convinced that Merima's father had been flown on a Medivac flight to the UK for emergency treatment. I couldn't breathe. I mean, what if her parents were actually in England?

I waited for what seemed like an eternity as files were scrutinized and names and photographs were cross-referenced. Finally positive identification was made and a driver for Islamic Relief chauffeured me to the General Hospital in High

Wycombe, an hour north of London. There I found Merima's father, still a very sick man, with her mother and younger sister at his bedside. Then came the problem. *How was I to break the news to them?* In the back of the car on the way to the hospital I had rehearsed again and again what I planned to say to them but now, faced with delivering the message that Merima was still alive, I was struck dumb.

In the end I couldn't seem to find the right words so I simply hugged Merima's mother and pressed photographs I had taken of her lost daughter into her hand. With tears in my eyes I made a rash promise, a promise I doubted I could fulfill, a promise I knew I would instantly regret. I promised her I would return to the refugee camp and bring Merima back to the UK with me.

Eight weeks later I arrived at Culineca. I was horrified by what I saw. The place now resembled a bomb site. I was told the camp had been declared a health hazard by the government, and just the day before I arrived it had been razed to the ground by bulldozers. The refugees had all been rounded up, loaded onto trucks and transported, yet again, to various other camps around Croatia. I panicked. *Oh, my god, what if Merima was lost? What if I couldn't find her? What would I tell her parents?* I couldn't bear to think about it. Amid the rubble, I sat down and shed tears of utter despair.

But, suddenly, as if by some miracle, there she was standing right in front of me, a mere child but one of the handful of refugees who had stubbornly refused to leave. I rushed towards her shouting the good news as though she could understand. She threw her arms around me sobbing. I handed her a letter from her parents and a postcard of a bright red London bus from her sister.

Through the interpreter I explained that, in order to be reunited with them, she would have to travel with me through seven countries and seven borders and I only had a copy of her parents' papers and a letter from Islamic Relief Worldwide to get her through. I told her there could be very serious problems. We could well be turned back at any one of those borders. And, even if we did manage to pass through 6 countries successfully, it would be very likely that, at the final border, she would be refused entry into the UK.

I told Mick that Merima would be coming back to England with us in the back of my van. I was nervous about what his reaction would be. I was beginning to have my doubts about him. He had been behaving very erratically on this convoy, losing his temper with everyone, even the refugees, and seemingly unwilling to part with some of the medications we had brought for the hospitals. However, I decided it was not the right time to confront him. I would leave that until we were back in the UK. His response when I told him my plans about bringing Merima to the UK with me was shocking.

"She smells. You'll have to put up with that all the way home."

Merima had never travelled out of Jugoslavia before in her life. She was very car sick, terribly frightened and eerily silent the whole way. She knew so little about me and I realized it must have crossed her mind more than once that I could be kidnapping her. We had no interpreter on the journey home so all I could do was hug her, squeeze her hand and smile reassuringly despite the dreadful, lingering fear we would not succeed.

The British border was the one I feared most and, by the time we reached there, I had decided the only thing to do, if we were to have any chance at all, was to smuggle Merima through. At this final stage I could not risk her being interrogated by some unfriendly immigration officer and turned away because of her lack of papers. So, as we climbed into our truck after crossing the English Channel, I hid Merima under a pile of sleeping bags in the back. In sign language I told her to keep completely still, absolutely silent. I then held my breath as we approached immigration.

Fortune again was on our side. The officers on duty asked a few simple questions but failed to search the back of the truck and waved us through. Again, I hardly dared breathe. I felt the sweat pouring down the back of my neck. All I could think of was what if we had been caught. Merima would have been returned immediately to Croatia and I probably would have ended up in jail.

But we had made it, the final hurdle. A few miles down the road, when I was sure the coast was clear, I called Merima to emerge from her hiding place.

"We are going to find your Mummy now," I said, hugging her as she clambered over the seat to join me in the front. I think she understood me for this was the very first time I had ever seen her smile.

Finally, two hours later, on the concrete steps outside number 48 Dersingham Road in High Wycombe Merima and her family had a tearful reunion. Merima's first words to her mother were: "I'm sorry".

Merima and I had both been extraordinarily lucky. On an illegal operation such as this any amount of things could have gone disastrously wrong. But it helped that she was a very trusting and very brave young girl.

Chapter 32
The Stalker

By this time, I had met up and discussed future plans with Gill and Shirley. They had also met Mick Roberts and Gill had suggested to him combining the efforts of Crisis Support and Brit-Aid. It was to be an unfortunate collaboration. Although none of us had, as yet, any hint of the devastating trouble we would face around the corner.

In the honeymoon period, everything appeared fine, on the surface. But, as I said, I began to have my doubts on our second convoy. I relayed my concerns to Gill and Shirley. I told them supplies had gone missing. But Mick always had a plausible excuse. I told them his methods of accountancy, too, were very erratic and had become a source of serious concern. But, again, he always managed to explain them away. Although, we had received some clues as to his behavioural problems from Andy, we underestimated just how serious those problems were and how they would affect his subsequent conduct. It all finally came to a head when he lashed out violently at one of our younger volunteers. From that moment on, the three of us decided we would disassociate ourselves from him entirely.

We started to make enquiries about his background, something we should have done at the outset. What we found out was, frankly, frightening. It turned out he had been in and out of borstal and prison since the age of 9. He had several aliases. And we discovered that many of the supplies we had gathered for the refugees were ending up in a bogus charity shop in North London and he was pocketing the proceeds. We learned that from Andy and another of Mick's young associates. But there was much, much more that we would learn later.

We suggested to Mick that he remove himself from charity work altogether and, if he failed to do so, we would have no alternative but to report him to the police and to the Charities Commission. We thought we had offered him the kindest option.

But, after telling us all to go to hell, Mick proceeded with a vendetta that showed no signs of ever abating. On the contrary, over the following two years the vehemence and vengeance with which he conducted it only increased alarmingly.

After a lifetime of exemplary behaviour, of never having broken the law, of always having been a 'model citizen', I was suddenly accused by Mick of being a "drug smuggler", a "gun runner", a "black marketeer", a "blackmailer" and a "Serbian spy". On top of these allegations, I received countless death threats on my answering machine, nuisance visits in the middle of the night and a seemingly endless stream of vitriolic letters and faxes addressed to me, to Gill and Shirley, to my friends, to newspaper editors, politicians and the police.

And that was not all. I was, according to Mick's letters, "being investigated by Special Branch, MI5 and Scotland Yard, being interrogated by the FBI for 'drug-related' dealings, that my children were all confirmed 'drug addicts' and that I should be 'immediately arrested for my past and future crimes." My life turned into a living nightmare. And there appeared to be absolutely nothing I, or anyone else, could do about it.

At the same time, Gill, Shirley and I were raising funds to set up a rehabilitation centre at Makarska on the Dalmatian coast for children from all sides of the conflict. Our "Children's Village" project had got to the point where the United Nations High Commission for Refugees (UNHCR), the Croatian government and the Variety Clubs International were supporting it and it had been designated a "priority medical need" for former Jugoslavia by the World Health Organization (WHO).

And yet, Mick was doing all he could to sabotage the project and to blacken our names. And there was still nothing we could do to prevent it. In 1992 there was no law that could protect us from his dangerous vitriol.

Police, politicians and lawyers alike told us that, unfortunately, he was so obsessed by us that we would probably never get rid of him entirely. Taking him to court, the lawyers said, would not work, because he was "so unhinged" that no lawyer would agree to represent him. He would have to represent himself and he would ramble on for days in court. He would get legal aid. But, we, as a charity, would not. We would definitely win but we would not get any compensation because he didn't have any money. And, thus, we would be left with substantial lawyers' fees to pay and nothing to show for it. And, most importantly, even if he was found guilty and with the risk of imprisonment, the lawyers said, it would probably not stop him from continuing his campaign anonymously.

His aim was to destroy Brit-Aid completely and to destroy me personally, since I had been the highest profile representative for the group and, as such, I felt responsible to safeguard the funds and supplies that had been raised through all our friends and contacts. When we decided to confront him, therefore, I volunteered to be the spokesperson. This turned out to be a mistake, because I had no husband to confront the bully, whereas Gill and Shirley were both married to men more than willing to defend their wives.

From that moment on, Mick conducted a campaign of slander, harassment and death threats against me personally. At 3am I would be woken by the telephone, either there would be nobody there or a menacing voice would whisper,

"I'm going to get you, you evil lady, just you wait!"

This might appear amusing in retrospect but, at the time, it was both sinister and very threatening. I then turned off the telephone so it didn't ring beside my bed. In the morning, I would play back the messages,

"I'm going to come and cut you into fucking pieces, you fucking bitch!"

Sometimes there would be up to 11 calls in 24 hours. When I was not at home, my children were also harassed by these threats. During the night, too, our doorbell would ring and a taxi driver, a pizza delivery man or a glass salesman would be standing on our doorstep telling me I'd ordered a cab, a pizza or an emergency replacement window pane!

Again, the police seemed powerless to act. This is just one more instance, they would moan, about the law in England designed to protect the perpetrator and not the victim. The only reassurance I received from them was that, "People who threaten other people's lives, rarely carry out that threat."

The police did, however, give me a special 'crime number' to dial just in case Mick showed up in person on my doorstep. By that time, however, he had changed his course of action. He got his friends or family members, to pretend they were supporters of our charity and to call us up to ask about our future plans. In this way, he was kept informed as to when our convoys were leaving, what fundraising events we had planned and the names of our supporters. On one occasion, our vehicles were searched at Ramsgate by the Customs on a "tip-off" that we were carrying "illegal drugs". Naturally, nothing was found and, after several hours of being wrongfully detained, our drivers were invited to tea with the Customs officials who, although they said they were not obliged to do so, apologized profusely.

Mick also sent the police around to Gill's Brit-Aid office on several occasions to interview her about "stolen funds" and "stolen vehicles". Each time the police left satisfied there was no substance in his allegations. This did not deter him. He simply went to another police station and lodged the same complaints but without informing them of his previous unsuccessful attempts. Yet, not one police officer cautioned him for wasting valuable police time, even though they all agreed that was precisely what he was doing.

Meanwhile, we remained committed to our cause and our convoys continued unabated. And Mick, who had surreptitiously found out what dates we were leaving, arranged to leave on the same date every time and tagged along behind us. A Jugoslav friend of mine, Ivana Stancomb, who was married to a British TV reporter, called me up one day.

"Caroline, the hospital in Zadar, my home town, desperately needs more incubators for their premature babies! Because of the stress of the war, the mothers are going into labour early. Please, if you can do anything, I would be so happy!"

On a previous trip the year before, we had delivered one incubator to the hospital, much to the delight of its medical director, Dr Martin Mikecin. Now, on our second visit to Zadar, and thanks to Shirley's medical contacts, we were given two more incubators, some battery/mains operated theatre lamps, anesthetics, intravenous antibiotics, heart monitors, ECG machines and a great deal of surgical and sanitary equipment that we could donate.

This time, my son, Elisar, accompanied us to film the work we were doing. And my co-driver was another young film-maker, Sonja Phillips, who I had known since she was sixteen. Despite their youth, both Elisar and Sonja, convinced me that they wanted to see the situation in Croatia for themselves. Elisar wanted to make a film about my work. And Sonja was keen to make a short documentary film on the effects of the war on the women and children.

On this second trip to the Zadar hospital we arrived at a time of great confusion. Ten minutes earlier a shell had hit the house directly opposite the hospital, across the street from the ward we would be staying in. People were screaming hysterically. Confused, panic-stricken and traumatized, they were rushing in all directions unable to predict where the next bomb would fall.

"What's happening?" I asked our interpreter.

"For the past 12 months, Zadar has been shelled like this on a daily basis," she replied. "When the panic is over, everyone is very calm and philosophical. But, when the bombs are falling" she grabbed my arm and choked back the tears, "we are terrified."

I nodded. "I've seen the same fear in Dubrovnik," I said.

"The hospital, airport and bridges are the main targets," she continued. "But many bombs go astray".

When I spoke to Dr. Mikecin later, he told me. "The bombs are devised to cause the most panic. Life during the shelling can never be lived normally. For two years all the schools and colleges have been closed down. Cinemas and restaurants only operate intermittently and at their own risk. And swimming has been banned because, just a few days ago, several rockets fell into the sea killing many people, mostly mothers and small children taking their afternoon swim."

"And you?" I asked. "And the hospital, how are you coping?"

"We have no choice," he replied. "We have been working round the clock, operating on the wounded from the front line. Our hospital has been hit several times."

"So how do you manage?"

"You will see," he said. "All our patients are now housed in the basement, either on rough mattresses on the floor, or in hammocks suspended from the ceiling. "

In these most appalling, distressing and stressful conditions, it seemed, Dr Mikecin and his team were amputating limbs, delivering babies and performing life-saving surgery - without electricity, without water - and without privacy.

The next day, at his suggestion, Dr. Mikecin, arranged for Elisar, Sonja and me to be escorted by two military officers to the front line, 10 kilometres inland from Zadar. Driving in zig-zag formation along the pockmarked roads, we visited the ruins of Crno, Dracevac and Murvica, once prosperous rural villages – but now devastated beyond recognition. Elisar and Sonja filmed everything we saw – the burnt shells of houses, the scorched fields, the massacred livestock, the desecrated churches and the graves that had been ripped open, their bones scattered and their epitaphs erased by vulgar grafitti. What was left was eerie, haunting - silent. The three of us hardly breathed a word to each other as we took it all in.

Fresh laundered shirts, encrusted by soot, were still hanging on a washing line. A child's kite dangled from the scorched branch of a tree. Carcasses of what were probably once cows lay rotting and fly-infested in the fields. A rusted tank, a trophy of war, provided a temporary makeshift playground for two little boys with plastic guns. A frightened dog and her pups cowered and whimpered in the ruins of what was once their family home. Grass and flowers, blackened and brittle underfoot, crackled as we walked.

We stopped for a moment and lit a candle on what remained of the altar in the small, gutted church at Murvica, only a week before, apparently, the scene of a joyous local wedding. The soldiers crossed themselves and knelt down in front of the broken altar. They mouthed a silent prayer. As I bent down to retrieve a charred candle from the ground, rockets streamed over our heads in search of their targets. We watched mesmerized as one landed near the airport, another near the main bridge and a third somewhere in the residential area of Zadar.

By the time the young officers returned us safely to the hospital, more wounded were being brought in for surgery. Bodies of young children, swathed in makeshift bandages, carried by parents, themselves bleeding and wounded. One child, playing on his own, had accidentally shot himself with his soldier father's gun. Another young boy, walking his dog in the field, had unwittingly stepped on an anti-personnel mine. A little girl, no more than three years old, lay bloodied and twisted in a cardboard box outside the hospital's main gate along with a mounting pile of rubbish. A small, limp, lifeless body - now just no more than a statistic.

Reluctantly we said goodbye to the soldiers. They were going back to the front line and, although unspoken, we all knew - maybe tomorrow it could be their lives ended prematurely, their broken bodies lying on the hospital floor, their children's corpses discarded in a cardboard box. I promised them I would take the candle home to my Croatian mother and, together, we would say a prayer for them - and for their ravaged country.

Chapter 33
A Campaign of Terror

Once we were back home Mick's campaign of terror began again in earnest. He managed to sabotage our first major fundraising event that was to be held at Sotheby's in late 1994 by leaking information to them that we were "being seriously investigated by the Charities Commission and Scotland Yard" which, of course, was entirely untrue. There had been complaints about us to the Charities Commission and to the police but all the complaints they received, the police informed us, had originated from Mick. Neither organization had any intention of investigating us. And, even though Sotheby's knew me and my family, they got cold feet and backed out. A few weeks later, once they realized their mistake, I received a letter of apology from the Chairman and an offer from the Board of Directors to reschedule the event for early 1995. Sadly, it was too little too late.

It was around this time, too, that my father's house in Hampshire was burgled. Although I had no absolute proof, I immediately suspected Mick or one of his cohorts was responsible. Realizing Mick could continue not only do serious damage to Brit-Aid's reputation but was now also capable of hurting members of my family, I asked my father to approach his MP, Michael Mates, to see if he could do anything to put an end to Mick's dangerous campaign.

Michael Mates was extremely sympathetic and immediately wrote letters to the Metropolitan Police, the Charities Commission and to the Attorney General on our behalf. At his suggestion too, we agreed to extend an invitation to the Charities Commission to look into Mick's allegations about Brit-Aid. And, as we all had expected, we were immediately cleared and informed by the Commission's officials that, if faced with a similar situation in the future, we could point to the fact that these accusations had been dealt with and dismissed by them. Armed with the letter of support from the Charities Commission, we made plans to reschedule our fundraising event in two parts. The Fashion event would be held at the Park Lane Hotel in December 1994 and the art sale would be held at Christies in early 1995.

Designers, artists and celebrities all remained wonderfully supportive. Michael Jackson, Angelica Huston, Marlon Brando, Gregory Peck, Tony Curtis,

Annie Lennox, Tony Bennett and Jack Lemmon, were just a few of the celebrities who very kindly donated to our project. Fashion designers and artists too were very generous and extremely patient. Cancellation of the event had meant we had to store the artists' works for a couple more months. But none of them complained or withdrew their donations.

Finally, on December 12, 1994, with 30 of the world's top fashion designers, our fashion event was held at the Park Lane Hotel. Several days prior to it, I received a letter from Mick.

"I know about the event," he wrote. "And I am going to destroy it. I am going to tell the Press that you are pulling off a grand deception involving thousands of pounds from the unsuspecting public."

True to his word, Mick telephoned the hotel PR department to inform them that our charity was involved in "gun smuggling" and "black marketeering". He then telephoned the police telling them there was going to be a demonstration outside the Hotel and asking them to arrest me "either before or during the event".

Both the police and the hotel security were extremely sympathetic to us and provided ample measures to deter any demonstrator. At the end of the evening, one of the police officers on duty that night told me there had been no demonstration.

"But," the officer said, "we did see the man in question alone outside the hotel. But he slunk away as soon as he saw our presence."

On the day preceding the event Mick had sent out a ten page fax to Eric and Julia Morley of the Variety Clubs International. It read, in part:

"Caroline Kennedy is a drug smuggler, a gun runner and a blackmailer. She paid me large sums of money to keep my mouth shut. She is living a lavish lifestyle, driving a smart car, dining at expensive restaurants and attending nightspots, while being investigated by MI5, the FBI and Special Branch. She should be arrested for her past and future crimes."

At around the same time, Mick eventually managed to convince one publication that his lies were worth printing. He had already contacted the *Mail on Sunday*, the *Jewish Chronicle* and the *Sunday Times* with his stories. All these publications had the decency to contact the charity with his allegations. Once they had spoken to us and received copies of his faxes threatening to destroy me and our charity by any means possible, plus the letters from the Metropolitan Police and from the Charities Commission clearing us of any wrongdoing, they sympathized with us and refused to publish any of his lies.

Time Out magazine, on the other hand, decided to give Mick's stories credence. And, although encouraged several times by my friend, Derek Addams, a member of *Time Out's* editorial staff, to phone our charity or its representatives for our comments, the journalist, Julian Kossoff, refused to do so. Kossoff simply went ahead and published an article, described by the lawyers and police as "obviously malicious" and "exceedingly defamatory" by juxtaposing it against a list of charities that had previously been convicted of fraud.

Kossoff, who later described himself on the professional network, Linked In, as "committed to high production values and accuracy" had got in touch with almost all of our contacts, including our medical suppliers, the Variety Clubs International, the Croatian Embassy and the Director of our Children's Village project repeating many of the slanderous accusations that had been spoon-fed to him by Mick. All these contacts, without exception, informed him that they supported us 100% and if he really was convinced the charity was acting illegally then he should send them some proof. Naturally, they never heard from Kossoff again, nor did he add any of their supportive comments to his extremely vicious article.

When we tried to contact *Time Out's* editor, Tony Elliott, with proof that what his magazine had published was totally wrong and grievously damaging, he neither bothered to apologize nor, even, respond. He took it for granted that a small charity wouldn't have the funds to take legal action and that, if they did, the trustees themselves would be responsible for any legal bills. Our lawyers and counsel felt we could win substantial damages but that if *Time Out* was willing to go to court it could drag on and take us up to at least two years before receiving any compensation.

We tried to put it all behind us and focus our attention on our next fundraising event, the art sale at Christie's. Everything was going smoothly and amicably. As I had done with Sotheby's a couple of months earlier, I warned Christie's director, Charles Hindlip, that some "nutter", either Mick Roberts or one of his cohorts, would make an attempt to sabotage the evening. I warned him of the allegations Mick would make, giving Christies' lawyers ample time to check up on our charity's credentials. I also gave Hindlip the findings of the Charities Commission and the letter from the Metropolitan Police confirming that Brit-Aid and its trustees had been cleared of any wrongdoing.

The day before the exhibition opening, I arrived at Christies to help hang the paintings. I was received by their lawyer who guided me into a small interview room. She handed me a letter stating that the exhibition had been called off. No explanation. No reason. Nothing.

"We are not at liberty to divulge the information," she told me.

Hindlip later informed me that it was someone who telephoned Christies saying he was a researcher for an investigative radio show, asking for an invitation because he was "conducting an expose on the charity for his programme". The phone caller also mentioned we were being "investigated by Scotland Yard" and gave the name of a police inspector with whom complaints had been lodged about the charity's "illegal" activities.

"It was our lawyers who made the decision to call off the event," Hindlip told me. "The phone-caller, who refused to identify himself, then stated you had stolen all the supplies from a Jewish aid organization and sold them on the black market."

The caller obviously didn't dare give the name of the Jewish organization, the World Jewish Relief, because he knew that had he done so, that Christies would find out from them that all their supplies had been delivered intact by us, and on time, to their representative in Split, Croatia. And, although it was, sadly, too late to salvage the exhibition, the World Jewish Relief wrote to Charles Hindlip informing him of this fact.

This whole episode was extremely upsetting considering how much time, effort and goodwill had been given by so many supportive individuals towards us and our very deserving cause. The fact that one man could be responsible for fostering so much damage and, not only get away with it, but manage to convince enough people that his lies were true, was, I believe, reprehensible. The law badly needed to be changed because people like Mick were so easily able to ruin so many lives by their mendacity. They knew they were protected by the law. They were ignored by the police while they continued to make people's lives a misery, safe in the knowledge that no one could or would do anything to prevent them.

The threatening phone calls and messages persisted. But I was not about to be deterred. My family and friends kept advising me to change my phone number or move home. But I was determined not to give in to Mick's intimidation.

Finally, on New Year's Day 1995, a police inspector, Detective Superintendent Kit Bentham, contacted me asking if he could come to my apartment to talk to me urgently. I agreed and he showed up at my door that afternoon. As he sipped on a cup of tea, Bentham told me the reason for his visit.

"Yesterday evening, New Year's Eve, we arrested a young man in this vicinity. He was driving erratically and it aroused our suspicions. We stopped and breathalyzed him. When checking his car, we recovered two full cannisters of petrol. When we took him down to the police station for questioning, he admitted he had been sent by a certain Mick Roberts."

I gulped. I didn't want to hear what was going to come next.

"I'm sorry to tell you this," Bentham continued. "But, he said he had been instructed to break into your apartment and to steal any incriminating evidence about Mick Roberts that you might have gathered. He was then ordered by Mick Roberts to burn down your apartment to cover up the burglary."

I was now, more than ever, convinced that it was Mick Roberts who had burgled my father's house. And I mentioned that to Det. Bentham. In response, Bentham informed me that, apart from our charity's complaints, they had accumulated a great many charges against Mick Roberts, and that a related case also involving Mick's bogus charity work was pending against him in Lewes Crown Court, Sussex, near where he lived.

"Apart from other dubious activities, Mr. Roberts has been involved in trying to prevent live animal exports to the continent. He has, allegedly, threatened people with guns and knives. He has carried out an arson attack on a local premises owned by the transport company carrying these animals. And a stockpile of drugs had been confiscated from his house. Do you know anything about any of this?"

"I had heard rumours," I replied, "but I didn't know any of the details."

I was still in shock from the news that Bentham had just given me.

"Oh, and also," Bentham continued, "your assertion that Mick had many aliases was right." Between us, Gill, Shirley and I had uncovered about nine aliases.

Bentham enlightened me. "Mick Roberts has changed his name and his location over 60 times!"

"Why did the police not do anything about him all this time then?" I asked. "There must have been records about this available?"

"I'm afraid he was being protected." Bentham said. "Mick Roberts, or whatever his real name is, has been a police informer for the past 19 years. There are many people in jail because of him and they probably shouldn't be there. Someone high up in the Force has been protecting him."

That finally answered so many questions that had been nagging me for so long.

"But it's over now," Bentham went on, "this has changed everything. He's in very serious trouble. What we'd like you to do, if you agree, is become a state witness against him in this related case. Would you do that?"

I shook my head.

"I'd prefer not to," I said. After having been told that Mick had been quite prepared to burn down my apartment where I lived with my children, I was naturally terrified of putting their lives in more danger.

"I understand completely," Bentham replied. "But I am confident Mr. Roberts will be found guilty and will end up with a substantial jail sentence. Your testimony will be a vital addition to the current charges he is facing. We will protect you, I assure you."

So, very reluctantly, I agreed. Over the next couple of weeks I compiled a dossier with copies of every single letter and fax I had received and a complete list of every phone call, message and threat that Mick or any one of his cohorts had made over the previous 36 months.

And a few weeks later, for the first time in my life, I found myself as a witness in a court case. Needless to say, I was extremely nervous as I entered Lewes Crown

Court. But Det. Superintendent Bentham and his deputy, Det. Sgt. Stuart Parsons, never left my side and I was well protected. When my name was called, I was ushered into the courtroom and, without looking over towards the defense table, I entered the witness box, took the oath, and told my story of three years of harassment by Mick Roberts. Mick's defense lawyer, for whatever reason, decided not to cross-examine me which was a relief. My testimony and my dossier of all Mick's offences were then entered into the Court record. Finally, the Judge told me I could step down.

Det. Superintendent Bentham wrote to me later to thank me for appearing and said that I had "acquitted myself before the Judge very well indeed." He told me Mick Roberts had been sentenced to six years.

The nightmare was finally over. After three years of living in constant terror, I was now free to return to a normal life.

Chapter 34

An Honorary Man

The war in Jugoslavia had ended. 20 year-old Mayumi had already left home to pursue her modelling career in Los Angeles. It was time now to concentrate on Elisar and Jasmine, who, through the whole distressing experience, had been extremely supportive of me.

Whether Jasmine had been affected by Mick Roberts' campaign against me or not, I didn't know. But it was around this time that she started displaying signs of mental health issues. As soon as I recognized there was something wrong, I got a referral to a psychiatrist for her from our family doctor. He told me Jasmine had a chemical imbalance and she was given a prescription for pills to help it. Looking back, I realize I should have got a second, and even a third, opinion. But I was so unfamiliar with mental health problems that I simply assumed if Jasmine took the pills, her issues would go away. Well, I was wrong, and for the first of several times over the succeeding years, Jasmine ended up in rehab. It took a good two years before she was correctly diagnosed with bi-polar and prescribed the correct treatment. But, even then, to get her to stay on the meds proved incredibly difficult.

But for now, satisfied that Jasmine seemed to be in capable hands, I started to look for work again. And, within a matter of weeks, I received a phone call from the Director of Leonard Cheshire International and former head of MI5, Sir Patrick Walker, offering me a job helping to set up the Leonard Cheshire Chair of Conflict Recovery at University College London.

A new door in my life had opened. A new chapter was about to begin.

I always believed very strongly that all my children should have the opportunity to understand the reality of life as a refugee. As I recounted earlier, Elisar had accompanied me on one of my trips down to Zadar in Croatia. Now I felt it was time for both Mayumi and Jasmine to learn, not just from listening to me and their brother, how fortunate their own lives were compared to the lives of so many young people living in hostile environments or refugee camps around the world.

"It's so easy," I told them, "to take a warm home, the ability to attend school, regular meals, a hot shower and, even, a flushing toilet, for granted."

My first assignment for the Leonard Cheshire Chair of Conflict Recovery was as the In-Country Manager of our programme with refugees with disabilities in Azerbaijan. Following its defeat in the territorial war with Armenia over the disputed Ngorno-Karabakh region, Azerbaijan, a country of just 7 million people, now had an extra 1 million displaced people living in abandoned buildings, disused factories and refugee camps across the country. My direct boss, Professsor Jim Ryan, Chair of Conflict Recovery and head of trauma surgery at University College London Hospital, had been invited by the Deputy Prime Minister and Head of Humanitarian Affairs of Azerbaijan, Dr. Izzat Rustamov, to help the plight of these displaced people, particularly those with disabilities. After an initial visit to some of these camps in 1995, Jim Ryan asked me if I would be prepared to live in Azerbaijan for a year to oversee our programme there.

I consulted with Elisar and Jasmine who were both still living with me at home. I asked them how they would feel if I left them to fend for themselves. They replied they felt very confident they could "survive" without me!

Thus I ended up in Baku, Azerbaijan. A few days after my arrival, I found myself an apartment and met up with Dr. Rustamov to plan our programme. Since he told me that the two camps I would be working in, Saatli and Sabiribad, were a three hour bus ride south from Baku, down near the Iranian border, I realized it would be far more sensible for me to live closer to the refugees. And so I left the apartment in Baku and settled at Echo House, a rundown single-storeyed wooden structure situated just outside Saatli, between the two camps.

Echo House was slap in the middle of a typical rural setting - green fields stretching out to the horizon, grazing cows switching their tails to ward off flying insects, geese scratching in the yard, ducks weaving in and out of the bullrushes in a nearby pond, the odd turtle sunning itself on the banks of a fast-flowing river. There was little there to break the silence, except the evening chorus of bullfrogs searching for a twilight romance, the distant whistle of a train passing beyond the meadows, the occasional bark of a startled dog woken from its slumber by an approaching shepherd and his unruly flock. From this rural scene it was hard to tell which country I was in.

But, as I looked out of the bus window, the closer I came to Saatli, the more clues I saw as to which country it actually was. There were men, in groups, sitting idly under the shade of an overhanging tree, sipping black tea and playing dominoes. There were women, gaily-coloured, in the fields, backs bent double, picking cotton. And then there were the sun-scorched domes of a local mosque shimmering silver and ready to topple down in the midday heat.

But behind this pastoral scene another, grimmer, image emerged. Even Echo House itself, at the centre, was deceptive. It was not someone's rural hunting lodge but a rundown, disused, guest house offering but the barest accommodation and an alarming lack of sanitary and hygienic facilities.

To its left was what remained of a Soviet oil exploration site. Dilapidated buildings, crumbling masonry, a huge, tangled web of corroding pipes, metal ropes and disintegrating pulleys. Antiquated, rusting machinery lying idle. Gaping, cavernous pits filled with rotting refuse, discarded tins, broken glass and stagnant, festering water - a breeding ground for the local malarial mosquito. This, I soon found out, was the playground of the refugee children who, with their families, were squatting in the decaying buildings around Echo House. This was my place, the place I was going to live, on and off, for the next three years. This was to be my home away from home.

My first mission was to find a reliable full-time interpreter who spoke, not just passable English, but extremely proficient English, as he or she would be required to understand and translate medical terminology. My guardian angel was, once again, on my side. Within my new home at Echo Camp, I found a refugee, Sevinj Rzayeva, a highly intelligent and compassionate high school graduate with impeccable English who offered to be my guide, companion and full time paid interpreter. I couldn't believe my luck. And throughout the next year, Sevinj was by my side continually, even though the work was exhausting, she never complained. As she told me, "I am always happy to help my fellow refugees."

I was soon to discover this new "home" of mine held many uncomfortable secrets, had tragic stories to tell, had painful memories to share. At the main gate as I entered, I found Abil Aliyev, a young man who, day after day, stood sentry there. I would watch him walk valiantly towards me, agonizing step by agonizing step, his legs forming a figure of eight. Courage, resilience and a determination not to be beaten by his own disability compelled him to carry on - to heroically resist a walking frame, a pair of crutches or, even, a walking stick to support his body. But he knew - and I knew, because he told me, that like his older sister, Gamila, and older brother, Azef, he would eventually succumb to the genetic disorder that had savagely claimed first their limbs and then their minds.

And what of Abil's family? What of his mother and father who could only watch helplessly as, at the age of 13, first their daughter and then their two sons had begun, stumbling, falling, losing control of their legs. These were my new neighbours now, internally-displaced people driven out of their homes in the Nagorno-Karabakh by the invading Armenian army. There had been no time to collect their belongings, no time to think where they were heading. No time for anything but sheer panic. Abil's father, alone in his car at the time, was unable to find his wife and his three totally dependent, disabled children. Scouring the countryside, searching everywhere, looking for a familiar face in the straggling line of refugees fleeing down the road, he was driven mad by fear of never seeing them again, of losing them forever in the desperate scramble to get out of the way of the approaching enemy.

This was the Aliyev family. They were my new friends. They had finally been reunited after that dreadful night two years earlier. Abil invited me to visit them. They were all living in one room, one flight up in a disused and abandoned factory building. Lumps of masonry were falling down as Sevinj and I climbed the stairs. On the first floor, Abil's sister, Gamila, sat on a chair by the door, day after monotonous day. In the same place, never moving, never seeing the outside world. She had just been sitting in the same spot for two years. Abil's mother, her back aching from carrying her sons up and down the stairs, generously prepared tea and homemade peach jam for us.

But I felt ashamed. I felt helpless. There was nothing I could really do for these children. The father told me I had done enough. That I was the only person to have cared about them, to have listened to their story, to have shown them compassion, to have lent a shoulder to cry on. It turns out none of the other NGOs operating in Azerbaijan had yet visited either Saatli or Sabiribad.

"But in my heart," Aliyev told me through Sevinj, "I always knew there would be no magical cure, no miracle treatment, no new surgical intervention that could ever help improve my children's condition."

Sevinj told me he blamed himself for their disabilities, believing that his work in a Russian mine for decades was the cause. He knew at the time how contaminated, how poisonous and how dangerous the place was but he could not afford to give up the work.

"And now they are condemned," Sevinj said. "and having lost them briefly once, he would never contemplate placing them in an institution. He and his wife will look after them as long as they are able to do so." Abil's mother nodded her agreement.

"I can provide wheelchairs for them," I said, "but that's about all I can do."

Over the months that followed, Shirley came out to join me on several occasions. And she and I, along with Sevinj and a medical team from University College Hospital, visited every single dwelling, hut, tent, or building that housed refugees. We took down the refugees' names, gave them on-the-spot health checks and made a note of those with particular disabilities that we believed we could either operate on or provide support to, and sent the information back to my boss, Jim Ryan, in London.

Jim, in turn, made contact with the top orthopedic surgeon in Baku, Professor Bagirov, and I made arrangements for Bagirov to come and visit those refugees with disabilities who we thought could be operated on and, thus have their lives substantially improved. When word spread through the camps that Professor Bagirov would be visiting, dozens of hopeful families approached us to please make sure to put their disabled son, daughter, mother, father on the list for a visit. We assured them we would not miss any of them. Professor Bagirov was a trooper.

He trudged through the camps visiting every single family on our list, made notes on each disabled individual, discussed ways he could help improve their condition and agreed to perform surgery on many of them.

Now with the agreement of Professor Bagirov and his medical team in place, we arranged for rotating teams of doctors, nurses, surgeons and physiotherapists from the UK to visit Baku and work alongside him to help lessen his workload.

I was shocked on my first visit to the main hospital in Baku. There were piles of stinking, rotting rubbish outside the main door. There were hordes of desperately ill patients waiting to be seen. I saw some intravenous liquids being dispensed into patients' arms from disused plastic coca cola bottles. I saw sterilizing machines that were completely rusted and falling apart. And, I witnessed someone waking up in the middle of his operation because patients were required to bring their own anesthetics to the hospital. But this poor man, like many others, could not afford to buy a sufficient quantity to last through his three hour surgery.

We were very fortunate in our choice of Professor Bagirov to be part of our Leonard Cheshire team. He was compassionate, hardworking and determined to help the refugees for no additional pay. He was already working long hours for a very low salary but now, with the refugee patients we were bringing to him for surgery, he worked until well after midnight every night of the week.

"Until you and Shirley brought me down to the camps," Bagirov told me, "I had no idea we had so many refugees in our country. And it certainly would never have occurred to me to visit them. So I am very grateful to you both."

Apart from identifying refugees with disabilities, Shirley, Sevinj, and our hardworking team of volunteer nurses that included our friend Zeb, a top grade emergency nurse from University College Hospital and Shirley's daughter Elizabeth, a nursing student, also became famous for locating men with undiagnosed hernias and sending them to Professor Bagirov to be operated on. Soon it became a standard joke that whenever we entered one of the refugee camps, men would approach us and drop their trousers! Inexplicably, there were many men with hernias, some fairly advanced cases, and we treated as many as we could. There were also patients with regular illnesses like cancer, kidney disease and heart failure. Sadly, there was little we could do to help them. And it was very sobering to realize that, without their necessary medications, they would probably not survive. But we had to concentrate on what we were there to do, what was in our power to do and the positive difference we could make in the lives of those whose disabilities we could improve by surgery and physiotherapy.

When the programme was running smoothly, I invited my daughter, Mayumi, to take time off her modelling career in Los Angeles and come out to Echo House, to help with the younger refugees who were either bored and restless or listless and introverted. Mayumi, who had been studying Wing Chun, the form of kung fu made popular by Bruce Lee, gave lessons to the children to help rid them of some of their excess energy and pent up anger caused by the hopeless situation they were in.

At the same time, I also set up a long-term project with Central School of Speech & Drama in London to send out some of their second year drama education students to work with the children, writing plays, making puppets, performing theatre, painting and creating gardens. Helped by the drama students, the children, wrote a play based on one of their Azeri folk tales about a wounded bird, which we performed in the camp. Whole families took part in this production. Mothers made the costumes. Fathers and older brothers built the set and the children acted. On their return to London, the students performed the play at the London International Gallery of Children's Art, alongside the art work the refugee children had produced during their time there.

After Shirley, Elizabeth, Zeb, the other nurses and drama education students left, Mayumi and I were left on our own for a few weeks until their next visit. Sevinj told me about a large group of refugees living in abandoned railway carriages nearby. I asked her to take Mayumi and me there to visit them.

The heat was intense that day. And the haze reflected off the carriage roofs as we approached. We squinted as the belching smoke from the nearby asphalt factory and the dust from the arid ground was whipped into our eyes by the unpredictable winds. As the air cleared briefly, I saw the silhouettes of children approaching us, seemingly hordes of them, though, in reality, probably far fewer. Their arms were outstretched towards us. Their clothes were ragged, their hair matted, their limbs encrusted by soot. But it was their eyes that caught my attention. Not the normal eyes of children. Their eyes were unresponsive, dulled by hunger, by lack of motivation, by boredom. They were the lustreless, unflickering eyes of young children, old beyond their years - some born, some growing up, all living on the railway lines of Saatli.

Their homes were abandoned railway wagons, no more than corroded metal junk heaps, destined decades ago for the scrap merchant's yard. They were windowless, airless and dank. There was no ventilation, no light, not even the fierce winds penetrated these dark hovels. As I stepped up inside one of the carriages, I could see that the occupants inside these improvised dwellings lived in perpetual darkness.

"They are stifling in summer," Sevinj told me. "And freezing in winter."

The only shade were not trees, for I noticed there were none there - but the back-breaking space beneath the wagons. Here the weak ones sat, day after day, singly and in groups, hunched up, cramped, listless, pitiful. The lack of animation was evident in their dispirited expressions, their vacant stares and their inability to brush away the invading army of flies which voraciously sought out their eyes, their mouths and any available open sore on their bent and feeble bodies.

Under a white shroud, like a mummified corpse, we saw an old woman the impoverished medical system in the country had forgotten, neglected or, deliberately, ignored. Her mind was confused, her right side was paralyzed by a minor stroke. She lay there mumbling words only she could understand. A despairing old man, her husband, put his ear to the faintly moving lips beneath the veil covering her face, vainly trying to interpret their meaning. He shook his head, desolate, for he could do nothing for her but watch over her and caress her shriveled hand. A small disabled boy lay next to her, dribbling, moaning, wretched - his unfocussed eyes infested by the voracious flies.

Mayumi, Sevinj and I watched this scene, moved and saddened, yet somehow transfixed. I was reluctant to intrude but, nevertheless, I wanted to be a part of it. I moved closer. At the same time, I became voyeur and participant, observer and player, detached yet intimately involved.

And, as I squatted down beneath beside the track, a cast of characters crawled in and out from under the wagon. A heavily pregnant mother, panting furiously, brow sweating, her swelling belly draped in purple nylon, heaved her weighty body under the train and settled herself gratefully in the shade. An old woman, doubled up by age and defeated by years of arthritis, dragged her distorted limbs painfully under the carriage, sinking, with a sigh, onto the temporary coolness of the metal track. A young man, a soldier from the war with Armenia, his left leg blown off by a recent encounter with a landmine, discarded his ancient crutches, stumbled forward, then flopped inelegantly down onto the ground beside her. Turkeys, geese, hens, ducks, cats and dogs, ever eager to fill their empty, worm-infested stomachs, scratched for crumbs of food among the feet of this motley cast.

Word about Mayumi's Wing Chun classes with the Saatli refugee children had obviously preceded our visit. The railway children came hurtling up the track towards her, pursuing her with chants of "Arnu Swarznegger, Bruze Lee, Junclode Vundam!" Simulating karate chops, high kicks and beefcake muscles, they suddenly came alive. For one brief moment, no different from children anywhere. For foreigners were few here and so aroused immediate curiosity. Those that did come rarely stayed. Few had time to sit for a while, to chatter, to play and, above all, to listen. They came with nothing and they left with nothing, for the railway wagons were inhospitable, uninviting and offered little in the way of comfort to the visitor.

The children, their dead eyes sparkling briefly, jostled around us, pushing, shoving, touching, eager to get a closer look at us. One or two grasped my hands, helped me to my feet, led me on. Others, naturally shy, held back, quietly observing us from a distance.

We spent some time there, with our new friends. But could we really call them our "friends" when we knew we would soon be leaving them? We would go home and, in all probability, we would forget them. And yet, there was this feeling, they would continue to haunt me, those railway children of Saatli, those images of despair, so young, so vulnerable, so needy.

Evening came quickly. Dusk's shadows, distorted and kicked in all directions by the unpredictable winds, threw dancing patterns over the broiling, dusty ground, flickering images, like a monochromatic kaleidoscope. The sun, was falling in the west, vast, shimmering and aflame, painted the sky cinnamon. Plumes of cinder smoke, gusting from the factory chimney-stack, released a delicate network of fluffy ashen threads across its sinking path.

We watched in silence. I held a child's hand, as the gently fading rays turned to a soft, golden apricot before finally being swallowed up by the welcoming earth. I squeezed that little hand in mine. I had to go back to Echo House. Night came swiftly there in Saatli. But no matter where I am, wherever I go from now on, I will still see those children's eyes. Not normal children's eyes. Eyes of children, old beyond their years.

Mayumi returned to Los Angeles soon afterward. She told me the experience was something she would never forget. Her favourite memory was of one little boy in her Wing Chun class that came every day with a pair of scissors in his pocket. He acted very aggressively, threatening the other children. But, after a couple of weeks training, he left the scissors behind and really threw himself into the class, becoming one of her better students. It also made her want to work with autistic children and, once she got back to LA, she applied to study at the Lovaas Institute for Early Intervention and, while still studying acting, went on to become a Lovaas Case Manager, working with autistic children, which made me very proud.

Now it was Jasmine's turn. I invited her and my stepmother, Daphie, to join me at Echo House. Daphie had persuaded all her friends around Hampshire to make soft toys for the smaller children. So, when she arrived, she had suitcases full of handmade stuffed dolls and animals. Sevinj gathered all the toddlers of Saatli and Sabiribad camps and Jasmine, Daphie and I handed them out to each one.

Following Daphie's brief visit, Jasmine immediately befriended our Echo House "gatekeeper", Abil. She also became friends with a young woman, named Ruggia, who had lost both her legs after being run over by a train on her way to school one day. Unlike the refugees, Ruggia was a local girl and lived in a house in Saatli. But her mother approached us one day asking if we could help her daughter. Through Sevinj, I told her that, sadly, there was little we could do for Ruggia, since both her legs had been amputated to the top of her thighs and there were no existing prosthetics that would work for her. All we were able to offer her was a brand new wheelchair that was a lot more comfortable, more mobile and more versatile than the decrepit one she was currently using.

During the following weeks, I managed to introduce Ruggia to other girls I had met with physical disabilities. And, after discussions with them, I went out and bought several sewing machines in the a market in Saatli. Sevinj then helped me locate a seamstress who lived close to Echo House and who was willing to teach them all how to cut cloth and make simple clothing. With the agreement of Ruggia's mother, we set up a twice-weekly sewing circle in Ruggia's house. Ruggia's father volunteered to act as driver, to pick up the other girls and bring them to his home. This activity, though small, gave me tremendous satisfaction. I had visited all these girls individually and seen them sitting in their huts or tents doing nothing day in, day out. Now they had friends they could share their personal stories with while, at the same time, producing clothes they could sell in the local market. The first blouse that Ruggia made, a bright red one with gold trimmings, she gave to Jasmine as she said Jasmine was the first person who had taken time to befriend her and she was grateful.

I was proud of Jasmine, too. She was so at ease with these young people with disabilities. She had shown that capacity from an early age when one of her best friends at primary school was a young girl with Down's Syndrome. Whereas other children in their school shunned or avoided the girl, Jasmine became her best friend. So it was not a surprise to me that she would immediately befriend both Abil and Ruggia. After she left, Abil never stopped asking about her and even wrote some poetry to her that I promised him I would send to Jasmine in London.

Within a few weeks, Shirley, Zeb and the medical team returned to Echo House. By this time I was able to show her our "brand new" toilet. The one in Echo House was beyond filthy. And the washbasin only produced ground water, dark brown from decades of flowing through corroded metal pipes. I used to joke to my friends that I was brushing my teeth in vodka because, in the local market, a bottle of Stolichnaya was cheaper than a bottle of water. Then, to my delight one day, my friend Mr. Mehman, a local man who cared for the refugees living around me, surprised me by producing a full height metal school locker which he converted into an outside toilet. He dug the deep hole himself and produced a mountain of sand and wood chips. Needless to say, I was very proud of it.

Now, with Shirley, Zeb and the medical team back, it was time to take another survey around the camps. In the pouring rain one day, on one of our walks around Sabiribad camp looking for possible patients, we came across a young boy, Mushvig, whose legs had been severely burnt several months earlier when he had fallen onto the camping stove that his mother had been using to cook on. Without medicines or antibiotics and with no hope of getting Mushvig to a hospital, Sevinj explained, that all his mother had been able to do since then was attempt to clean his wounds with rags and boiled water several times a day. So, by the time we came across him, Mushvig was close to dying of sepsis. We knew we had to get him to a hospital very urgently.

Shirley contacted Khalid Khan, the local director of Save the Children, and showed him photographs of Mushvig's extensive injuries. He immediately offered to provide an ambulance to take Mushvig to Baku. With no bandages available locally, Shirley swathed Mushvig's legs in cling-wrap plastic to avoid further infection and accompanied him and his mother on the three hour journey to the hospital. Professor Bagirov recruited a friend of his, a burns specialist, to operate on Mushvig and his life was saved.

When Shirley, Sevinj and I visited the little boy in hospital just a week after his operation, he was running up and down the hospital corridor playing football. Considering how close to death he had been, it was no less than a small miracle. I asked Mushvig if he wanted to be a footballer when he grew up. He shook his head.

"I want to be an English teacher," he said through Sevinj, "because my life was saved by two English ladies!"

When my year's residence in Azerbaijan came to an end and it was time for Shirley and me to return home, the men in Sabiribad camp invited us for a meal. We were the only women at the makeshift dinner table that night. At the end of the evening, one by one, the men stood up and toasted us as "honorary men" because we "worked so hard" and we were "so brave". I wanted to remind them that their women worked harder in the cotton fields or in the local jam factory and, at the same time, cooked for them and looked after their children, all the while living as a refugee in a tent. And while the women were doing all this, the men were doing nothing but sitting under the shade of an overhanging tree, drinking tea and playing endless games of dominoes. Although it was probably the highest honour these men could bestow on me, I wanted to say I was not sure I was so proud to be called an "honorary man"!

On the last day before we left Echo House, Shirley and I delivered three shiny new wheelchairs to Abil and his two siblings. Asef, the older brother, wasted no time trying his out, Suddenly, for the first time, he experienced the thrill of independence. Mobile, carefree and proud. We watched him as he was immediately surrounded by curious, jostling children all eagerly begging their turn to push him around in his new machine. His mother, Shirley, Sevinj and I stood off a little from the crowd, watching silently this excited, chattering, laughing group, our arms around each other, shedding tears. This was an emotional moment for all of us.

As I waved goodbye for the last time, young Abil, aloof and brave, was still standing defiantly, sentry at the gate, refusing to acknowledge the wheelchair that waited for him but knowing, one day soon, he would have no choice but to use it. And as I said goodbye, his sister, Gamila was still sitting by the door of her first floor room, in her brand new wheelchair, and I wondered if she would ever emerge to see the outside world, ever touch the grass, ever watch the birds fly, ever see the men playing dominoes under the overhanging tree, ever hear the women singing in the cottonfields or ever see the sunrise over Echo House.

Chapter 35
Why Newfoundland?

Our next two projects with the Leonard Cheshire Chair for Conflict Recovery were working alongside the Landmine Survivors Network, with landmine victims in Bosnia and restoring the emergency surgery department of the main hospital in Pristina in Kosovo that had been destroyed by the war. The Leonard Chair of Conflict Recovery also published a handbook for medical and NGO personnel delivering medical aid in hostile environments. I was asked to write the final chapter, *"Coming Home",* how to adapt to home life after working overseas under stressful and conflict conditions.

Since neither Shirley nor I were required to go out to either Bosnia or Kosovo, Col. Alan Hawley, an Army friend of my boss, Jim, invited us to be the two civilian 'guinea pigs' on a Disaster Relief Operations Course he had devised for British Army personnel. Since Col. Hawley surmised that troops would increasingly be called upon in the future to do humanitarian work rather than go to war, he felt they should learn how to work alongside and compliment work being done by NGOs helping refugees in conflict environments and victims of natural disasters.

So, for three extremely tough weeks, Shirley and I lived in the Army barracks at Aldershot, alongside soldiers who had volunteered to participate in this highly intensive new Course. We learned how to triage patients after an attack or following a disaster, such as a train derailment. We learned how to provide clean drinking water for 100,000 people in a conflict zone. We learned how to diffuse a hostage situation. We learned how to cope with victims of floods, earthquakes and famines. And we learned how to distinguish between airborne, waterborne and vector-borne diseases and how to treat them.

At the end of the three week course, we each had to give a presentation to the top military brass at the Army HQ at Aldershot about the particular subject we had been given to study at the outset of the course. My subject was how to deal with victims following a famine. And Shirley's subject was how to help victims following a volcanic eruption. We both passed and received our certificates. Our names and contact details were automatically forwarded to disaster relief organizations in our neighbourhoods, in the event there were any local disasters in the future and the organizations required trained volunteers.

It was also around this time that my father fell ill with late onset leukemia. So, after nearly a decade working with refugees, I decided it was time for me to take a sabbatical.

Over lunch at the Travellers' Club, I told my boss, Sir Patrick Walker, of my plans to step down. He had been an inspiring boss and I was truly sorry to leave. Later he wrote me a very touching letter, stating:

"I would like to place on record the enormous debt the Leonard Cheshire Chair of Conflict Recovery owes you for your remarkable work over the last few years. Your willingness to travel in often uncomfortable conditions, your ability to establish good relations with people at all levels in other countries and your skill as a writer and speaker about the Centre's work, have been a major element in the amazing progress made by the Centre since it started. Yours will be a hard act to follow."

A month or so later, Daphie and I were at the hospital in Midhurst when Daddy's test results came in. The Macmillan cancer nurse was very direct but very delicate in how she conveyed the news to us.

"Mr. Kennedy will require complete blood transfusions every so often as the increasing presence of the white corpuscles in his blood will make it harder and harder for him to breathe. Sadly, there is nothing we can do. Intervals between the transfusions will become shorter and shorter. Until, I suspect, one day he will say that is enough. And he will pass away."

This news was devastating. Daphie, now aged 71, had been with my father since she was 18. And, apart from her children and her local community in Hampshire who loved her, he was her whole life. She took the news very stoically but I could see she was breaking up inside. We hugged each other.

"We will all be there for you," I whispered as I hugged her tightly. "You have always been there for him and for us. We will be with there for you."

I was grateful that my overseas work in Bosnia and Azerbaijan had ended so that I could keep that promise to her. And, over the next year, as much as I could I spent almost every weekend down in Hampshire with them. We even found time, between his blood transfusions, to take a holiday, by road, to some of his favourite places in France. We drove into the French Alps and then down to the coast, to spend time on his boat, *The Blue Dolphin*, that was moored in Juan les Pins. It was on that trip that I found him weeping on his hotel balcony, overlooking Lake Lugano. This was the moment he finally expunged the ghost of my mother when she had informed him the marriage was over those many decades ago. Despite normal problems, disappointments and setbacks, my father was one of those stiff upper lip people who always managed to find something to smile or joke about. So, to see him so frail, and in tears was a very unfamiliar image to me. Underneath it all, I realized he was fragile and brittle, like we all are.

When we got back home, I wheeled him out into the garden, along the paths leading into his fruit orchard. We stopped to admire the numerous Admiral butterflies feeding on the lavender blossoms. It was always the small things like this that had given him the most pleasure in life. As we stood there, I probably didn't say half the things I should have said to him, and later wished I had. But I did tell him how much I loved him. He squeezed my hand and said he knew that. I apologized for not always heeding his wise advice over the decades, that I knew he had given it honestly and for the best reasons. I thanked him for bringing Daphie into all our lives and told him it was the best choice he could have made, not only for himself but, more especially, for us children. I assured him we would all look after her. And I told him again, as I had many times before, how grateful and how fortunate I and my children were to have him as my father and their grandfather. He was silent during all this and just squeezed my hand tighter. And, when I wheeled him indoors he insisted on sitting down at the piano to play some of his favourite tunes, as he always had done all his life. But, this time, quietly cursing his ageing fingers for hitting the wrong keys.

As the Macmillan nurse had predicted, after almost a year, the transfusions had now become a bi-weekly necessity and my father decided he had had enough. He died in Daphie's arms a few nights later. I think he wanted to be alone with Daphie at the end because about two weeks before he made the decision, he insisted we all go on holiday with my mother. We were very hesitant but he was adamant. So, when Daphie relayed the news of his death, we were on a gulet sailing along the Turkish coast. We all wanted to fly home. But Daphie refused to allow us to cut our holiday short. In the end, my brother Alexander, flew back to be with her and help with the funeral arrangements. Daddy's loss was felt by us all, children and grandchildren alike. And it left a gaping hole in our lives to this day.

Following the funeral, I arranged to take Daphie on a trip to Antarctica in a small group led by my friend, wildlife photographer and BBC TV presenter, Mark Carwardine. Since Daphie had always loved animals, I thought the sight of baby penguins cavorting on the ice, would instantly cheer her up. It was probably the best thing I could have done for her. The pure magic of seeing so many animals in their natural habitat up close, had an extraordinary effect on both of us. Elephant seals, leopard seals, huge colonies of gentoo, chinstrap and adelie penguins, pelagic birds such as, petrels, shearwaters and skuas, pods of orcas, dolphins, several species of whales, humpbacks, minkes, southern rights and the comedian of the southern seas, the blue-footed booby.

And then out of the blue, in May 1997, I heard from Rita again. Joe had just died and she called to give me the news. We both wept a little over the phone. He had been a good friend to us both.

"I really wish you had married him, Caroline," Rita said. "He really wanted to marry you but you were so young then that he felt he would be clipping your wings if you settled down with him. He really loved you."

"Yes, I know," I sobbed, suddenly feeling very guilty.

I always felt guilty when I thought of Joe. I knew how he felt about me. I had been very tempted to marry him when I was about 21. But I also desperately wanted to travel the world. And so he had reluctantly let me go with a fervent promise that if I ever wanted to return he would always be there waiting for me. He would repeat that whenever we spoke or saw each other over the ensuing decades. But the guilt I harboured most was that I had never made time to go and see him when he was seriously ill the year before he died.

Talking to Rita only made me feel worse. During the phone call I unburdened on her the same way she had so many times, over the decades, unburdened her feelings on both Joe and me. And, for the first time, I realized that Rita could be kind, compassionate and understanding.

During our hour long conversation she never once talked about herself. She simply consoled me, told me that Joe had understood all the decisions I had made in my life, even though they excluded him and that, in her last phone call with him, he had told her again that he still loved me and how proud he was of me and what I had done in my life, my work in Bosnia and Croatia during the war, my recent work with refugees in Azerbaijan and my best-selling book that had been published a decade earlier. He had followed it all with great pride, she told me.

"I beat him to it, didn't I?" I sobbed.

"Beat him to what?" Rita asked.

"Writing a best-selling book. All these years he promised me that one day he would sit down and write a blockbuster. I convinced him he had a great story to tell. From being a US Marine Colonel in the South Pacific where he was awarded a Bronze Star and in Iwo Jima during the Korean War to becoming New York's top society columnist. It was a great story. But he was the world's worst procrastinator."

"Yes," Rita agreed. "I kept pushing him to do it too. He just kept putting it off and putting it off."

I told her about my last phone call with him about two months earlier.

"He was crying. I think perhaps he knew he was dying. But, just as he always did, he still promised me that as soon he got off the phone he would sit down and write his best-seller. And this makes me feel really bad because, for the first time in our long relationship, I didn't believe him."

I was actually pleasantly surprised that Rita didn't immediately take the opportunity to remind me about her book, *"Actress to Actress"*, that had recently been published. Under normal circumstances she would have done so. Somehow I was touched by her self-restraint. I felt it demonstrated her real affection for Joe and her gratitude to him for being her sounding board all these years.

When I eventually replaced the receiver, I searched for Joe's last letter to me. In it he had written many of the things that Rita had just told me.

I cried some more. Joe had been a lover, a mentor, a cheerleader, a father figure and a guardian angel in my life. He had always been there for me and, somehow, losing him was like losing part of who I was as a person. Coupled with the death of my very special father, I now felt a deep sense of personal loss.

To cope with this void, I knew I wanted to spend a little time in peace and surrounded by beauty. I was determined to spend more time with whales. I had already taken Mayumi on a whale research project in Maui, and I had truly become hooked by these amazing creatures. So, in July 1999, I took Elisar on another whale research project, this time in Newfoundland, with a well-known local marine biologist and whale enthusiast, Dave Snow.

Most of my friends back in the UK thought I was mad. Believing Newfoundland was somewhere in the Arctic Circle, they thought I would probably freeze to death on a summer holiday! How wrong they were. That summer turned out, not only to be unseasonably hot, but the whales were plentiful. The gannet, puffin, kittiwake and guillemot colonies were thriving. And my initial fascination with whales and seabirds soon became an obsession. So much so, that once the two week holiday was over, I decided to buy a house there. At that time property prices were low and I ended up with a 3 bedroom, 5 reception room house overlooking the ocean and islands in the heart of the Witless Bay Ecological Reserve, for the equivalent of around 25,000 pounds.

I loved everything about Newfoundland from the outset. I loved the people. I loved the informality. I loved the wildness of the vast landscapes. I loved the vast panoply of the night sky. And I even loved the ocean fog, the way it hovered, floated and danced over the ocean as it made its way to shore. I knew this new home could be a much-needed bolt hole, somewhere I could write, watch the antics of the whales and seabirds from my window, and marvel at the passing icebergs tinged fuchsia pink in the early morning sunrises.

And so I made my move. Some of my friends thought I would die of boredom living in such a remote place. Others smiled cynically, silently keeping their thoughts to themselves. And yet others predicted, I would be back on the next flight back home. But there were those, just a handful of them, who patted me on the back, said I was being typically courageous, typically independent, said I had guts, said I was doing the right thing. They even said they would do it too if only they were daring enough.

Why did I do it? Probably because, to me, it presented just one more challenge to what had already been a very varied, well-travelled and adventurous life. Since my childhood days when I was able to look at an atlas and discover there was a whole big world out there waiting to be explored, I had always had "itchy feet". In fact this need to travel had, at times, been so overwhelming that the only way to quench the thirst for adventure it produced was just to get up and go. This move to the wilds of Newfoundland was just such a moment.

So then the question - why now? That question was, probably, the easiest to answer. Over the past eight years as my work took me to the refugee camps, orphanages and rehabilitation homes of countries such as Bosnia, Azerbaijan and Croatia, all wrecked by war, natural disasters or ethnic conflict, I felt the need for a little beauty in my life. My job involved providing desperately needed medical and surgical attention to refugees and displaced people with physical disabilities. But, despite a wise, well-meaning and oft-repeated warning never to get emotionally involved with the people I was working with, it would have taken a cold heart indeed not to be affected by the many tragedies I witnessed and the many heartrending stories I listened to during this period. Also my children convinced me that, after so many years of looking after them and others, it was time to look after myself. Time to give myself the space, the tranquility and the opportunity to meditate, on paper, on a life that had been both fun-filled and action-packed. Time to reflect on a life that, like all others, despite its successes and rewards, had also had its share of disappointments and failures.

In Newfoundland I found the peace, the stark natural beauty and the warmth of the local people I had been hankering for. I realized instinctively that here was a place I could write my book undisturbed by the intrusive distractions of city living. Here was a place I could spend countless hours watching the whales cavorting without even stepping out of my front door. And here was a place I would never feel like a stranger, where I would be welcomed, without exception, by people in my local community. And, above all, here was a place that could offer a home for my children where they would be free to enjoy the beauty of nature in all its many varieties, in one of the last unspoiled natural refuges on this planet. I had always felt a little guilty of not really providing them a stable home all these years. And now, here was the chance to remedy that.

So I began to settle into my new home. Familiar things I had gathered from my wanderings came with me. Textiles, fabrics, baskets, tribal objects, carpets, buddhas and prayer mats all finally found their natural home. The vibrant colors of India, Nepal, Thailand, Burma, Indonesia, the Philippines, Patagonia and Tanzania vied, harmonized and blended as they draped over my furniture, spread over my bed and hung from my walls. Ethnic baskets for rice, sweet potatoes and betel nuts all found a niche of their own. Bronze buddhas from Tibet, carved ivory santos from Manila and ancient tribal figures from Kalinga stood side by side on my shelves.

The views from the windows on all sides of my house offered an almost unrestricted panorama of the bay, illustrating an abundant choice of natural wonders – whales, seabirds, rugged coastline, pristine water, undisturbed islands, pine forests and rocky shores. A kitten kept me company, an occasional moose came down to feed in my garden and a family of otters cavorted in the pond behind me.

When I first arrived I looked around and thought, perhaps, I had never actually lived. I had never before been able to slow down the pace of my life. Just the normal everyday pressures of living had taken their toll. And I came to the realization that, for one precious moment, I would no longer have that insatiable urge to travel. I felt completely content. The contentment came from being surrounded, for the first time, by people who appeared to be innately happy. The contentment came from being immersed in the natural beauty of my surroundings. And the contentment came from spending full days out on the ocean with my friend, Dave Snow, among the numerous species of whales that visited their summer feeding grounds around Newfoundland every summer. So, despite no longer earning a salary, I never felt so rich.

And the funny thing was that – even in the first two months living there – three city-dwelling friends came to visit me and they all ended up buying properties near me too. They fell in love with Newfoundland, just as I had done. They no longer teased me about the cold, the isolation and the boredom of living alone in remote places. They immediately understood.

But I did say to myself maybe things would be different with the approaching winter. With the prevailing northeast wind howling through the eaves of my wooden house, with the ice settling on the windowpanes and with the winter fog enveloping my home for days at a time, maybe the honeymoon period would be over and maybe, just maybe, my innate wanderlust would return.

Over the years, my love of Newfoundland and its people has never diminished. But enduring my first long winter there, I do have to admit, was indeed a shock to my system. And I never found the courage to repeat it. So Newfoundland became my summer home, somewhere I would return to every year in June, July, August and September, to renew friendships and to soak up the rugged beauty of the place I wanted to call "home".

On September 11 2001, I was in Newfoundland when the attack on the World Trade Center took place. In fact, Shirley and Zeb were visiting me at the time and we were out on an early morning hike together. When we returned, I found my daughter Jasmine watching television. I admonished her for not being outside on such a beautiful day but she simply pointed to the television without saying a word. Like everyone else around the world, we watched in stunned silence as we saw the second tower explode and crash to the ground.

Shirley suddenly screamed. "My daughter, Sarah! Her office is in the World Trade Center!"

Of course, there was no way of communicating with Sarah. So, Shirley with Zeb in tow, decided to fly home immediately. But that was not an easy thing to accomplish. All the transatlantic flights had been diverted, most of them to the safe airports of Newfoundland - Gander, Stephenville and St. John's and none of them were leaving. I drove them to St. John's airport and it was chaotic. On the city's tiny airfield, international planes were sitting wing tip to wing tip. Their passengers were forced to remain on board for five days, being fed by the hospitable Newfoundlanders who collected food, diapers, baby formula, clean clothing, sanitary equipment and anything else that was required to make the passengers' lives more comfortable. Once they were permitted to disembark, the Newfoundlanders took the stranded passengers into their own homes and allowed them to stay until the planes were given permission to make their onward journey to their original destinations.

It was an extraordinary and heroic time. Friendships forged between the travellers and their local Newfoundland families remain strong to this day. Many of them contributed to an education fund to give Newfoundland students scholarships to US Universities. Others have returned for holidays there. And even an award-winning play was written about this incident, entitled, *Come From Away*. It was proof, once again, that something positive and good often comes from something bad.

Thankfully, Shirley's daughter, Sarah, turned out to be fine. She happened to be late to work that day. But it was during this visit that Shirley also talked about her son's recent trip to Costa Rica. It was somewhere I had never been so I listened intently. Later I read up about it and, of course, my feet started to itch again. *Maybe I had room in my life for one more adventure?* I decided to check it out, little realizing that I would find a new home and a new purpose for the next fifteen years!

Chapter 36
Farewell to the Pearl of Dubrovnik

So, after the summer when I returned to London, I checked out Gap Year projects in Costa Rica. I thought that if I arranged to work on a few projects in different parts of the country, I would get to know it, at least superficially, and decide whether I would like to live there more permanently. It suddenly seemed like a good idea. Elisar and Jasmine were living in London and Mayumi was still living in Los Angeles. Costa Rica was conveniently placed, halfway between the two. I had missed having all my three children together with me and imagined that we could, perhaps, establish a home base in Costa Rica where we could all gather in the holidays.

And so, for the next three months, I watched over leatherback turtles nesting and hatching on a remote beach in Guanacaste, I looked after orphaned and injured animals in a wildlife refuge in Santa Ana and I helped build a kitchen in a biological station in Cabo Blanco National Park. And when it was all over, a friend came to pick me up from Cabo Blanco and brought me to a beautiful guest house, Casa de las Tias, in Escazu, owned by Xavier and Pilar Vela. For the first time in three months, I was able to look in a mirror and I didn't recognize the person who looked back at me. Not only was I very suntanned and in desperate need of a haircut, but I had lost close to 20lbs. The following evening, Pilar took me to a performance at the nearby Little Theatre of Costa Rica, the local English Language theatre. And, without the slightest hint of anything momentous that was going to happen, a seed had been planted in my brain and an idea for a new career was germinating and about to take centre stage in my life.

And then, of course, there was Michael Cannon. Michael had been at Marlborough School with my brother, Alexander. Michael had been living in Costa Rica since 1971and owned a small hotel near Poas Volcano, one of the main tourist attractions, just north of San Jose. Michael had been separated from his wife for more than ten years by the time I met him, and although he returned to the UK every year to visit her and his four adult children, he told me the marriage was over. He called me several times once I was back in the UK, expounding the virtues of Costa Rica and the many reasons I should opt to live there. But my mother was getting frailer by the day. She had started refusing to eat and I spent the next few months looking after her, all thoughts of moving to Costa Rica, pushed to the side.

The one thing my mother yearned to do before she died, was visit Dubrovnik and see her family houses one more time. Following the removal of President Tito, citizens who had formerly been banned from the country, were now allowed back. Mummy had taken Elisar, Jasmine and me to Dubrovnik two years earlier. She had reconnected with many of her relatives she hadn't seen for decades. It had been an emotional visit, her first in 60 years. Now, this time we all knew it would be her last and we were determined to make it special. Marina, Tessa, Alexander and I brought her there and even managed to get her into her former house, situated in the centre of the bay of Cavtad, south of Dubrovnik, that had been taken over by the Communist Party as a guest house for holidaying officials and their families.

As she sat in her wheelchair on the balcony of her house, gazing out over the Adriatic Sea, as she had probably done so many times in her youth, she announced, "Now I can die happy!"

And, within a day she fell very ill and, against her wishes, we had to bring her to the local hospital. The doctor recommended very forcefully that she stay where she was but she was determined to die at home in her own bed. She begged us to ignore the doctor's wishes, and to bring her back to London. We were very concerned lest she die on the way home. But we also wanted to carry out her one last wish. So we cut short the holiday and brought her back to London. Within a month she was rushed by ambulance to the Chelsea & Westminster Hospital where she died of pneumonia. We buried her alongside her beloved Billy in the cemetery at Mortlake.

My mother had been such a sweet, giving person, that she left another big hole in my life. She had, uncomplainingly, supported me and my children financially for decades, since Ben had failed to help us. A good friend of mine, a barrister, had often advised me to report Ben to the CSA to force him to pay, at least, child maintenance. But, I had no wish to cause any animosity between him and our children so I never did. What had upset me more than that though, was that Ben had never bothered to fly to England to visit Jasmine in hospital during the several times she had been admitted for her mental health issues. In those times, too, my mother had always been there for both Jasmine and me.

In 1995, eight years before her death, my mother had decided to sell her house in Mallorca. As her energy had declined with her advancing age, it had become too much of a responsibility to her and too much of a drain on her resources. For us all, it was an end of a glorious era and a time to look back on our shared memories of many happy summers. Once sold, she generously divided the proceeds between me and my siblings and I gratefully lived off the income it provided for several years. And then, within a month of her passing, I had sold my apartment in London, I had helped Elisar and Jasmine move into their own rented accommodations and I was packed and ready to leave for the next adventure in my life, in Costa Rica.

Chapter 37
Theatre In My Blood?

It was my father who said to me, "If you want something to happen, you have to make it happen yourself. Don't expect others to make it happen for you!" I have embraced this religiously all my life, whether it was to do with work, to do with travelling or to do with the raising of my children. I made things happen. Sometimes, obviously, I made the wrong choices and regretted them. But, very often, I made the right ones. The move to Costa Rica was the right one. Even Elisar and Jasmine told me that.

"If you hadn't decided to sell the apartment and leave," he said. "I would still be living at home in my thirties. It was time for me to move on. But home was so comfortable that I just stayed on."

And, Jasmine, who had been very much dependent on me due to her mental health issues, was equally sanguine. "You moving out was probably the best thing you ever did for me. I needed to make a life on my own. I needed to know I could be responsible for myself. And you helped me do that."

So, rather than feel guilty, I actually felt good about selling up and leaving London.

The next thing on my list was to find somewhere to live in Costa Rica. After two rather miserable short-term rentals, I found a great apartment in an old converted house, quite rare to come by in Costa Rica. It was in Escazu, a place where, apart from the coastal areas, most of the expats were settled. But I liked the fact that the house was in a very Costa Rican neighborhood and the local "king" of my street was a huge Costa Rican, Asdrubal, with bulging muscles and a smile for everyone. And he just happened to be the porter/handyman/gardener/security guard for my house. No one dared cross him. And no one was stronger than him. A couple of times someone tried to break into the premises while I was living there, but Asdrubal saw them off in seconds flourishing a broom in one hand and a machete in the other. So I felt extremely safe from the start.

The question that arose was, now that I had arrived, what was I going to do? So, when Pilar brought me to a board meeting of The Little Theatre group a couple of weeks later, I immediately jumped in and offered to join as Secretary. And the following year, I even put my name forward for President. I think, possibly, many of the people involved were glad for some new blood and accepted me immediately. I soon discovered there was a mountain of work and a lot of parties, associated with being a member of the theatre group. We put on five productions a year, mainly with expats, both professional and amateurs, but also with Costa Ricans wanting an opportunity to improve their English.

Again, as I had done so many times before, I jumped in at the deep end. One play I had really loved was Ed Graczyk's *Come Back to the Five & Dime, Jimmy Dean, Jimmy Dean*. I decided to direct it, little realizing at the time what a complicated piece of theatre it was. It involved two casts, one younger group from the 1950s and another older group from the 1970s. Occasionally, the two groups had to be onstage at the same time. To distinguish between the two, I used blue lighting for the 1950s cast. Fortunately, I had plenty of support from other, seasoned, directors. Part of the fun I had was finding items on Ebay for the James Dean "shrine", which made up an elaborate part of the set. I even found a nude photo of James Dean that I placed strategically in a 1950s fan magazine. At one point the cast was supposed to gather around and look at photos of Dean in the magazine. I kept the photo back from rehearsals, preferring to use it on opening night so it would elicit the most natural shocked reaction from the cast. It worked!

Following the success of this production, I now had the directing bug. But, as President of the Board, I helped in all areas of our productions. So at different times, I was stage manager, I was prop master, I searched for costumes in local flea markets and I did sound and lights. I also oversaw the transfer of the theatre from a private house in Escazu to the Lawrence Olivier Theatre in the capital, San Jose. This was not only a much larger venue but also had proper theatre facilities, like dressing rooms, tracker spotlights and a sound booth.

My second attempt at direction was *Calendar Girls*. I had written the script myself based on the British film of the same name. I was told by more experienced directors that having the stage go dark and then having a camera flash for the "nude" scenes wouldn't work. But, in fact, I proved them wrong and it worked out even better than I had hoped. The third play I directed was *Steel Magnolias* and, although challenging, it also worked pretty well. I even took on acting roles myself in several productions, including as Marguerite in *An O'Henry Christmas*, Megan in *84 Charing Cross Road* and, my favourite of all, as Eleanor, the mother-in-law from hell, in *No Sex, Please, We're British!* I could never claim to be a natural actor but I enjoyed performing and was more than willing to learn from the professionals in our theatre group.

I also found time to get involved with several other projects during this time – The annual Queen's Birthday Party at the British Ambassador's residence, to raise funds for needy schools across Costa Rica. My job every year was finding enough acts to perform on the two stages throughout the day. Along with my friend, wildlife artist Didi Hyde, I also helped to publish Costa Rica's first green guide, *Paginas Verdes de Costa Rica*, a directory of green businesses and services throughout the country, that we gave away at local supermarkets. I started a film club screening mostly foreign and arthouse movies, first at a private home in Escazu and then at the North American Cultural Center. I became a prison visitor to two English girls who were imprisoned on drug-related charges. And I resurrected the arrangement I had in Azerbaijan with the Central School of Speech & Drama by bringing their second year drama education students to work with the indigenous Bribri tribe in the Talamanca mountains.

When I had visited the Bribri, on one of my first trips to the Caribbean coast of Costa Rica, the women there had told me they feared losing their culture due to the influx of tourists. They needed help to write down their history and their legends so their young children could learn about their past. This was at a bad time for the tribe as there was a disease affecting their banana and cacao plantations and, thus, the families were suffering from lack of income. On my return to England I discussed all this with Sally Mackey, head of the Drama Education department at Central and, just as we had done in Azerbaijan, she agreed to send out four second-year students on a 6-week rotating basis, to help the Bribri put their lives and legends into dramatic form.

All the drama students who came out and stayed, in fairly primitive conditions, among the Bribri, raved about the experience. Most of them cried when they left. They had forged a strong bond, particularly with the children of the tribe. I also arranged for one of the students, Christina, to work with a local indigenous theatre group, the Pa Blu Serke, to perform a production of one of the historical pieces the students and the Bribri children had worked on. I then arranged for it to be performed at our theatre in San Jose and it was a much-publicized sell-out. The Bribri were happy with the result and I was happy for them. They realized that, not only could they could make people more aware of their history with this play but they could also earn some money by performing it in colleges, universities and museums around Costa Rica.

Chapter 38
Paradise Lost

As a prison visitor, I created a bond with two young English girls who had been caught as drug mules and were imprisoned in El Buen Pastor prison in Desamparados, on the outskirts of San Jose.

El Buen Pastor was nestled into the lush foothills of the massive southern mountain range, overlooking Costa Rica's Central Valley. It was obvious from my first glimpse of it that the ramshackle building had fallen on hard times. It was visibly falling apart and there were no funds, so the Director told me, to repair it. Some months before I started visiting the girls, Chris and Jo, the building had been deemed unfit for its current use and condemned for demolition. So, further down the road, a more modern extension was being built to take its place. But this too was faced with a major problem. There was a severe shortage of potable water on the new site and so it was only being used as a temporary "protection" unit to house those girls whose lives were considered to be in danger. This was where I found Chris on our first meeting. But Jo was in solitary confinement.

The girls, Chris from a middle-class neighbourhood of Leeds and Jo from a depressed inner-city area of Wolverhampton, were lovers. But it was because of their love for one another that they found themselves serving a five and a half years prison sentence without the possibility of parole. Both were very young, 22 and 23. Chris, soft-spoken and more talkative of the two, was the quintessential English rose, voluptuous figure, porcelain complexion, auburn hair and green eyes. Jo, the amateur poet, was part Jamaican, more introspective, with dark eyes and an ever-ready smile that radiated warmth.

On my first visit I was subjected to a body search and then required to wait in line for a couple of hours in the hot sun while my ID was being processed. Finally, I was given permission to enter the prison compound. There were actually four English girls serving sentences at El Buen Pastor at the time and I was taken to a separate room where they had all been assembled to meet me. Two of them were very defiant and told me pointblank they weren't interested in anyone visiting them. But Chris and Jo immediately grasped the opportunity. This first visit was to begin a routine of twice-weekly visits, every Sunday and Thursday, until a year later when they were finally released back to the UK to finish serving out their sentence there.

As we sat under the shade of a tree that first Sunday, I asked them how they came to be incarcerated in a country they weren't even interested in visiting. Theirs was a long and tragic story but not dissimilar from the stories of many young people who get used as drug mules around the world. It was a sobering lesson on how desperation for money to simply live a normal life can often lead people to do something so dangerous and so risky.

"I was to blame," Jo told me, "I'd had a previous drugs conviction in England. I was caught at Heathrow with 92 kilos of cannabis that I was paid to bring in from Jamaica."

"So why did you make the same mistake again?" I asked.

"Because Chris and I were in love. We had put a deposit down on a place together. We needed money to buy things for it, furniture and stuff. They offered me $15,000 for one trip to bring in 10 kilos of cocaine from Costa Rica. It was tempting."

When Chris found out about this plan she was fuming. "I called Jo and threatened to break off our affair."

So, not wanting to lose Chris, Jo relented. She told her "recruiter", that she would find someone else to take her place as the drug mule. But this proved impossible.

"Since Jo was constantly being threatened," Chris said, "we finally we said, if it's got to be done, it's got to be done. But I didn't want Jo to go alone."

"When we arrived in San Jose, the "recruiter" was there at the hotel waiting for us." Jo said, "I recognized him immediately from my last drugs trip to Jamaica. He told me he had drilled the bottoms of our suitcases and put the drugs inside. He assured us everything would be fine."

Their return trip, they were told, would take them through Caracas and then on to Paris where they would disembark before heading on to the UK.

"That way," Chris explained, "they said we could mingle with thousands of football supporters who would be making their way back to England from an international match in France."

In the morning a taxi picked the girls up from the Hotel Europa and took them to the airport.

"I wasn't particularly frightened," Chris said, "but just very sad. I knew something would go wrong."

"We walked into the Departure Lounge, hardly daring to breathe," Jo said. "We sat down and I said to Chris, 'We're going to be OK! We're really going to be OK!'"

When their flight was called, the girls, much relieved but still nervous, joined the queue to board the Taca Airlines plane. But just as they were about to enter the plane they felt someone tapping them on the back. They turned around to face a large unsmiling man with greying hair and sweating temples.

"You no fly!" he announced.

"What do you mean? What's going on?" the girls asked.

Inside the office of the airport police Chris and Jo were handcuffed. The girls watched as an officer picked up their suitcases, opened them, removed the contents and proceeded to rip away the linings.

"We were terrified," Chris said, "but then we saw there was nothing there. I couldn't believe it. We were so happy."

Their sense of relief didn't last long. The officer reached into his pocket, drew out a screwdriver and drove it hard into the base of each suitcase. They watched as he extracted it covered in a fine white powder.

He warned them, "You're in BIG trouble. BIG trouble!" They were escorted to the local police station in Alajuela.

A welcome visit that evening from the British Consul, Sheila Pacheco, raised the girls' spirits somewhat but her message brought them little cheer.

"Sheila was really kind and sympathetic to us," Chris told me, "and it felt so good to speak English with someone again. But she warned us we would be going to prison in Costa Rica, possibly for a long, long time, between 8 and 20 years. We were utterly devastated."

I asked them what contact they'd had with their parents.

"At first I was too upset to call them," Chris replied, "I thought they'd be horrified and angry with me. But when I did finally speak to them they were so relieved to hear from me. They said they would support me 100%. I was phoning them reverse charges to begin with until they ended up with a phone bill of nearly two thousand pounds!"

The court case that swiftly followed their arrival in "El Buen Pastor" found them guilty and sentenced them each to 5 years and 4 months.

"I wanted to tell the court it was all my fault, that Chris wasn't guilty of anything," Jo explained. "I wanted to take the blame myself. But my lawyer warned me if I did that the judge would probably increase Chris's sentence to 8 years. I had no choice but to plead guilty."

In fact, my first meeting with the girls took place while Jo was in solitary, a separate derelict block surrounded by a high wire fence situated at the far end of the prison grounds. Despite the appalling conditions there and the fact that, for a first offence, she had been sentenced to 18 days, Jo still managed to smile when I arrived. I asked her how she came to be there.

"I caught a girl stealing Chris's trainers," Jo explained. "I guess I should have just walked away from it but I didn't. We'd already had so many of our clothes stolen. You see you can't leave anything out here, not even for a second, otherwise it'll be taken immediately, even our toilet paper. Anyway the girl pulled a knife on me. And then someone informed the officers and we got caught."

Although most of what I had heard so far about the treatment of the prisoners by the officers was negative, I asked Chris if there were any instances of kindness that she had received from them.

"Well, yes," she said, "one or two have been very nice to me, the ones that speak a bit of English. They have posted letters for me, arranged for me to see the Director and the doctor, that sort of thing. But mainly here prisoners run the prison, the guards are easily intimidated, that is well known by everyone."

"A lot of the tougher prisoners pay the guards to turn a blind eye," Jo added, "they can then bring in almost anything they like, including drugs, knives and alcohol. And then they either use them themselves or sell them off to the other girls."

I asked Jo what were her plans were if she was allowed to go back to England.

"I would like to study law," she said, "so I can help other prisoners abroad. But, with my two convictions, I don't know if they'd let me."

"In my way of thinking," I said, "that would make you particularly well qualified to help others who find themselves in the same situation as you."

"But the very first thing I want to do," Jo continued, "apart, of course, from seeing my family, is to apologize to Chris's parents. I feel really guilty and I want to tell them I'm truly sorry she got into all this because of me."

I suggested they make the most of their time there by teaching English to other inmates, by painting, keeping journals, writing poetry and staying busy. So, over the ensuing weeks, I brought them all the materials they would need plus books, sanitary supplies and, of course, chocolates! I was proud of their resilience. I doubted very much I would have survived a similar experience. With their permission, and with their names changed to protect them, I wrote an article about them and it was published in the Independent on Sunday.

A few times I brought Jasmine with me to visit Chris and Jo. When she had completed her 8 week massage course in Guanacaste, she came to stay with me in Escazu. Just as she had done when she met Ruggia and Abil in Azerbaijan, Jasmine immediately struck up a close friendship with the two girls. And, being around the same age as them, she realized immediately how fortunate she was that she had never been forced to make the life-altering decision in her own life that they had been forced to make in theirs.

Chapter 39
A Difficult Romance

That Christmas, in 2004, I finally had my wish, when all three of my children, accompanied by their partners, visited me on holiday. I took them to the islands of Bocas del Toro in Panama. Sadly, though we didn't know it at the time, it was to be one of our last gatherings all together.

The following summer I flew to London for Elisar's wedding, taking a taxi directly from Heathrow Airport to the registry office. I had never seen Elisar so happy. At 35 his personal and professional life was just taking off. After years of working with one film company, he had decided to branch out, set up his own production company and work on his own projects. From the age of 23, he had already made a few low-budget films, but he was now determined to help resurrect British wrestling that, after a few scandals in the late 60s, had disappeared from TV screens, with his friend, Elliot Grove, he wanted to help create a British Film Festival, Raindance, to complement the US Festival, Sundance, and, with a group of friends including Edgar Wright, he wanted to help promote the British independent film industry by setting up the New Producers' Alliance.

In my after-wedding speech, I reminded everyone of the time when Ben was celebrating his 35th birthday, and Elisar, at the age of 6, had blurted out, "35? 35?"

And Ben had replied, "Yes, 35, what's wrong with that?"

And Elisar had replied, "Well, 35 that's really, really old. That's the end of that then, isn't it?"

Yet, here was Elisar, aged 35 and his new life, both personal and professional, was just beginning.

After the wedding I returned to Costa Rica where my relationship with Michael Cannon was continuing to blossom. Although it was constantly fraught with problems, we had managed to ease into a routine where I drove up to the hotel every Friday night and spent the weekend with him at his lodge. Or we would drive down to Puerto Viejo together, one of our favourite destinations in Costa Rica, and spend long weekends there with our many Caribbean friends. We also took side-trips to Cuba to stay with my friends Nicolas and Rosa Porro in Havana, two trips to the Isla de Cocos, where we swam with shoals of graceful Moorish Idol fish, schools of hammerhead sharks and the occasional solitary whale shark. And another up to Northern Labrador, with my Newfoundland friend, Dave Snow, to see polar bears in their natural habitat.

But, despite the fact that Michael's children all lived in England, they continued to voice their disapproval of our affair and did everything they could to put an end to it.

"Their main concern," Michael told me, "is that I will change my Will and make you the beneficiary of the farm and the hotel."

"That's ridiculous," I said, "I wouldn't even want either. I don't know the first thing about farming or running a hotel!"

"I know, it's preposterous," he said. "Plus they know very well my Will is watertight and they will inherit everything. Which will, in fact, be a joke on them because neither the farm nor the hotel are making money and they will have debts to pay!"

Michael's children still constantly reminded him he had a "wife" in England, from whom he was not yet divorced, and they warned him that I was probably a "gold digger"! Michael was a highly complex man and he was torn between them and me. Sadly, he never was able to summon up the courage to stick up for me and, thus, I realized the affair was doomed from the start.

I found this hard to understand. My children were happy for me that I had found someone to share my life with in Costa Rica. Why did his children not feel the same way about their father? Were they secretly hoping he would get back with their mother, Cherida, after over a decade of living, not only apart but on different continents? He was hesitant to show me a very unpleasant letter one of his daughters had written to him about me, for fear of upsetting me. But I insisted because I wanted to know what I was up against. Even his close friends of many years were appalled at his children's attitude towards me. One of them told me, "It was a standard joke amongst all Michael's friends in England that if their family home was being burnt to the ground, Cherida would first save the horses, then the dogs, then the children and then, lastly, Michael! That's how much she cared for him!"

Whatever their reason, his children managed to make Michael's life miserable and refused to accept my role as his girlfriend. They made him feel guilty by constantly telling him that his brother had been a better father to them than he had been.

At one time, we bought 25 acres of land together, with a waterfall behind it, in Bajos de Toro. He told me he was buying it with me in secret and, together, we would develop it into an artists' retreat and he wouldn't tell his children because it was "none of their business". Of course, they eventually managed to coax the information out of him and forced him to sell his half. Yet again, he couldn't stand up to them. He told me they said, "You're not going to invest any of our money with her!"

So, as he always did, he backed down and did their bidding.

Yet, when a major earthquake struck, in January 2009, and Michael's hotel was completely destroyed, not one of them flew over to help him. I was the one who walked through the rubble with him, day after day, picking up and binning literally tons of broken glass. I was the one who bought him dozens of plastic boxes and retrieved as many salvageable items as I could find from what was left of his house and hotel. And I was the one who stood by him and advised him to take a break after I saw he was close to a nervous breakdown.

Meanwhile, his children were constantly calling him, writing to him, badgering him, insisting that he start rebuilding the hotel immediately from scratch. They didn't take into account that he had no money to do so. And, since neither his house nor his hotel had been insured, he wasn't about to receive any compensation from an insurance company for their loss. So, by insisting he rebuild, they were forcing him to borrow large sums of money both from friends and from banks, money that he knew would take him the rest of his life to pay back. His mood changed dramatically. All our friends noticed it. The stress was taking its toll and he began taking it out on me.

I had been seriously considering ending our relationship before the earthquake but, once it happened, I thought it would be unfair to make him suffer another blow. He was counting on me to be there for him. So the affair continued. And, to his credit, he did rebuild the hotel. Within less than two years, Poas Volcano Lodge, was reopened, not as a converted family home as it had been before, but as an expensive boutique hotel.

At this point, again, I thought he was back on his feet and it would be a good moment to end the relationship. But then he was diagnosed with prostate cancer that required immediate surgery. Again, not one of his children bothered to come to visit him and to make sure he was recovering. I visited him every day, even though the hospital was on the opposite side of the town from where I lived. Thankfully, he did recover and was soon back at the new hotel greeting and entertaining the guests, as he so loved to do.

Out of the blue, within weeks of the hotel opening, my phone rang. It was Rita.

"Darling, I'm here in Costa Rica!" she announced. "I'm here to do some interviews for my documentary, *World of Film* about the movie business around the world. When am I going to see you?"

I was about to answer. But then Rita being Rita, answered her own question.

"I'm here with my producer, Peter," she continued. "We'd love to stay with you. We wouldn't get in your way. We'll be out all day. It will just be a place to sleep."

I smiled to myself. In a way I was relieved. Rita was still the same. But, at least, this time she hadn't just turned up on my doorstep in the middle of the night in the pouring rain!

"I'm not living in a house any more, Rita," I replied. "I am in an apartment with only two rooms."

"Oh, that will be fine," Rita gushed. "Peter can sleep on the sofa. He won't mind."

"I think you'd be far more comfortable in a hotel," I said, desperately trying to avert a difficult situation. "My boyfriend, Michael, has a small hotel. I'm sure he would love to have you to stay."

Fortunately she agreed. At the age of 82, Rita's energy had not dissipated, her passion had not waned and her beauty, although faded, was still arresting. As I had imagined she would, she instantly charmed Michael. Within seconds of meeting her he was in her thrall, bending over backwards to make her comfortable and to cater to her every whim.

Instead of ordering a taxi for them, Michael drove Rita and Peter to see Poas Volcano, then to the massive waterfall at the Waterfall Gardens and, when he was free, even to some of their business appointments during the following week. He made sure they occupied the best rooms and even laid on packed lunches for them.

When I joined them for dinner the first night Rita and I gossiped about the past over a few drinks. I had warned Michael that Rita would probably not eat dinner though she might steal a few morsels from our plates. Actually, I thought that by the age of 82, Rita might finally have allowed herself to indulge in a proper meal.

Michael asked her if she'd prefer fish or chicken.

"Oh, Michael," she replied, "how I wish. But I can't afford to put on another pound. I am filming this series. But don't let that stop you from eating. Peter's very hungry. He can eat for two of us!"

I ordered the fish and the two guys ordered the chicken. We sat down to eat. You can probably guess what happened next.

Rita speared mouthfuls from all our plates and Peter, who politely refused a second helping, probably went to bed hungry.

When offered Tres Leches for dessert, again Rita declined.

"Darling, I can't touch milk. But you go ahead. Don't worry about me!"

Needless to say when she saw us all relishing the dessert, she picked up a spoon.

"I'll just try a tiny bit, if I may?" she said to Michael.

"Go ahead," he replied indulgently and pushed the dessert closer to her.

"No, no. Only a tiny bit!" she said, pushing the plate back to him.

"Are you sure?" he asked. "We can always order another one!"

"No, no. Absolutely not!" she replied, smiling sweetly, her spoon hovering like a circling hawk over the Tres Leches. "I couldn't possibly eat a whole one. But it's so good. So possibly just one more spoonful won't hurt."

She then turned to me and stuck her spoon into my dessert, then Peter's, then back to Michael's, snatching his last mouthful before he had a chance to swallow it.

"I'm so full!" she announced. "You're a naughty man, Michael. You shouldn't have let me do that!"

A few hours later there was the familiar knock on my door. Somehow, I had almost expected it.

"Caroline, are you asleep? I need to talk to you!"

I rolled over and nudged the sleeping Michael.

"I told you," I whispered. "I haven't seen her for ages and I just knew she would wake me up to talk!"

"OK, Rita," I said, "Give me a minute!"

It was icy night up in the cloud-forest of Poas, so I borrowed Michael's thick dressing gown, cocooned myself inside it and opened the door. I followed Rita to her room. She was shivering, obviously unprepared for the bitterly cold, damp nights in the mountains.

"Can I share that with you?" Rita pointed to the voluminous bathrobe I was wearing.

I couldn't say no. So I opened the bathrobe and she snuggled up beside me.

Then the two of us sat there, swaddled in Michael's bathrobe, and reminisced. Although her mother was long dead, I was touched to see Rita was still wearing the fluffy pink slippers, much-worn now, but still functional.

I realized I had known her now for 48 years. We were "old mates", "buddies", "comrades-in-arms". Our characters and lifestyles could not have been more opposing and yet, strangely, life had chosen to throw us together at different times and in different places. She was not even a best friend. And yet, here she was, popping in and out of my life and making her mark on me. We were joined through our love for Joe, who had been a huge influence on both our lives and who was a shared anchor to both our pasts.

We chatted effusively into the early hours of the morning like two excited teenagers after a date. We had so many combined memories to explore - about Princess Grace, about old friends we had known in New York, about plays on Broadway we had seen together, about movies old and new, about her failed love affair with Ian Black, about motherhood, about our lives in the intervening years and much, much more.

We giggled helplessly as we remembered how incapable Rita had been after her two broken marriages, her ignorance about paying household bills, her inability to book a flight, her fear of being without a man in her life to maintain her, indulge her and take care of her. And we marvelled at how the traits that Rita should have had in her 20s and 30s, like independence, focus and self-confidence, had suddenly blossomed in her 60s, 70s and 80s.

And then, of course, there was our guardian angel, Joe. We both acknowledged we owed him a huge debt of gratitude.

I wondered aloud what Joe would have said had he seen us both together 48 years after that dinner in her Park Avenue apartment.

Rita smiled. "He would have said. Don't worry about her, darling. It's only Rita being Rita!"

We spoke a few times after this visit. But that night would be the last time Rita would turn up in my life. She died in 2016, two years before I moved to the US with my own plans to show up on her doorstep unannounced one rainy day! I always wondered what her reaction would have been had I done so.

Now that Michael was more busy running the new hotel, it seemed like a good opportunity to finally break free from the relationship. It was a relief, I think, for both of us. He no longer had to justify the affair to his children. And I no longer had to put up with their mean-spirited attitude. Ironically, his youngest daughter, who had been the most vocal of the four against me, held out an olive branch after our split and, while not actually apologizing for her prior behaviour, did invite me to stay with her and her new husband if I ever visited the UK. Although I never took her up on her invitation, I was grateful for her change of heart.

A few months earlier, Jasmine had left Costa Rica to live in the Philippines and had found a new boyfriend there. She was working in Ben's museum up in Baguio, in the Mountain Province, but was, once again, forgetting to take her meds. As a consequence, she had a very bad episode and ended up in hospital, followed by rehab. I flew out to the Philippines to visit her there and was appalled at the facility she was housed in. The old house itself was made entirely of wood and was, thus, a firetrap. And the area around the house was fenced and padlocked. So, if there had been a fire and even if the patients had managed to get out of the house, they would still have been trapped as they were entirely fenced in with no possibility of escape. I couldn't wait for her to be discharged because I truly feared for her life.

The split with Michael also freed me up to spend more time with Mayumi and her partner, John, in LA. My visa allowed me to stay up to 3 months in a year and so, rather than actually live with them, I bought my own condo in Culver City which I lent to friends in the months I wasn't there.

In 2012, while visiting LA, I offered to work for the Obama reelection campaign. When asked if I had any experience canvassing during elections, I was able to say "yes". I had campaigned with Billy several times while he was an MP, and had knocked on many doors. So I was sent to Las Vegas twice to knock on doors there and encourage people to get out and vote. The reception I received was vastly different from the reception I received while canvassing Inverness-shire. Instead of being offered a cup of tea, I was faced with barrel of a shotgun.

Las Vegas, I discovered, was a place of enormous contrasts. The doors I was knocking on belonged to a wide variety of people, from the tacky multi-million dollar homes of the very rich to rundown bedsits shielding the illegal relatives of, mainly Latino, casino workers. Then there were, too, the white supremacists, who either refused to answer the doorbell or, once they realized why I was on their doorstep, slammed the door in my face. One even went back inside his house and came back out armed with a loaded rifle and chased me off his property.

Another white supremacist who, at least, bothered to exchange a few words with me, said, "You come over here from England and tell me how to vote! How dare you? Your whole country is Muslim. And now you want America to become Muslim too! Obama is Muslim. I know that, because he wears a Muslim ring! Michele gave it to him! Look, here!" And he proceeded to extract a crumpled magazine article out of his back pocket and pointed to a photo of a ring on the finger of an unidentifiable black man that certainly did not resemble President Obama.

"There, you see! He's wearing a Muslim ring! He's going to turn us all Muslim, that's what you want, isn't it? Now, get off my property!" He then turned around, walked back inside and slammed the door in my face.

But I did make some new friends in LA. I joined hiking groups, writing groups, improv groups and play-reading groups. And then there was one of my oldest and dearest friends, JJ, an LA resident for decades, who patiently sat with me for hours in St. John's Hospital in Santa Monica, while we waited for Mayumi to give birth to my first grandchild, Ronan. Mayumi had hoped her baby would be born on September 21ˢᵗ as that would have been my father's death anniversary and Ronan's second name was Geoffrey after him. But the labour was long and Ronan did not make his appearance until the next day.

But my friend JJ never gave up. She rushed out every so often and bought us drinks and sandwiches and stayed on, determined to hold my hand, until after the birth. It was a thrilling moment to hold my grandson in my arms as I instantly remembered holding my own babies, each one for the first time, and marvelling at their tiny fingers and toes, their perfect noses, lips, ears and eyes. Each one a very special gift. A tiny helpless little creature and, yet, each a person in their own right. And, at that moment of wonder, I speculated on what their future might hold. I experienced the same at that moment with Ronan.

Too soon my three months was up and it was time to return to Costa Rica, to the theatre and to rehearse my lines for the next production, playing Eleanor in the British farce, *No Sex, Please, We're British!* It was my largest role to date and it tested my skills as an actress. It involved several quick costume changes backstage. I thought I had got it down to a fine art but, on one occasion, I simply couldn't find my next costume in time for my entrance and had to appear on stage in my bra and pants, much to the amusement of the cast and the audience. I was acutely embarrassed, of course. But, since it was a farce, it didn't really matter. And I doubt many in the audience that night even noticed, thinking it was all part of the normal show.

Something I had been longing to do since I arrived in Costa Rica in late 2003, was to take part in the annual Romeria pilgrimage. I wanted to know what it felt like to walk among hundreds of thousands of devotees, from all backgrounds, from the capital San Jose, to the Basilica of the Virgin de los Angeles in the old capital Cartago, a distance of around 25 kilometres. I was thrilled when Hannia, the wife of my actor friend Joseph Loveday, who had just appeared with me in *No Sex, Please, We're British*, offered to accompany me.

"I do it every year," Hannia told me. "And we can stay at my sister's place in Cartago overnight and then Joseph will drive down to pick us up the following morning."

It was an offer I couldn't resist. Another actress friend, Lisa de Fuso, decided to join us. And so, the three of us set out, armed with walking sticks and backpacks stuffed with snacks, water, change of shoes and raingear. Thankfully though, despite the pilgrimage being held at the height of the rainy season, on August 2nd every year, it didn't start to rain that day until we reached the Basilica in Cartago.

The walk itself was an extraordinary experience. Mothers breastfeeding their babies while walking along the road. Toddlers holding their mothers' hands, desperately trying to keep up. Complete families, with their pets in tow, eating picnics as they walked. Elderly people on crutches or supported by walking frames, determined to walk the distance, straggling at the rear. Some people chatting excitedly all the way. Others playing loud music to help them along. And many walking in silent prayer, meditating on the religious meaning of the pilgrimage they were taking part in. Red Cross tents had been set up along the route as waystations for the bruised, the blistered and the infirm. And there was even a massage tent, run by massage students eager to hone their skills on the aching limbs of the many pilgrims, ourselves included. Needless to say, we were immensely proud of ourselves when we reached our destination because, although 25 kilometres is not a huge distance, the topography of Costa Rica meant that most of the walk was uphill. The last couple of miles was the best part as we descended into the valley of Cartago and, in the far distance, we could make out the glinting spires of the ancient Basilica – our destination.

Before long I was back in Los Angeles for the birth of my second grandchild, Ione. Mayumi had been determined to have two children before she turned 40. She just made it. There was more reason for me to be in Los Angeles now, so that I could help her and her partner, John, with the babies. They suggested they petition me to come and live in LA permanently. I had loved my life in Costa Rica but I had probably indulged myself too much. It was time, I realized, to settle down and be a committed grandmother.

Costa Rica, too, at the time was going through a massive change, not only of government but of laws, of lifestyle and of the cost of living. And, with these, came a rapid change of rules regarding foreigners. Whereas before, as an expat, it was much cheaper to live there than in the US or the UK, it was also fairly simple to circumvent the red tape. Now it was now becoming increasingly challenging. The new changes in the law brought with them new taxes and a more complex bureaucracy to navigate. These were designed to root out those foreigners who were living there illegally, by not bothering to apply for a resident's card or pay their social security taxes. The new government was determined to address this. So, after twelve great years, I felt it was the right time for me to leave.

Me and Ben in London

Ben, Elisar & me in the Philippines

Caroline Kennedy

Jasmine, Mayumi, Elisar and me in our London garden

Staff at the Hobbit House, Manila

Phillip Knightley and me going over my research materials

Stephen Ward and Pelham Pound

Collecting prosthetics for delivery to the hospitals in Jugoslavia

The stalker, Mick Roberts

Julia Morley and me at The Children's Village at Makarska

Mayumi and the railway children of Saatli

Caroline Kennedy

Mr. Mehman, Shirley Ludlow and me with our new outside toilet at Echo House

Ruggia and Jasmine in Saatli

Shirley Ludlow and me consulting with refugees

The Aliyev family in Saatli

Caroline Kennedy

My friend in Newfoundland, marine biologist Dave Snow

Farewell to my mother, Daska

I'll Be There

Drama students from Central School of Speech & Drama in Costa Rica

The cast of Calendar Girls

Caroline Kennedy

Ben and me reunion in 2016 in Manila

Mayumi and Jasmine

Working on the Obama reelection campaign in Nevada

Elisar & Lisa

Caroline Kennedy

Matt Devlen, Elliott Grove & Elisar at Raindance

Elisar, my niece Milica and me in London 2019

I'll Be There

Me with my grandchildren, Ione, Ronan and Sienna

Chapter 40
The Bombshell

While John and Mayumi began the initial paperwork for my green card application, I took time off to go back to the UK to visit Daphie, who had been diagnosed with non-Hodgkins lymphoma and was becoming increasingly frail. I stayed with her for 8 weeks, keeping her company and making sure she got the right at-home nursing care.

During this visit, I teamed up with three friends to produce an anti-Tony Blair CD. Back in February 2003, Elisar, Jasmine and I had attended the march in London against the Iraq War. And watching the television news later that day, seeing the millions of people all around the world marching for the same cause, had affected me deeply. The fact that not one of the politicians who had taken us into the illegal war on the bogus claims of "weapons of mass destruction" had since paid a price for that deliberate and reckless decision was, in my opinion, monstrous. And Tony Blair, in particular, one of the principal architects of the war, had not only refused to apologize for his part in it but had gone on to exploit his role by increasing his wealth and influence around the world. My friends and I wanted to make our voices heard. We wanted to show that twelve years after that worldwide demonstration, we still supported the people of Iraq. And the one way we felt we could raise funds for them was by producing a CD of original songs and poems read by celebrities, entitled *Not In Our Name* and donating the proceeds to an Iraqi NGO helping the children affected by the war.

At the end of the 8 weeks, it was immensely sad saying goodbye to Daphie, realizing it was probably the last time I would see her. Elisar and Lisa promised to keep checking in on her to make sure she had everything she needed. And my brother, Christopher, flew over from Philadelphia to take my place.

From London I flew to the Philippines to be with Jasmine who was about to give birth. Daphie had told me she was determined to stay alive long enough to learn about the baby's safe arrival. And, indeed, on April 3, 2016, Christopher was able to whisper in her ear that Jasmine had delivered a healthy baby, Sienna Daphne. Two hours later, Daphie died. Sadly, since Sienna developed several serious complications soon after her birth, she was held in the ICU for almost two weeks and I was unable to return to the UK for Daphie's funeral. I needed to hold Jasmine's hand as little Sienna fought for her life.

Once Sienna had recovered and Jasmine had taken her home, and when I was confident she had found a reliable home helper and settled into a routine, I left for my summer in Newfoundland. My time spent in Manila had been very fraught for all of us. So, combined with my sadness over Daphie's death, I was all the more ready for some alone time by the ocean.

But then the bombshell hit. News that no parent ever wants to hear. Elisar and Lisa called me one day in August and, in tears, told me that he had just been diagnosed with Stage 4 metastatic colon cancer. The doctors no longer called it "terminal cancer". They now referred to it as "incurable" which basically meant the same thing - Elisar's cancer was too far gone to be treated with any success. All the doctors could hope to do was to extend his life for a few months longer than he would have without any treatment. Elisar, who had been my firstborn, my only son, a wonderfully caring, calm, thoughtful, generous, talented and compassionate person – the shock was unbearable. I wanted to go to him immediately. But he didn't want to see me in distress. And I couldn't blame him. So, almost as a penance, I spent the rest of the summer gathering beach stones to make into a stupa, or shrine, to him in the desperate wish that by doing so, it would display some miraculous powers and he would live.

I admit it was a crazy idea and, although I created a beautiful structure, complete with three raised flower beds and a small Chinese pagoda that I discovered, discarded, on top of a metal heap in the local recycling centre, it attracted a lot of tourists with their cameras but it did nothing for Elisar's cancer. For some reason, I got some masochistic pleasure, too, from the persistent pain in my leg that only got worse every time I gathered stones from the beaches and carried them home. Somehow, I believed that the pain I was experiencing, might help alleviate Elisar's pain and overcome his disease. But, all it did was rip the main tendon in my leg to a point where I needed surgery, although I didn't realize that was what was happening at the time.

Since I was not allowed to visit the US while my green card application was pending, I decided to accept an invitation to New Zealand from my friend and former "calendar girl", Carol Marianne. She and another "calendar girl", Dale, had both left Costa Rica for Auckland. Dale was originally from there and wanted to return to spend more time with her daughter and granddaughter. And Carol who, like me had been a wanderer much of her life, was keen, in her own words, "to find a New Zealand apple farmer and settle down."

I flew to Auckland in late February 2017. Carol was there at the airport to greet me. She had not yet found an apple farmer but she had bought herself a beautiful home, set among rolling hills and within a couple of miles from the beach.

Being the effervescent type, Carol immediately launched into a barrage of shared Costa Rican memories. And, in no time at all, we had picked up where we left off and were reminiscing all the way back to her house.

Dale joined us a few days later and the three of us resurrected our *Calendar Girl* days – recalling the moment Dale accidentally let go of her towel, during a publicity photo shoot, revealing her bum for all of us to see. And the moment Carol's strategically-placed iced buns dropped, almost exposing her tits to the startled audience! It's always a blast seeing old friends after so many years. But seeing these two was, for me, a real tonic. I realized then I had not really laughed since Elisar's diagnosis six months earlier. His imminent death had been all I could really think about.

Carol and I took a "Thelma and Louise" car trip for a week criss-crossing our way around the North Island, stopping off to lunch among lavender fields, pausing for hikes along the beaches, driving through the Hobbit Village and ending up in New Plymouth at the raucous WOMAD Festival (World of Music and Dance) in New Plymouth. Too soon it was time to head back to Auckland and for me to board the Dutch vessel, the Noordam, for my first (and, considering how dreadful it was, probably my last), cruise that would take me across the Pacific to Vancouver. The only reason I decided to book a cabin on the Noordam was because I needed a slow way to get to Newfoundland. Another reason was that I had never visited Polynesia and, having told James Michener all those years before that I would definitely do this at some point on my life's journey, this 46-day cruise presented that opportunity.

Within a few days, almost everyone on board had got sick with flu. I understood then that cruise ships were nothing more than floating sanitoriums. They also presented a form of assisted living accommodation for some who, rather than living in an old folks' home for the rest of their days, took back-to-back cruises until they literally died on board.

The ship's doctor told me, "On a month's cruise we average at least two deaths."

"But then what happens when you're out at sea?" I asked. I was intrigued. I had never actually thought about this aspect of cruising before.

"Well, the florists get mad because we put the bodies in the flower shop. It's the only place that's cool enough all the time to prevent the corpses from decomposing. And then we call their next of kin to make sure there is someone at the next port of call that can identify the body and take it off the ship."

Well, that was a revelation! And, since I was now on a cruise of 46 days and everyone appeared to be sick, it was not hard to work out that, by the time we reached Vancouver, there would be at least two bodies lying below decks among the vases of roses, proteas and arum lilies. That was a sobering thought and was enough to put me off ever taking a cruise again. So I was very grateful when it ended and I was able to make my way across Canada to Newfoundland for the summer. Reluctantly, after seventeen years, I made plans to sell my house, as I knew I would be spending as much time as I could from then on with Elisar and Lisa.

Once a buyer was found at the end of that summer I returned to Costa Rica and to a mountain of paperwork for my green card. That took up much of my time for a while so, despite the pain in my leg increasing by the day, I put off seeing a doctor until it was so unbearable that it prevented me from doing my daily two hour walk. At first I was given cortisone injections to limit the pain. But, by this time, even these did not help.

So I decided the time had come to get a proper diagnosis. I needed to find an orthopedic specialist to discover what the problem was. In this I was extremely fortunate. I was given the name of one of the world's best foot and ankle surgeons and he just happened to be a Costa Rican. He immediately diagnosed a snapped tendon. So, within a few weeks, I was in hospital for surgery. A tendon from my foot was removed, stretched to fit from the arch of my foot to the back of my knee and sewed into place. Although I had several scars on my leg following the operation, within a few weeks they weren't even visible. And now it was time to learn to walk again. First I used a knee scooter, then crutches and finally I was able to discard both. Mayumi and Jasmine both came to look after me for the first couple of months while I was recuperating, although I was not able to do much with them as my lack of mobility destroyed any plans I might have of actually having fun with them and my grandchildren.

Chapter 41
Losing My Son

When I had recovered sufficiently from the surgery and was back on my feet, I rushed to England to be with Elisar for his first operation to remove part of his colon. Following the surgery, instead of recovering, he appeared to be fading fast as, one by one, his organs started shutting down. Lisa and I were at his bedside when he woke up from the surgery and we immediately alerted the medical team that something was drastically wrong. The nurses pumped him with drugs in a desperate effort to revive him and rushed him to the emergency room while his medical team tried to work out what was causing this drastic reaction. His surgeon finally realized that Elisar was allergic to the antibiotics he had prescribed for him post-surgery. Thankfully, once this was figured out and his antibiotics replaced, Elisar started to make a slow recovery. It was a terrifying time and I couldn't help but think that, from here on, there were going to be many days like this when his health would rapidly decline only to be revived again.

Elisar's resilience and positivity, considering his near death experience, was astounding. And every one of the medical staff at the hospital on the cancer ward fell in love with him. Like my father, he never complained. He just accepted everything stoically and with his own brand of understated good humour. It is hard to describe how immensely proud of him I was.

Once Elisar was discharged, I returned to Costa Rica, but received daily updates from him or Lisa about his various treatments – and there were many. Most of them, of course, came with hideous side-effects. So, although his medical team were, as they had promised us, keeping him alive, the physical cost to Elisar was becoming enormous. He lost his hair. The skin on his face and hands became discoloured. He got restless leg syndrome which prevented him from sleeping. He lost a dangerous amount of weight. And he was regularly throwing up and having panic attacks.

For a mother it was unbearable to think about. Imagining him suffering so intensely was intolerable. It made talking to him very difficult because I didn't want him to see how deeply it was all affecting me. I desperately wanted to be strong for him. He was also adamant that he never wanted to discuss his illness. But there was little else to talk about. We could share memories. We could talk about family. We could certainly talk about politics as we were both political junkies. We could talk about television programmes. We had to avoid all talk about work or work plans because we both knew there wouldn't be any. But, whatever conversation we started, even though neither of us intended it, the discussion always reverted back to his cancer. It was an all-consuming topic. And it was a no-win situation. I knew that if I avoided the subject then it would look like I didn't care. If I did speak about it, it would upset him. As a consequence, we spoke less and less and we simply messaged a lot. That way, too, he wouldn't see my tears and I wouldn't see the terrible effects the treatments were having on his body.

In retrospect – and even at the time, it is not something I am proud of, I know I should have been a rock for him. After all, it was him that was fighting for his life, not me. I should have been able to hold it all together. But I was a mother. His mother. And all I wanted to do was hug him, tell him everything would be alright, that it would all be over, that he would survive this. But both of us knew, that would all have been lies. There was no surviving this. That had been made abundantly clear to us from the start. And to prolong the pain and suffering just seemed so cruel. Although it was Elisar who was prepared to try anything in order to stay alive for just a few more months or weeks, desperately hoping that, in the meantime, there would be a new drug trial he could take part in or that a new miracle cure would be found.

To this day, I haven't been able to go back to read through our messages from this period. I know there are some that I dare never read again, particularly those that he continued to type even though he was either so affected by the medication he was on or he was delirious from the illness affecting his brain, that he was actually writing complete gobbledygook. Had he known that was what he was doing, he would have been absolutely mortified. I just hope he never reread them himself in his more lucid moments.

Elisar and I were both political animals. He was devastated by the vote on Brexit. And then, when the news came through of Trump's election, we were both convinced it was the end of the America that we had both grown to love. For a brief moment, I was not so sure I wanted my green card after all. But then, as I wrote to Elisar, we were both born fighters. And, once I got my permanent residency, I assured him I would fight, as best I could, to help restore someone with morals and compassion to the White House.

But to obtain my green card under a Trump administration was destined to take much longer than the 18 months my lawyer had predicted. And, since my final interview was slated to be at the US Embassy in Costa Rica, it meant I would have to stay in Escazu until it took place. It also meant I couldn't visit Mayumi, Ronan and Ione in Los Angeles. In the end, it took three years to process my card, not helped by the fact that the US Immigration Service mistakenly sent my file to the US Embassy in Manila for my interview, rather than the US Embassy in San Jose. It then took the Embassy in Manila four months to forward my file to Costa Rica. Finally, in August 2018, for the second time in my life, after an interval of 55 years, I got my residency. I felt like I had come full circle. After a month of goodbye parties in San Jose, of selling and giving away a lot of my collectibles, I arrived at LAX on August 26th, 2018 as a permanent resident.

As soon as I arrived, I started looking for an apartment. This time I fixated on Raintree Circle, the old MGM, Lot 3 in the old movie capital of Culver City. It was 37 acres of natural landscaping, immense trees, a huge lake, an island and plenty of wildlife. After living in Costa Rica, I thought it was the only place I could possibly adapt to, an oasis in the heart of West LA. On top of that, I had hoped it would be somewhere Elisar could come to spend his last months or weeks with me, sitting peacefully by the lake enjoying the antics of the ducks, the pelicans, the geese, the herons, and the rest of the wildlife that considered Raintree Circle their home.

While improvements were being done to the new apartment, I visited Elisar and Lisa in London for Christmas 2018 and helped them with their move up to Liverpool. Both of them had long wanted to move out of London and, now that he was ill, it seemed to be imperative for his wellbeing, physically and mentally. I totally endorsed their decision. Ben, Mayumi and John helped them financially to make the move possible and we were able to spend their first New Year in their new home together.

But the stress of the move inevitably took its toll on his failing health. On days that he felt well, he overdid it by helping Lisa and me to put the house in order, unpacking boxes, erecting shelving units, preparing his games room and rushing around with us to order new furniture. Sadly, a fire at their storage warehouse in London two years earlier had consumed all the furniture and many of their own personal effects they had hoped to bring with them to their new home. Much of the furniture he had received from Daddy and Daphie's estate, as he had loved the home they had provided for us, and he felt very nostalgic about the items he'd inherited from them. The fire, occurring just a couple of months following his original cancer diagnosis, had been a huge blow.

When the time came for me to leave, Elisar and Lisa drove me to Liverpool Station. In my heart, I knew it would be the last time I would see him. I think he knew it too. We hugged for a long time in silence. What could we say? Just that I loved him beyond measure. But even that sounded too trite. I didn't want to let go of him. But my train was waiting. I turned around, picked up my suitcase and walked away. But then, as I reached the entrance of the station, I turned back for one last look. At that same moment, as he was getting back into the car, he turned too, and we hooked onto each other's gaze, just for a second. And that was the last time we saw each other. I cried all the way back to London. And then, I cried on the plane, all the way back to LA.

But I couldn't have stayed with him any longer. I had to leave because Jasmine and Sienna were arriving for a holiday in March and I had to prepare the new condo for them. I stayed with John and Mayumi until the improvements on the condo were completed. In mid-February, I came down with what I thought was bronchitis. No matter what I took for it, it didn't seem to get better. I stayed in my room to avoid passing it on to Mayumi, John and the children. But, eventually, I had to ask John to take me to the nearest Urgent Care Clinic. I couldn't breathe. I was quite scared. What I probably had, after travelling from London a couple of weeks earlier, was Covid. But, at that point, very few people knew about it. It was only about a month later, that Covid was heralded as a pandemic that was spreading across the world.

Jasmine and Sienna were due to arrive on March 26th. But, as the pandemic got worse, President Duterte announced that the Philippines would completely shut down on March 20th. No one would be allowed to arrive or depart after that date. I panicked. I stayed up all night trying to change Jasmine's flight. For exactly thirteen hours, I hung on the phone waiting to speak to a Philippine Airline representative. Finally, my persistence paid off. I spoke to an agent who managed to change their flights to March 18th. Now I had to rely on Jasmine to make arrangements at her end to actually get to the airport and get her and Sienna on the plane.

Thousands of Filipino nationals and foreigners, terrified of being stuck indefinitely in the Philippines were desperate to leave and were prepared to take extreme measures to do so. And then, of course, there were the road blocks that had been set up to prevent the spread of the virus. Jasmine was terrified that even if she and Sienna were prepared in time, that they would be turned back at one of the road blocks on their way to catch their flight. Fortunately, a friend of hers had connections in the police force (something everyone needs and relies on to accomplish anything in the Philippines.). He sent his car and a police motorcycle escort to pick them up from their house and bring them to the airport.

At one point while she was waiting in line, Jasmine called me and said, "I can't do this! There are too many people! The lines are huge. It's taking forever. Sienna's fallen asleep and I am having to carry her and carry the luggage. It's crazy!"

I had to cajole her just to focus on the end result. There was no way she or I wanted her to stay in the Philippines. She would not have survived as the lockdown was so strict nobody was allowed out of their houses. And only one person was permitted, once a week, to go out and buy groceries, which would have meant she would have to leave 2-year-old Sienna in the house on her own while she went shopping. It would have been an impossible scenario.

I said, "You can do it! You've got to do it. And in less than 24 hours it will be over. You will be here and you will be safe!"

I was just scared that, in the panic and confusion, the airline might have oversold the tickets and she and Sienna might not even get on the flight. But obviously I couldn't say that to her. Despite the chaos and the delays, it eventually went smoothly and the two of them arrived in LA the following day.

And we were lucky too. This was just a week before the US lockdown. I had moved into the new condo just in time. Now we had this beautiful 37 acre property we could walk around every day. There were tennis courts and a swimming pool. And we could simply order groceries to be delivered. So we really had no need to venture out.

Due to the pandemic, Elisar and Lisa were confined to their new home too and, because of him being so vulnerable to any illness, they weren't even allowed to take a walk on the beautiful long stretch of beach behind their house. The proximity of this beach was one of the main reasons for them buying it and they had been looking forward to walking there every day, so it was yet another blow for him. He told me they managed to sneak out at night a couple of times just to stand on the beach and breathe in the sea air. But that was all he was able to do. By now he was receiving mainly palliative care so we all knew the end was close.

On July 20, 2020, Mayumi received the dreaded phone call from Lisa in the early hours of the morning. About ten days earlier Lisa had told us he had been transferred to a hospice near them. She told us the move was to tweak his meds. But we all knew what it really meant. And, from then on Elisar was in and out of delirium. It was a very hard time for Lisa. And, through it all, she had been amazing, disregarding her own health issues and her work to look after him and be his sole carer for four years. We owed her a huge debt of gratitude. Now, due to Covid none of us were able to travel to London to be with her and say goodbye to him. We were denied the opportunity to hug him one last time and tell him what a very special son and brother he had been. We all felt cheated. But then, at the same time, because of Covid, we realized there were so many people around the world experiencing the same loss, the same grief and the same barriers to saying goodbye to their loved ones. We were not alone.

Elisar's last wish was that his ashes be scattered in the bay in front of my mother's house in Mallorca where he had spent every summer of his childhood. It was a wish we were determined to fulfill. But, again, with Covid restrictions, we were unable to do carry it out until September 2022, over two years after his death.

Six months after he died, my niece, Milica, who also had Stage 4 metastatic cancer succumbed to her disease. Elisar had been her rock. And she told me before she died that she couldn't have faced her illness without his help and support. She said that when he died, she knew it was the end for her too.

"I felt that if Elisar could stay alive, then I could too." She told me. "When he died, I just gave up all hope and I hid myself away for a week."

They had both been extraordinary examples of courage. Losing them was a terrible blow for our family, particularly for Mayumi and Jasmine. They had lost a brother who they adored and a cousin who they also adored. There was no explanation, no consolation, no silver lining. It was brutal. We still talk about them both a lot. We are not yet over the grief. Perhaps the grief will never fade it will only recede.

In retrospect, I have had the life Elisar couldn't have. I have been blessed with just enough money to be able to support the itinerant lifestyle of my dreams. Elisar loved travelling too. But, unlike me, he was very much a homebody. And, his dream was to buy his own home. Not simply a small apartment but a real home where he could have cats and dogs, where he could cook for his friends and play board games with his family. And it's sad to think that when he finally got the home of his dreams, he was unable to enjoy it the way he should have done.

In 2021, just a day before my 77th birthday, I, too, was diagnosed with cancer. All my life I have lived in many countries and been fortunate to have good health. But I arrived in the USA, the most expensive country in the world to get ill, and I get cancer. Sod's Law, I guess. My right kidney had to be removed immediately as the tumour was already too big to cut it out. The bills for surgery and subsequent treatment were enormous. I had no health insurance yet and was faced with mounting debts to the hospital and to my medical team. Thankfully, my son-in-law, John, came to my rescue, spending days on the phone working out an arrangement with the finance department of Cedars-Sinai Hospital to cut my bill by two thirds and then finding me a health insurance package that would cover the vital post-op treatments.

I realize I am still blessed. I have my two daughters and three grandchildren, all of them talented, all of them loving and all of them around me.

I know Elisar, Mayumi and Jasmine wanted me to finish this book that I started decades ago. And, in a way, it has been a cathartic exercise. I have laughed through parts of it and cried through others. I have included things long forgotten and forgotten things I should have included. I have revisited old friendships and have mourned those no longer with us. I have opened new chapters and closed old ones. And, fortunately, despite a lifetime of packing and unpacking suitcases, I have never thrown away the things most valuable to me, my papers. Whether on trains, planes or buses, whether setting up temporary homes in the UK, America, the Philippines, Azerbaijan or Costa Rica, whether visiting remote places or familiar ones, I have kept my writings, my journals, my letters, my articles and my press clippings for when, one day, I would need them. Some of them are faded. Others are yellowing. And many are brittle to the touch. But, amazingly, most of them have remained intact. And together they tell a story of a wandering life. My wandering life.

Chapter 42
The World is a Book

And, right now, as I think back on my life, I remember the last production I appeared in on stage in San Jose. It was entitled, *The Stuff That Dreams Are Made Of*. It was a series of personal stories by members of our theatre group. And the one that I wrote and performed, I think, summed up my life perfectly. So, to end my story, I add it here. Entitled, *The World is a Book*, after the saying by San Augustin.

"Since I was very small I have always had an innate wanderlust. Day and night I would pore over books with photos of strange places, wild topography, fascinating people and exotic flora and fauna. These pages excited me like nothing else. Forget *Alice in Wonderland*, forget *Winnie the Pooh*, forget *Little Women*. As I grew up it was the writings of T.E Lawrence, Wilfred Thesiger, Gertrude Bell, Francis Younghusband, Freya Stark, Margaret Meade and others that fired my imagination and became my Bibles. And it was the words of San Augustin that became etched in my mind: *"The world is a book. And those that do not travel read only one page."*

Even at an early age I dreamt of writing a best-selling book about my about my wanderings, to write about people who didn't resemble me, to learn about cultures different from my own and to live among tribes from as far afield as the mountain ranges of S.E. Asia to those of the Brazilian and Amazonian rainforests. And I secretly hoped that someone, someday, would describe me as, "eccentric", "fearless" and "inspiring".

I wanted to be like Freya Stark, aged 85, astride a donkey, riding across the Himalayas. Her words resonating in my ears: *"To awaken alone in a strange place is one of the most pleasant sensations in the world."*

And I made up my mind there and then that all my travels would be on my own.

It's funny looking back. I was single-minded. I was determined. And I was supremely confident. The type of arrogant self-belief that only comes with youth, ignorance and inexperience. I was so certain that I, like the renowned Arabist

Gertrude Bell, would feel as comfortable sitting in a palace with kings as I would be squatting with nomads in a tent in the desert.[

Over the decades I have travelled extensively - to the Soviet Union, India, Nepal, Africa, South East Asia, North America, Canada, Australia, Japan, the Middle East, the Caucasus, Eastern Europe, the Antarctic, the sub-Arctic and Latin America.

During those travels I have shared an hermetically-sealed train compartment for 2 long weeks with three very drunk and very smelly Russian men as we crossed the vast Siberian tundra. And I have had to demonstrate how tampons are used to four extremely perplexed male customs officials at the Siberian border who had never seen one before in their lives! They were convinced I was a spy and the tubes were mini telescopes I was using for my espionage work!

I have been robbed by a band of criminals as I walked alone to see the temples of Cheng Mai and I have been used as a police decoy to catch a serial rapist in Hong Kong. I've been toasted as an "honorary man" for my work in the refugee camps of southern Azerbaijan and I've been transformed into a living goddess by a remote Ifugao tribe living high up in the Cordillera Mountains of the northern Philippines.

I've illegally smuggled a terrified young Bosnian refugee girl in the back of my truck, away from the war zone, across 6 countries and into the UK, to reunite her with her parents. And I've been mistaken for the Maharishi Mahesh Yogi by a large group of very curious, but obviously very ill-informed, Chinese journalists in Hong Kong!

I've taken and passed a Disaster Relief Operations Course with the British Army and I've delivered lectures aboard the luxury liner, the QE2, about the hidden wealth of Ferdinand and Imelda Marcos of the Philippines.

I've hosted a birthday party in a prison cell for the Bolivian painter, Benjamin Mendoza, who was incarcerated for attempting to assassinate Pope Paul VI. I've played chess with Marlon Brando, played tennis with Al Pacino, sang on stage with Tony Bennett and giggled into my napkin as Monica Lewinsky dipped a cigar in brandy and rolled it seductively across her thigh at dinner. I've dined with King Hussein in Jordan, played charades with Princess Grace in Monaco and I have even sipped tea and watched horse-racing in front of the TV with our late British Queen.

And what have I learnt from these unique, and somewhat surreal, experiences? I have learnt not to take myself too seriously. I have learnt that listening to people is far more valuable than talking to them. I have learnt that a notebook and a pen is far more reliable than memory. I have learnt that refugees who have little or nothing to offer are far more generous than people who have plenty. I have learnt that, in the words of the author James Michener, *"If you reject the food, ignore the customs, fear the religions and avoid the people, you might just as well stay at home.*" And I have proved to myself that Freya Stark was right all along – that travelling on one's own opens up many more doors than travelling with others.

As you have read parts of my dream have come true. I have indeed written a best-selling book although, sadly, it was not about travels. And to my delight I have, in fact, been dismissed as "eccentric" or just plain mad by many of my friends and family who watched me set off alone by train, at the height of the Cold War, across East Germany, Poland, Russia and Siberia. I have indeed been described as "fearless" by my fellow journalists in Manila. And I have been told I am an "inspiration" by the three people who matter most in my life – my children.

My dream has been to travel the world. And I still have new places to visit, new horizons to explore, new adventures ahead. But San Augustin's words remain as relevant to me today as they always were: *"The world is a book. And those that do not travel read only one page."*

He was right, of course. To me the world has been a book and there may still be a few more chapters to write.

Printed in Great Britain
by Amazon

4ad7533c-3b80-4f6f-9606-c03e8ce4f81aR01